Von Abele, Rudolph
    Alexander H. Stephens,
a biography.

DATE DUE

MAR 23 '88			

NOV 28 '78

Alexander H. Stephens

STEPHENS IN MIDDLE AGE, PHOTOGRAPHED IN
WASHINGTON ABOUT 1858.

(*Liberty Hall collection, Crawfordville*)

TO MARK VAN DOREN

Preface

THIS book might easily have been twice as long as it is; but the importance of its subject would not have stood the strain—nor, very likely, would the mythical reader to whom it is addressed. The significance of Alexander Stephens as a man, a problem in the psychology of personality, motivation, and behavior, is both greater and more exciting to study than is his meaning as a public figure in the American past. But that is not to say he has no such meaning. He has; and, after all, no man is capable of division into two, one private and the other public. He is public and private equally in everything he does. Stephens, in his political career, was a representative of the South, and stands—cannot help standing—as one among many symbols of a civilization. Sometimes he acted with his colleagues, sometimes against; but in either case he cannot be dissociated from his section. He was an individual and a Southerner, himself and a stone in the pattern, sharing with the multitude of other stones a certain irreducible minimum of beliefs, ideas, points of view, environments, and conditions. There is a borderland, dim and elusive, where the unique in any man is joined with the typical, and the two streams, by either conflict or agreement, rush together into the open world as words and deeds. To understand Stephens is to understand something of the South; to understand the South is to understand much that is in Stephens. But Stephens is not all South either; he is a person. And his importance, to historians and readers in any age, lies in both directions—in himself, and in the light he points upon the history of his time. It is my hope that some glimmering of such light may have found its way into these pages.

The making of a book always entails obligations which it is a delight to record. I wish first to acknowledge my debt to Mark Van Doren, without whom, in a very real sense, this book could never have been written. The debt I owe him is an honor to bear, and one in payment of which a lifetime's work—or pleasure, rather—would not suffice.

To Professor John Allen Krout of Columbia University, under whose guidance the actual work was done, I am deeply grateful for patient and helpful criticism. Professor Allan Nevins, also of Columbia University, read the manuscript and gave much encouragement and sound advice. Professor Louis M. Hacker, of Columbia University, pointed out a number of flaws in my handling of the subject, and I am indebted to him for making me rewrite the book. Professor Roy F. Nichols, of the University of Pennsylvania, read the manuscript and was generous with time and criticism.

Miss Elizabeth Gunn, in charge of Liberty Hall, allowed me to wander at will, and was constantly helpful in research. Professor Raymond B. Nixon, of Emory University, pointed out sources I might otherwise have overlooked. I must also thank Mrs. Sarah White and Mr. Ralph Golucke, of Crawfordville, Ga., Mr. Frank A. Holden, Mrs. Myrta Lockett Avary, and Mrs. John S. Spalding, of Atlanta, Dr. Robert G. Stephens of Washington, Ga., Mother Claude Stephens of New York, and Mrs. W. F. Bushnell of Harrisburg, Pa., for information kindly given.

Mother Gertrude Buck and the staff of the library at the Manhattanville College of the Sacred Heart, New York, made months of reading easy and pleasant. Mrs. J. E. Hays and the Department of Archives and History, Atlanta; the

Library of Congress; the University of Texas Library, Austin; the Manuscript Division of the Pennsylvania Historical Society, Philadelphia; the University of Georgia Library, Athens; the Emory University Library, Decatur; the Manuscript Department of the Duke University Library, Durham, N. C.; the Carnegie Library, Atlanta; the Ordinary's Office, Augusta; and the Columbia University Libraries, were all generous with manuscripts, newspapers, and assistance.

Columbia University provided the means, in the form of two fellowships, by which I was enabled to work uninterruptedly for two years. To my parents I owe far more than I can tell; without their patience, understanding, and faith I could not have completed the book at all.

RUDOLPH VON ABELE

New York, 23 October 1945

A Note

THERE may be those who in reading this book are disturbed both by its treatment of certain personal incidents in Stephens' life, and by the apparent freedom with which it explores his unconscious. In regard to the first point I should like to say that every anecdote, however embellished, has a documentary basis in fact, and that the embellishments have been added, with a strict eye to the maintenance of truth, upon the time-honored principle of "what is plausible in the circumstances." As for the second point, I do not deny that I have a theory of Stephens' character. It may be utterly incorrect: but it is the result of much thought, based upon the study of a remarkably revealing correspondence. Every one of my guesses roots itself in the hard soil of fact.

Contents

Illustrations

ALEXANDER H.
STEPHENS

𝔄 𝔅iography

BY

RUDOLPH VON ABELE

"VIRTUTIS AMORE"

Motto of the Stephens coat of arms

NEGRO UNIVERSITIES PRESS
WESTPORT, CONNECTICUT

Originally published in 1946
by Alfred A. Knopf, Inc., New York

Reprinted with the permission
of Alfred A. Knopf, Inc.

Reprinted in 1971 by Negro Universities Press
Division of Greenwood Press, Inc.
Westport, Connecticut

Library of Congress Catalogue Card Number 74-135614

ISBN 0-8371-5201-1

Printed in the United States of America

Alexander H. Stephens

Eighteen-Sixty

VOICES in the smoky crowded chamber; rise and fall of conversation beneath the yellow lights as the hands of the clock move steadily forward. At the Speaker's desk a man sits waiting, now turns to talk with those about him, now draws a clawlike hand across his pale forehead to brush away wisps of untidy chestnut hair that keep falling into his eyes, now stares sharply out into the chamber, or pulls his awkwardly fitting coat back into place, or crosses and uncrosses legs that, to judge by the way the trousers flap and crease, are thin and bony. Outside the chamber the open area on the hilltop round the ugly Gothic Capitol building is filled with carriages. Some hundreds of yards below, through leafless trees, the red Oconee mutters toward the sea, minute by minute licking Georgia soil down with it. Latecomers hurry up the hill and into the Capitol, men dressed in brown or black, surtouted, perhaps carrying canes, taking off tall hats as they pass through the doors, their faces sober and intense, their tones excited. The calendar says it is the fourteenth of November, eighteen-sixty. The Georgia legislature is in evening session, having special business before it. (America, this evening and the next, and for many evenings to come, has special business before it.)

Then all the latecomers are in, and the man at the Speaker's desk is introduced to the crowd, though in more than a facetious sense he needs no introduction: "The Honor-

able Alexander H. Stephens," and so on, but none who
have come could have failed to recognize the tall and
angular figure on the dais which now unfolds from its chair
to full height and stands a moment, waiting for applause
to die away. Under the flaring lights the color of his face
is an unhealthy yellow splotched with brown. His smolder-
ing black eyes turn slowly this way and that as he waits; a
hand caresses the huge gold fob dangling from his watch
pocket, or hangs loosely at his side. Then bloodless, ascetic
lips, pulled awry, one cannot but imagine, by some great
secret agony, part themselves, and a shrill voice says: "Fellow-citizens—" After a second or two he proceeds, speaking
slowly and without notes.

"I appear before you tonight at the request of members
of the Legislature and others, to speak of matters of the
deepest interest that can possibly concern us all, of an
earthly character. There is nothing—no question or subject
connected with this life, that concerns a free people so
intimately as that of the Government under which they
live. . . ."

Motionless, the lanky scarecrow figure stands on the dais,
addressing the gathered legislature of the state of Georgia
and as many private citizens of Milledgeville and the neighborhood as have managed to push into the hall, saying:
"My object is not to stir up strife, but to allay it; not to
appeal to your passions, but to your reason . . ." and
urging: "Let us therefore reason together." Not far away,
in the Executive Mansion, the Governor of Georgia, Joseph
Emerson Brown, is preparing for the military defense of
his state. He reasons no longer; his mind is fixed.

"The consternation," Stephens continues, "that has come
upon the people is the result of a sectional election of a
President of the United States, one whose opinions and
avowed principles are in antagonism to our interests and

rights. . . ." A little more than a week ago his old friend
Abraham Lincoln has been made President-elect of the
United States, but not one vote from any Southerner has
helped to do it. And the question Southerners now ponder,
the decision they begin to think they will be forced to
make, is propounded by the tall orator in the state house at
Milledgeville: "Shall the people of the South secede from
the Union in consequence of the election of Mr. Lincoln
to the Presidency of the United States?" Many think so:
for the past week members of the legislature have received
dozens of petitions coming from county after county, demanding, in the most pompous possible language, the
prompt secession of Georgia from the Union. The people,
it seems, are loud for separation. But Stephens, as intensely
as possible, makes answer to his question: "My countrymen,
I tell you frankly, candidly, and earnestly, that I do not
think they ought. In my judgment, the election of no man,
constitutionally chosen to that high office, is sufficient cause
for any state to separate from the Union. . . . Let us not,"
he pleads, "be the ones to commit the aggression." There
are those in his audience who shake their heads and frown
at this; but if they disapprove, they cannot be surprised.
Never, during twenty years of political power in his state,
has Stephens been known to be one of the so-called "chiv-
alry," the "fire-eaters," meaning the aggressive Southern
radicals.

He talks on, his voice gathering volume, charged with all
the conviction of which he is capable, echoing and blurring
against the back gallery of the hall, this chamber where he
first spoke twenty-seven years ago. When applause breaks
in upon his speech, he gives a magisterial rebuke: "I trust,
my countrymen, you will be still and silent. I am addressing
your good sense." If they are agitated, he is not. There is
no real danger, he argues. If Lincoln's purposes and policies

be opposed to the security of the South, yet the gains of the Democratic party have been sufficient to keep him from controlling the machinery of government. But should they prove insufficient? He yields the secessionists a grain of comfort: "I will," he admits, "have equality for Georgia . . . in this Union, or I will look for new safeguards elsewhere," immediately countering, though, that in his opinion those safeguards can be had in the Union. The government of the United States may not be perfect, he goes on, but he thinks it the best in the world, England's included. Under that government the South has grown in wealth, in commerce, in population, has erected a culture, has benefited in every conceivable way. Why, Stephens wonders, should we deliberately throw ourselves into the unknown? The America he knows is "the Eden of the world, the Paradise of the universe"; and if the Southern people leave it now they may soon become demons doomed to cutting the throats of their late brethren. (There are Southerners who would not mind.) Let the Southern people first send in a bill of grievances before they act; let them do the utmost that ingenuity can devise to settle the situation peaceably. Northern states have enacted laws designed to keep runaway slaves from ever being returned to their owners: very well, let the owners first demand the repeal of these laws before they wantonly disrupt the Eden of the world. Do nothing illegally. Above all, let the will of the people prevail. Some want the legislature to take Georgia out of the Union at once. This is wrong. The people, and only they, can do so irrevocable and fateful a thing. Should they decide for disunion, he, Stephens, can do nothing but bow to their decision and support their efforts; but he hopes they will not so decide. "I am for exhausting all that patriotism demands before taking the last step," he says, adding that if all such efforts fail, "we shall at least have the satisfaction of knowing that we have done our duty and all that patriotism could require." [1]

That is all. The shrill voice ceases; the speaker sits down; the audience slowly disperses, though some remain to congratulate or argue with the pallid, wearied, cadaverous orator until he leaves the Capitol. In a few hours the crenelated pile of stone on top of the hill is lightless and deserted; the carriages are gone; and the red Oconee, chuckling among stones, is almost the only sound in the cool November night.

Two months and two days later the Capitol building once again receives crowds of men, two hundred and ninety-seven of them, come to this place to do what Stephens had wished they would not do. The town, Milledgeville, the drowsy dusty dirty country village of perhaps two thousand, is living now in history, and is conscious of living in history despite its sprawling indifference and its seclusion in the midst of thick oak and pine forests through which wander turnpikes that are mainly wheeltracks, choked with reddish dust in summer, axle-deep in rainy seasons. The loungers who used to slump on the galleries of groceries and hotels, feet up on the unpainted railings, whittling, sending ten-foot arcs of tobacco juice in every direction, hats tilted over their eyes; the farmers who used to come into town, riding wagon beds or in spindle-wheeled buggies, to do their business at bank or store and gather on corners to talk about sickness, or cotton, or drought, or local politics; the lawyers who ambled from county seat to county seat on horseback or in buggy, carrying their inevitable green bags filled with books and papers; the plant-

1 The text of this speech may be found in Richard M. Johnston and William H. Browne: *Alexander H. Stephens* (Philadelphia, 1878) (cited hereafter as *J&B*), 564–80; and in Henry Cleveland: *Alexander H. Stephens, in Public and Private, with Letters and Speeches* (Philadelphia, 1866) (cited hereafter as *Cleveland*), 694–712.

ers in wide hats who were always worrying about making both ends meet, watching the price of cotton, watching the price of likely hands, reading their weekly newspapers and studying the state of the nation—all these are laboring under some powerful excitement. Something is going on which none of them, however stupid or lazy, can ignore. An election has been held, and a convention is meeting up the hill in the Capitol, to decide whether Georgia shall stay in or get out of the Union. Therefore every Georgian of any prominence is in Milledgeville this week, and you may at any moment, strolling along the streets, encounter the heavy, portentous figure of Herschel V. Johnson; or the little sly eyes and hedonist lips of Howell Cobb, encased in rolls of fat; or the tall, soberly clothed, pious Governor himself, in rusty black, looking like a provincial and talking with an upcountry nasal twang; or Robert Toombs, perhaps not altogether sober, booming along with his customary aristocratic scowl; or Alexander Stephens, muffled in shawls and greatcoat against the cold, carrying a light cane, walking carefully lest he slip and fall; his brother Linton perhaps with him, appearing almost stout beside the fragile semi-invalid. People here are wearing homespun as a gesture of defiance; or they flaunt secession cockades and badges. Young men are organizing companies of militia and drilling in the streets. Newspapers are devoured and passed from hand to hand until they fall apart. South Carolina has been out of the Union since December 20; Mississippi seceded just a week ago; Florida and Alabama within the past five days. Already there has been shooting: the steamer *Star of the West,* trying to enter Charleston harbor with provisions for the garrison at Fort Sumter, has been fired upon. The President-elect, silent, oracular, waits at Springfield, Illinois. Negotiations between South Carolina and Washington have broken down. Everyone here is waiting to see what the convention will do.

Behind closed doors two hundred and ninety-seven men assemble at noon on the 16th of January 1861. For a certain number of hours each day for the next four days they deliberate, come out, return, while everybody waits. In the chamber there is long discussion, sometimes heated, for these men are in deadly earnest. There is no time for attitudinizing now. Eighty years from this day no one will know just what is being done and said behind these noncommittal doors. A journal is kept, but it records no spoken words.

Alexander Stephens, expected to be leader of the opposition, has turned that job over to Herschel V. Johnson. When, on Friday the 18th, Eugenius Nisbet offers resolutions declaring Georgia's duty to secede, and Johnson counters with other resolutions aimed at holding Georgia in the Union until every thinkable conciliation has been tried, in the debate that follows Stephens claims the floor and briefly speaks in favor of Johnson's resolutions, little more than summarizing his speech of two months ago—as if he were convinced he can do no more. More talk; and then Nesbit's resolutions, as anticipated, pass.[2] That night a committee meets, Stephens being one of its members, charged with the task of drawing up the ordinance that will carry Georgia out of the Union it unanimously entered in 1788. The town is alive with rumor all day and the next morning; there is much coming and going, much deep consultation, at the Executive Mansion, in the Capitol, in hotel rooms. At twelve the two hundred and ninety-seven meet again. The ordinance of secession is reported. Johnson's resolutions looking to amicable settlement are moved as a substitute by young Benjamin Harvey Hill, with whom Stephens, though for the moment allied, is not on speaking

2 Percy S. Flippin: *Herschel V. Johnson, State Rights Unionist* (Richmond, 1931), 177–8, 185–6; *J&B*, 379; Alexander H. Stephens: *A Constitutional View of the Late War between the States* (Philadelphia, 1868–70) (cited hereafter as *View*), II, 305–7.

terms because of an old misunderstanding. The convention, which has not come together out of a desire to be
amicable, tosses Johnson's resolutions into the trash basket
and, amid vast excitement, votes to secede, two hundred
and eight to eighty-nine. Hill and his friends have swung
to the majority side at the penultimate moment; Alexander
Stephens firmly votes nay when his name is called. So does
his brother Linton. So does Johnson. The clock over the
Speaker's desk, the clocks in Milledgeville houses, clocks
all over Georgia, are striking two in the afternoon. It is
Saturday, the 19th of January 1861.[3] The Union is dissolved! *Le jour de gloire est arrivé!* Milledgeville gives
itself over to a weekend of celebration, as if there were
something to be happy about. Windows are illuminated
with candles that night; there are impromptu torchlight
processions; the little brass cannon belonging to the militia
are fired off; toasts by the hundred are drunk; every tavern
and hotel is jammed with singing, excited, happy men.

Alexander Stephens declines to join in the exultation.
He has pledged acceptance of whatever the people may
decide: now the pledge must be fulfilled. Yet it is difficult
to do. For him the Union has meant something more than
for these men and women who now so unthinkingly re-
joice in its destruction. If, as he has so often said, Georgia
is dearest to him and claims his first allegiance, the Union
nevertheless comes second, and closely. He is depressed
and thoughtful in the midst of revelry and the fever of
coming war, because he fears the future. Has he not said
it already, nearly ten months ago?—"Men will be cutting
one another's throats in a little while. . . ." And for what?
For the sake of the obsessions of a clique of radicals, South
as well as North.

But it is a strange decision he is making in choosing to

---

[3] Isaac W. Avery: *The History of Georgia from 1850 to 1881* (New York,
1881) (cited hereafter as *Avery*), 155.

oppose secession. Were he to ardently support it, as Toombs and Cobb, his cotemporaries for twenty years as leaders of Georgia have done, his position would be one of great power. A convention is to meet in a few weeks at Montgomery, Alabama, to form some kind of provisional government for the seceded states. That government will need a president, who might very well be a Georgian. But not a Georgian who has spoken against secession. Toombs or Cobb perhaps, but not Stephens. He is now nearly forty-nine; has lived a considerable political life; has dominated a large section of middle Georgia (the section he has lived in from birth, the section he knows best and loves most deeply) ever since the early 1840's: does it not now seem as though he were deliberately throwing away his future, making certain he can never again wield the power he once held? True, he has been out of politics since 1859, when he resigned, for various reasons, the Congressional seat he had held since 1843; but does he really want to stay in Crawfordville, the tiny crossroads village where he was born, tending to the house along the railroad he calls Liberty Hall, and to the plantation a few miles off, worked by thirty slaves? As his shrill voice responds: "Nay" to the clerk's reading of his name this Saturday afternoon, it is as though he were wantonly snuffing out the light of his career. What does he expect to do in the ten, fifteen, twenty years of life remaining? Or does he, continually attacked by illness of every conceivable variety, suppose he has not many years remaining?

Again, his decision is strange because it is not the decision of the majority of the class of men to which he belongs. Among them, by and large, he is an anomaly. His position in the civilization of which he is a member clearly shows him to be one of the Southern ruling class. He is a native of middle Georgia, the social and economic center of the state; he is a lawyer and a politician; he is a planter.

Though his thousand acres and thirty slaves form a small plantation when set beside others of ten thousand acres and a hundred slaves, his interests and the interests of the largest planters coincide; his troubles and theirs are the same. And they, in the main, enthusiastically support secession. His own section, for the first time in his history, has turned against him, returning to the convention now meeting seventeen delegates for secession and only ten against it. Not even his great personal popularity has been able to prevent defeat. Ten years ago, in a similar crisis, the people of the state overwhelmingly supported him in standing firm against disunionists who did not consider the Compromise of 1850 a compromise they could accept. But Toombs and Cobb had then been with him. Now they are opposed, and the people are opposed. Toombs and he, despite occasional irritations close friends for thirty years, are now not friends. Save for Johnson and Hill he stands quite alone, a reluctant looker-on at a play he does not like.

Somberly, heavy-hearted, he prepares to acquiesce in the people's decision. (Is it really that?) He has in the past been known to be rash, has been known to stand for Southern rights, has even been known to speak of disunion in moments of great anger. Not now. The men who have voted Georgia out of the Union are men of property and men of status, but at this moment they are revolutionaries. He, by contrast, plants himself upon the law; refuses to do anything the law does not permit or justify; insists a legal election is no ground for lawless action. He has always revered the law; has had almost fanatical devotion for legal justice and liberty under law—what he calls "constitutional liberty." Like Shylock, but in an opposite spirit, he jealously watches that the bond be kept. Since childhood it has been so. . . .

CHAPTER ONE

Youth (1812–32)

THERE were many trees and the house was hidden by trees. He knew their names, oak, short-leaved pine, hickory, red cedar, black walnut. Father told him the names of the trees and showed him how the leaves of different trees were different. In summer the woods were cool and shady and he could not walk there alone because they said he would get lost and never come back again. All around the farm, all around the land where father had cut down the trees and planted corn and potatoes and beans and peas and built the house out of logs from the trees he had cut down, all around was the forest. The earth was red when you turned it up with a plow. In winter it was cold and sometimes it snowed. Then he stayed indoors unless father told him to go and bring in the sheep. Father had sheep too, and it was nice to pat their sides before the wool was cut off from them, it was soft and warm. Not like the big old gray stone in the pasture where he and Aaron and John went to play. The stone was warm and rough and hard when he put his hand on it. Sheep were soft, stones were hard. Father would call that learning.

Past the trees that were on every side of the farm was the world. Father often saddled a horse and rode out through the trees, going to places where other people lived. Washington. That was one. It was over there, eighteen miles away. The place he lived in was Wilkes County. Washington was in Wilkes County, this place was in Wilkes

County, and Wilkes County was in Georgia. Georgia was very big and had more people in it than you could count. Sometimes some of them would come riding in through the trees to visit father. They came on the turnpike that ran from Washington to Greensboro. Once a week a man rode by with two bags hanging from his saddles, and he brought letters. In the West, where he went, there were Indians, Creeks and Cherokees, but they did not come here. Father did not like it when people came on Sunday because he said Sunday was a holy day and must not be profaned. What did that mean? It meant Sunday was different from other days so you could not do the same things on Sunday you did other days. You had to be very quiet and listen to father pray at table. He always prayed, but it seemed as if he prayed harder on Sunday. When people came to visit on Sunday he asked them in and had them sit down, and then he would talk to them about the efficacy of prayer and immersion and the Holy Ghost, and get up and bring down a book from the cupboard and read sermons to the people. They never stayed long to hear him because they generally had something else to do and so they went away. Then father was glad.

Father was a teacher. Mother, his mother, was dead. Father told him that, and in the old field behind the house there was a thin piece of stone standing up in the ground and it had mother's name on it, Margaret Grier Stephens, and the year she died, 1812. That was the year Alexander was born. His father told him that too. Aunt Betsey Grier came visiting one day and she took him and Aaron and John down the path to the grave, and she was crying. His mother was Aunt Betsey's sister. Now he had a new mother whom his father called Matilda. He wondered what his real mother looked like and sometimes went to the grave and wondered whether she would be there if he dug the red dirt away. She was dead, and father said she was in heaven, so she could not be here too.

Father would often sit by a knot light and write letters for other people. They said he had the finest handwriting of any man in that part of the country. People liked his father and said he was one of the most upright and honest and pious men they had ever seen. He rarely smiled, but he was not grumpy either. He said many times he did not really want to teach school but did it only because the neighbors liked him so well he could not refuse. He liked to grow fruit trees and cut off little stems from trees and peel the bark from other trees and set the stems into the trunks of the other trees and put clay around and bind the stems to the trunks. He called that grafting. And he liked to mix mortar and put bricks on top of each other to make chimneys, and he liked to sit by the fire in the evenings and make shoes for the children to wear. He never talked much, but he was always interested in what people were saying and doing. In school he never pulled the boys' ears and never raised his voice when he was scolding, but he was very strict all the same. Alexander loved him a great deal even though he was so strict. There was one time when he was watching sheep and it came on dark and he had to bring the sheep in. It was in the winter, and there was snow on the ground and it was cold and he was cold and shivering. When he called the sheep in they all came except one ewe, who would and would not come. It was so dark and silent and crisp, and he was afraid and lonesome, and when he thought of how far he was from the house it made little shivers go up and down him and he felt hot in his belly, and so he did not go looking for the ewe but went home and did not tell his father. Next evening the ewe was still lost, but he did not say anything. In the morning father came out with him to look at the sheep, and father saw at once that there was a ewe missing. When father asked, he said yes, father, she is lost, but when father asked why he had not told about it he was afraid to tell that it was because he did not want to have to go out into the woods looking for the ewe. Then father took him by the hand and they went up the fields in the snow look- ing for the ewe together. Finally they found her, and she was lying dead in the snow. Next to her lay a little lamb which she had borne before she died. Father looked and did not say anything, and he looked and felt sad because the ewe was dead and it was his fault. She was so cold and quiet it made him want to cry. When they came home again father whipped him very hard and talked to him in a stern voice. He thought he would never in his whole life forget the dead ewe in the snow and his father standing looking at it.[1]

Alexander went to school sometimes, but more often stayed at home, for there was much for him to do. Father was not a rich man and could not afford to keep Negro slaves, as some of the other people in Wilkes County did, and therefore the children had to help. Alexander was not always well, and not so strong as the other boys, but he did whatever father told him even so. Father did not make him do heavy work, but he had to fetch water, pick up chips at the woodpile, haul manure to the garden, walk barefooted behind the plow and drop corn seed into the furrow that it made, smelling the pleasant smell of damp red dirt turned up, feeling his feet sink into the coolness of the earth. Sometimes, after he was ten years old, he would even work the plow himself, though it was hard. And if there was nothing else to do he would take care of the babies. There were always new babies coming. When he was eleven and a little more, in July 1823, there was an- other baby for him to look at. They decided to name it

1 *J&B*, 23, 24, 35-7.

Linton. Linton would be his brother when he grew up, but
not a real *real* brother, only what father called a half-
brother, because they had the same father but different
mothers. Sometimes he wondered what it was that made
one man your father and one woman your mother.

When he was six he went to school for three months,
going two and a half miles through the woods to a clearing
called the Cross Roads. The teacher's name was Nathaniel
Day, and he was not so good as father. He drank whisky
as everybody else did except father. You could smell the
whisky on his breath sometimes when he came down the
schoolroom and looked at what you were doing. Father
never drank, he said it was a filthy habit. School was from
early in the morning until the middle of the afternoon,
with two hours out at noon for lunch, but since nobody
had a watch, not even Mr. Day, they would sometimes get
quite hungry before he would look at the shadows on the
grass and decide it was time to eat. In the schoolhouse you
sat on benches along the wall, with your feet on the bare
dirt, and when Mr. Day called on you to recite, you had to
stand up. Everybody studied out loud, spelling and cipher-
ing mostly. When you were learning the alphabet there
were five letters called vowels, and reciting them you had
to say: "A-bissel-fa, E-bissel-fe, I-bissel-fi, O-bissel-fo, U-bis-
sel-fu," which meant: "A byitself A," and so on. You had
to spell words out syllable by syllable, and it was easy to
make mistakes. But Alexander was a good speller and it was
fun to say: "I-m im m-a ma imma, t-e te immate, r-i ri im-
materi, a-l al immaterial, i immateriali, t-y ty immaterial-
ity." [2] At noontime, after lunch, girls and boys would play
games but not together. The boys would play townball or
bullpen or marbles, mumblepeg or leapfrog. Alexander
was not very good at games.

2 *J&B*, 24; Richard M. Johnston: "Early Education in Georgia," in *Report*
of the Commissioner of Education, 1894–5, House Doc. 5, pt. 2, 54th Cong.,
2nd sess., 1704–6.

Sometimes there was excitement in school, as the time when the older boys decided to turn out Mr. Day because he would not give a holiday at Whitsuntide. They were going to come very early, before him, and shut the door of the schoolhouse and wedge it tight with benches and keep him from getting in. But a few days before the turnout was to happen, Mr. Day scolded one of the older boys, Perkins. Perkins answered in a loud saucy voice, and Mr. Day ordered him up to his desk to be birched. Perkins walked up the aisle, but when he got near Mr. Day, instead of waiting for his whipping, he took the birch in one hand and Mr. Day's collar in the other. All the boys who knew about the turnout came running up, and they pushed Mr. Day down on the ground and held him there, while the other children screamed and cried because they thought Mr. Day was going to be killed. The big boys held the master down until he promised to let school out for several days. Then they had a boy go out for a gallon of whisky, which Mr. Day paid for. The little children were taken home.[3]

After Mr. Day there was no school for a while, except what Alexander could learn from father at home. In 1820, when he was eight, and for the next two years, he went with father to wherever he was teaching, and studied under him, learning how to read and write out of Murray's *English Reader* and Murray's *English Grammar,* learning how to cipher out of the *Federal Calculator,* learning geography out of Woodbridge's *Universal Geography.* He learned, among other things, that "diligence, industry, and proper improvement of time are material duties of the young," that Georgia was a state in a country called the United States of America, of which a man named James Monroe was the President, that the United States was bounded on the east by the Atlantic Ocean, on the north by Canada, on

3 *J&B*, 26–7.

the west by a line somewhere beyond the Mississippi River, and on the south by the Gulf of Mexico. Georgia was not so large after all . . . and yet it was large enough too.[4]

The boy Alexander could have learned too that there were in Georgia, in the year 1820, 340,989 people, whereas in 1790, twenty-two years before he had been born, there were only 82,000. He could have learned, had he been interested, that one of the reasons for the coming of this swarm of settlers out of the north was the invention of the cotton gin and the consequent facilitation of the production of upland cotton, a meager 1,000 bales in 1790 leaping to 40,000 in 1811. He could have learned, and perhaps did, that most of the people who lived in the region he knew had come down from Virginia, six hundred miles away; while those inhabiting the yet wilder and more sparsely settled lands in the hills to the northwest were emigrants out of the North Carolina mountain country. Between the two groups of settlers were many differences, in speech, in wealth, in breeding; and the advantage generally lay with the Virginians. He could have learned that what he lived in was called Middle Georgia; that the section so named ran in a wide belt in a southwesterly direction all the way across the state; that north of it were hills and then mountains; that south of it were dismal, endless stretches of dead and dying pine, growing out of a loose gray sand dotted with bunches of scraggly grasses; that south of the barrens, where almost nobody lived, was the seacoast country, warm and wet, thickly populated, and making its livelihood chiefly by trading and growing rice. Down there were the old aristocratic families, descendants of those who had crossed the ocean in the years before the Revolution; Savannah, the largest town in Georgia, was full of them. Up here, in the softly rolling country, fertile-soiled, not

---

4 He certainly used the *Calculator;* cf. *J&B,* 31; the other books were common in old-field schools.

damp, not rocky, was the real center of the state. To north
and south were extremes, here was moderation. Men who
could command this region could command the state. Scattered all through these counties, Wilkes, Oglethorpe,
Greene, Hancock, Warren, Columbia, were the farms of
industrious, if not wealthy, yeomen, owning their own land,
possessing few slaves, aspiring to the condition of the handful of rich men among them, the men of twenty thousand
acres and a hundred slaves. Already in 1820 there were
fourteen planters in Wilkes who owned between fifty and
ninety-nine Negroes. They were the squires, and their
Greek-revival houses stood monuments to their good taste
and conservative philosophies.[5]

The tone of middle Georgia society, though, was not determined by the nabobs—not, at least, while Alexander was
a boy growing up on his father's farm. This was quasi-
frontier, and its customs were not notable for elegance or
classicism. Nature was too close, and men needed all their
strength to cope with frost and drought and flood, to clear
the forests and to thrust their wretched turnpikes through
them, to get from one place to another and then stay there
in reasonable safety. Where sudden death was always hovering, life had to be large of gesture, expansive and careless, lest melancholy and perhaps even madness come. Men
drank by the gallon, wrestled and bit and gouged, were
handy with horse and gun. It was said, half-seriously, that
in one county, on the mornings after court days, when the
county seat was jammed with people from miles away, the
children would go around the square with plates, picking
up the eyes that had been gouged out. Force was admired
in this society, and so was craft. But piety and learning
were respected too, perhaps because so many lacked them.

5 Ralph B. Flanders: *Plantation Slavery in Georgia* (Chapel Hill, 1933),
66–70 et seq.; Adiel Sherwood: *A Gazetteer of the State of Georgia* (Athens,
1827, reprinted 1937), 18.

That was why Andrew Baskins Stephens, the schoolteacher, was so well thought of by his neighbors. In the midst of roughness he was quiet, even-tempered, sedate, and stern, a just man according to his lights, expecting prompt obedience from his children, wishing them to be "peaceable, friending and obliging, never fretting and finding faults of others to the neglect of their own, but by the faults of others correct their own." [6]

Standing by itself a few hundred feet up the field from Alexander's mother's grave was another stone, bearing the name Alexander Stephens, and the dates 17 March 1726 and 13 March 1813. Under this stone lay the bones of the boy Alexander's grandfather, his father's father, of whom Andrew Stephens probably had much to tell. Born in England, this Alexander Stephens, at twenty, was a Jacobite fighting with Prince Charles in his final battle at Culloden. Escaping the ferocious English pursuit that followed the defeat of Charles, he shipped for the colonies in the year 1746. His history in America is vague and shadowy; the first precise fact now known of him is that for some years he lived in Pennsylvania, among the Shawnee Indians, in a village near what today is Chambersburg, as far from white men as he could conveniently get. During the French and Indian War he enlisted in the colonial militia, was present at Braddock's defeat, and later served in an outpost garrison near Sunbury, Northumberland County, being discharged in April 1757.[7]

For another nine years there is no exact date in his life, as though between wars he would go into hibernation; but some time after his discharge he turned up in Rye town-

[6] Harry H. Hain: *History of Perry County, Pennsylvania* (Harrisburg, 1922), p. 617. The eye-gouging story is in George G. Smith: *The Story of Georgia and the Georgia People, 1732 to 1860* (Macon, 1900), 201.

[7] The dates of birth and death are on his tombstone. *J&B*, 17; Alexander H. Stephens: *Recollections of . . ., his diary kept when a prisoner at Fort Warren, Boston Harbour, 1865* (New York, 1910) (cited hereafter as *Recollections*), 3; Hain, op. cit., 616; *Pennsylvania Archives*, ser. V, i, 84.

ship in Cumberland County, at the junction of the Juniata and Susquehanna rivers. What he did for a living is unknown; all that is sure is that he made love there, and married. The owner of the ferry at this place was one James Baskins, who had a daughter, and her name was Catherine. While crossing the river on the ferry Alexander Stephens caught sight of the girl and fell in love with her. Perhaps he courted her like Othello, with tales of the strange things he had seen among the Indians; and perhaps, like Desdemona, she loved him for the dangers he had passed. However it was, the two soon wished to marry. Her father, however, like Brabantio, with the conservatism of respectability, failed to see in the forty-year-old adventurer what she did, and threatened to disinherit her if she persisted. Unintimidated, she did persist, and married Alexander Stephens in 1766. The couple settled five miles upstream, where they remained until after the Revolution. For a time the wanderer was domesticated to the axe and plow and house; and pretty thoroughly, for the family of two soon grew to one of ten.[8] Once there was a lapse, when Stephens enlisted in the Continental army and fought through the entire Revolution, coming out, it is said, with the rank of captain: as if the sound of bullets so pleased him that he could not resist their call. But at the close of the war he returned to the farm on the Juniata, where he remained for some years. Restlessness, apparently one of his root characteristics, soon overcame attachment, however; and at some time before 1792 Alexander Stephens took his family and set out for Georgia.[9]

[8] In 1781 Baskins owned 277 acres of land; cf. *Pennsylvania Archives*, ser. III, xx, 480. The pretty tale of courtship is in Hain, op. cit., 615.

[9] There is no evidence to prove Stephens' service in the Revolution, but all the biographers say so, and it may be true. The date of his removal to Georgia is vague, but must lie between 1790 and 1792; for Stephens' name does not appear in the *Heads of Families* of the 1790 census; and in 1792 his son Andrew was going to school in Georgia. Jessica C. Ferguson, of the Pennsylvania State Library, helped elucidate this point.

At first he stopped in Elbert County, on the edge of the state in the northeast; but soon he was at Kettle Creek, site of a bloody Revolutionary battle, about ten miles west of Washington, Wilkes County; and here, on rented land, he lived until 1805. Catherine died in 1794; not long after, two of his sons, James and Nehemiah, left him, one for Pennsylvania, the other for Tennessee. One by one four of his five daughters were married off, and the old man was left alone with a daughter and a son. That son was Andrew Baskins Stephens.

The boy had little of his father's temper. He remained most of his life quietly in one place instead of striding restlessly across half the world; he never fought a battle, not because he could not—he was, when young, a good wrestler —but because he would not. He was only thirty when the War of 1812 began, yet he took no gun. Blood held no magic for him. What he did like, even as a child, was farming and books. Whenever he could be spared he was sent to school; and by the time he was ten had made such progress that his father sent him to the academy at Washington. And when the people at the other end of the county wanted a school, and approached the Reverend Hope Hull, who kept the Washington academy, asking him to choose as a teacher that one of his pupils whom he thought best fitted for the work, he chose Andrew. This was in 1796: the boy was only fourteen.[10]

At the end of his first year of teaching he bought a hundred-acre tract just outside the future site of Crawfordville, paying part in cash and giving bond for the rest. He did not attempt to clear the land, but went on teaching, while his father, now seventy-one, lived out his age at Kettle Creek. Andrew was investing for the future.

In Wilkes County about this time there was living one

10 Louis B. Pendleton: *Alexander H. Stephens* (Philadelphia, 1907), 17; J&B, 19; *Cleveland*, 36.

Aaron Grier, member of a clan of Griers that had settled in Georgia in the 1760's, descendants of a Thomas Grier who had come to Pennsylvania from the north of Ireland. It was Aaron Grier's daughter Margaret whom Andrew Stephens married on July 12, 1806 and took to the land he had bought. How different from his father he was may be gauged by a circumstance of his courtship: on the 17th of May of the year he married he wrote Grier a letter asking his sanction of the union, enclosing a sketch of his history and antecedents, concluding: "The use of this written communication does not wholly originate in pusilanimity or in other sources that may be deemed timid, but in the intention to afford you requisite intelligence; and thereby to furnish you matter sufficient for absolute conclusion." He evidently believed in laying his whole hand on the table.[11]

Margaret bore him three children, Mary, Aaron, and Alexander. It is said that she was a mild, gentle, intelligent woman, but not very strong. Her delicacy of health was her most apparent legacy to her youngest son, who was born at about one in the morning of February 11, 1812.[12] Within a month she died, having been married not much more than seven years. Three young children could not without harm be left for long without a woman to take care of them. Andrew Stephens waited until 1814; then he married Matilda Lindsay, the daughter of a Revolutionary soldier, Colonel John Lindsay. This woman seemed not to have impressed the boy in any great degree: at least he rarely afterward spoke of her. He was eminently his father's son.

Coming of leaves and blossoms, long warm summers,

11 *J&B*, 19; Hain, op. cit., 616, quotes the prudent letter.
12 Alexander H. Stephens MSS., Manhattanville College of the Sacred Heart, New York (cited hereafter as *MC*), February 9, 1853. In citations from this source, if the date only is given, the letter is one written by Alexander to Linton Stephens.

months of deep blue, and green, and brick-red earth and
locusts singing, months of the falling of leaves and cornshucking days, months of frozen creeks and icicles hanging
from roof-edges and thin powdered snow sifting on wheeltracks and woodpiles, year followed year in a linked pattern. The boy was ten, then he was eleven, then twelve.
Then something happened one sleepy Sunday morning in
the summer of 1824. He was dressed up in his best woolsey
jacket and long trousers, given a wool hat to wear, and a
Bible in his hands, and his father took him to Sunday school
at Powder Creek meetinghouse. Here were about thirty
boys, divided into several classes. Alexander was assigned
to the class studying Genesis, but before the others had got
past that book he had finished the whole Old Testament.
He had never read so much in his life, and suddenly discovered that he liked to read. A boy who would read the
Old Testament because he wanted to, without prodding,
was a rare specimen in that region, and he set people talking. It was an important day for him, that Sunday. Until
then there had been movement but no direction; he had
merely been growing; but now there was something to do,
something with a purpose and an end. Under his father's
steady hand he might become a teacher—some such idea
may, indeed, have been at the back of the parental mind.

The steady hand, though, was not on him long. Two
years, and the boy was fourteen. A Saturday in May 1826,
he out plowing in the "new ground," a ten-acre field not
far from the house. Down in the house Andrew Baskins
Stephens lay in bed, sick with pneumonia. No sound here
but the plow whispering through the soil, the cries of occasional birds; then the pound of running feet, and he was
told to come back to the house. Leaving the plow stuck
where it was, he went, trying not to think of what he probably feared was waiting. Day before yesterday Andrew Stephens had made his will; yesterday he had called the boy

to him and talked for several hours, explaining that he was about to die and telling his son what he expected of him. Today, as Alexander went out of the bright day into the half-dark of the house, his father was talking again, lying in bed and talking; but after listening a moment the boy went cold with terror. The quiet, steady mind was stumbling in a fog of memory, could no longer tell the unreal from the real, or past from present, did not recognize persons or places, did not even recognize the frightened boy, to whom the fact of death was still incomprehensible, standing by the bed waiting to be seen and spoken to. If there had been hope that he would recover, there was none now. He had been certain himself it was his end. In another room his second wife, the boy's stepmother, lay ill with the same disease. The long day passed, laboriously climbed to noon, hung there, it seemed, for hours in a blaze of blank hot light, and then descended into shadow, twilight, night. Hours of darkness and shaded candlelight, hours of stirring grayness and the first faint notes of birds. Delirium had faded, giving way to stupor, loud breathing, closed eyes, unconsciousness. And the boy still waited in agony for the eyes to open and fall on him with recognition. But the eyes were shut; the breathing lessened, lessened; and in the morning ceased.

For some moments the event was too vast for understanding. To the boy his father had been for fourteen years his universe; and now the world had died. He turned from the bed and went out of the house into the fields, walking dumbly, anywhere, until he could no longer walk. There he fell upon the grass and buried his face in the wet grass and clutched rough bending grass in his hands and cried; while at a little distance another boy, a friend, stood silently watching him, not knowing quite what to do, having never seen his friend like this before. To the end of his life the boy would remember that 7th of May as the bitterest day he was ever to endure. "When I saw him breathe his last," he wrote, "it came near killing me. It seemed as if I *could* not live. . . . He was the object of my love, my admiration, my reverence. . . . His whole life, from the time of my earliest recollection, was engraven upon my memory. . . ." [13]

Andrew Stephens was buried beside his first wife. A stone was erected upon his grave, the inscription on which, in many respects, could have stood for the whole family:

HE WAS DISTINGUISHED AMONGST
HIS NEIGHBORS FOR MANY
QUALITIES OF THE HAND AND HEART
BUT FOR NONE MORE THAN FOR
PROBITY TRUTH HONOR AND
INCORRUPTIBLE INTEGRITY [14]

One week after his death the stepmother followed. The boy would willingly have made a third.

II

Near Raytown in Warren County lived a brother of Margaret Grier named Aaron, who had distinguished himself in the Indian fighting in Alabama during the War of 1812, and had come out a colonel. When, upon the double death, Andrew Stephens' children were scattered, those by Matilda Lindsay were sent to her relatives; while those by Margaret Grier, Aaron Grier Stephens and Alexander, were taken in by the ex-soldier. He offered Alexander a home without board, and this generosity was fortunate, because, when the Stephens property was sold for distribution, each of the children received but $444, and the eight

---

13 *J&B*, 22, 39–40.
14 The stone still stands in a grove of old oaks some yards to the right on the Sandycross road about two miles north of Crawfordville. Andrew B. sleeps between his two wives. Can the inscription have been composed by the boy Alexander?

per cent interest from Alexander's share barely paid for his tuition and clothing.

For five months or so in 1826 he and his brother attended a Catholic school, at a place called Locust Grove, kept by an Irishman named O'Cavanaugh. On the first Friday that Alexander went to school, spelling exercises were going on. The names of countries were being considered, and O'Cavanaugh, coming to Alexander, gave him the word "Arabia" to spell. But since he spoke with a thick brogue, what he said was "*Ah*-rabia," a noise that to the boy meant nothing. He answered: "I can't spell it, sir."

Flaring up, the teacher yelled: "You confounded little rascal! You tell me you can't spell the word? Spell it, sir—" grabbing a birch and waving it over his head—"*Ah*-rabia!"

The boy had stood up and moved to the door, looking down at the ground; but when O'Cavanaugh began brandishing his birch, the shame he had felt at missing a word was dissipated, and in its place came a "bold defiance"—which is to say, an answering flare of temper. "I had made up my mind," he wrote long afterward, "after my father's death, never to let any man lay violent hands on me with impunity." And so, raising his black eyes and looking the infuriated teacher full in the face, the slight, pale boy answered:

"Mr. O'Cavanaugh, I did not understand you, and I don't understand you now. I can spell every word in the lesson if it is pronounced as I pronounce it. But I thought it better to tell you that I could not spell the word as you gave it out than to say I did not understand you. It was bad enough for me to miss the word as I did; but, sir, you shall not speak to me in that way."

For a moment, with the rest of the school breathlessly looking on, the two stood motionless, while over O'Cavanaugh's face came a slow expression of amazement. The boy, watching him, thought he would lunge out with the birch as soon as he comprehended how he had been bearded, in which case he was ready to "let him have one of the stones lying at the doorsill." But, no doubt with a considerable effort, the teacher controlled himself and went on with the lesson. The boy's nerve probably impressed him, for he afterward made it a point to be attentive and pleasant to him; and for his part, Alexander "really got to like him very much" [15] —perhaps because O'Cavanaugh had been the first adult against whose authority he had been able to rebel, and not only rebel but conquer. "This was another epoch in my life," he thought in retrospect. "It was the first time I had ever faced a man as his equal." His father was dead; and in a subconscious and symbolic sense this episode was his triumphal dance of release. He, all his life, would have been trigger-swift in denying it; yet unconsciously he was forever trying to free himself of the hand which had been on him with a governing pressure during his formative years, and which went on clutching at him out of the grave long after the hand of flesh had rotted to grass. His conscious veneration of his father's memory was merely confirmation of a subterranean conflict.

While he was going to school at Locust Grove, in the autumn of 1826, one Williams, a Presbyterian minister, came to Raytown to establish a Sunday school. He called upon Alexander's aunt Betsey, she being a member of the sect, and the boy soon came to know him. When the Sunday school project was broached, Alexander was interested, took Williams around the neighborhood to meet the people, and, when the school was opened, entered as a scholar, becoming quickly, by reason of his proficiency, a teacher. The superintendent of the school, Charles C. Mills, took notice, as did Williams, of this sober, quiet, rather delicate boy, pious and a little inclined to melancholy

15 *J&B,* 44.

brooding. Such a boy would make an ideal minister; and in these terms Mills began to think of him, though the boy himself had no such notion, supposing that he would study to become a "merchant's clerk," and later on pursue his other talents if he could make enough money to afford it. It was by now obvious, if it had not been so for years, that he was incapable of hard manual labor. Desk work of some sort was the only alternative. His slender, tall figure and striking face would probably have looked well in a pulpit. For the moment, though, he went on going to Locust Grove, declining his uncle's offer to give him pay and hire him as a farmhand if he would abandon his education.

At the end of the spring term in 1827 he left the school, intending, if he could, to get a clerk's job, perhaps in Crawfordville. It was a hard decision: with the pessimism that was to be habitual for forty years he imagined at once it was "the last day I should ever go to school." [16] For a few days he stayed at home, doing nothing, thinking the best part of his life was gone, and the most he had to expect was some dull pen-pushing, with, if God was good, the chance to read a little, go to school a little—but by driblets at the most.

Mr. Charles C. Mills, however, was thinking otherwise. In the Sunday school he was keeping a quiet eye upon the boy as he taught his classes; and on the Sunday following the closing of Locust Grove he asked Alexander how his studying was coming on. The boy said he had quit: the term was over and it was to be, he had decided, his last. Mills expressed surprise and wanted to know what he was going to do. He spoke of his idea of becoming a clerk. Mills shook his head, clucked his teeth, and inquired whether Alexander would like to go to the academy in Washington and study Latin. He would like it well enough

16 Ibid., 43, 46.

if he had the money, he replied: but he had none. Thereupon Mills offered to send him himself.

To this the boy had no immediate answer. He said he
would first have to consult his uncle and aunt, which he
did; and, the former leaving him pretty much to his own
inclination while the latter strenuously urged him to accept, he accepted. On July 28, 1827 he and Mills got into
a buggy and drove the fifteen-odd miles north to Washington, the county seat of Wilkes and the center of fashionable
society for the surrounding region. It was a larger town
than when Andrew Stephens had lived in it and studied,
thirty years before; and it was more important. Save for
the relatively higher economic status of its inhabitants, it
was a typical middle Georgia village of about a thousand
people, sprawled athwart the Athens turnpike, with a courthouse, a jail, a branch of the state bank, two churches, and
an academy. Its private dwellings were then, as now, its
boast,[17] being somewhat closer to the romantic idea of
antebellum Southern houses than those of most other
towns. All in all it was the right place for a talented boy.

The academy was presided over by a young man named
Alexander Hamilton Webster, a Presbyterian divine who
was also minister of the Presbyterian church. Mills knew
Webster, and it was to the door of the preacher-teacher's
home that he and the boy drove that 28th of July. It had
been arranged for Alexander to board with Webster. "So
this," remarked the pedagogue when Alexander was presented to him, "is the little boy I have heard Mr. Williams
speak about so much." The remark carried implications
which the little boy very likely failed to grasp, but which
were quickly to become palpable.

Between Webster and the boy a warm attachment sprang
up within a few weeks, while the sultry days were spent

17 Ibid., 48; Sherwood, op. cit., 111–12.

in memorizing Latin declensions and conjugations. On August 18 Alexander was moved from a grammar class into a reading class, where he began studying *Historiæ Sacræ*. And then one day Webster took him aside and told him a story. It had not, he said, been Mr. Mills' idea that he should come to Washington to study at the academy, but really his, Webster's, own. And why? Because he had heard much from various people of Alexander's studiousness and good character, and had been led to believe he would make a fine clergyman. Having wished to test his impression at close range, he had arranged for Alexander to come and live with him. Now, after three weeks, he had seen and he was satisfied. He would undertake to prepare Alexander for college; and as for money, there was an organization called the Georgia Educational Society, which made a specialty of affording the means of education to boys whom it thought fit for the ministry.

This was an entirely new view, and the boy was embarrassed by it. "From very early in life I was strongly impressed with religious feelings; and after the death of my father this subject took deep hold of me. During the summer of 1827 I made profession of faith . . . but whether I should be fit to preach, or should feel it my duty to do so, when I grew up, I could not know." [18] It was not a question to be lightly taken. The world was pressing him to tell it what he wanted, and he was hesitant.

Until the end of September, while he continued to study, the subject was laid aside; but when he returned home he took Webster with him. Aunt Betsey upon being consulted doubtless urged him to accept the offer. The result, however, was a kind of compromise: he was to go on to college under the sponsorship of the Educational Society, and if, after graduation, he should decide against the ministry,

[18] *J&B*, 48–50.

such a decision would not be regarded as bad faith on his part. As for the money which would be advanced, that he would under any circumstances repay, especially if he were to decline the cloth.

So he went back to study with Webster, for whom his fondness was by now prodigious, so much so that, moved somehow to express it, and noticing upon a Latin grammar he had borrowed the owner's full name written out—Alexander Hamilton Webster—he determined to adopt as much of his benefactor's name as he could, and from this time signed himself Alexander Hamilton Stephens. But there was little time for gratitude. Just after his return, Webster was taken ill with "a malignant autumn fever," and died in October at the age of twenty-six.[19] If the boy experienced, as he probably did, another attack of overwhelming despair, there was reason enough: not only had a new and kindly friend died, but it might be that his future would be considerably altered by the event, possibly to the point where he would have to stop studying and go to work. He packed and prepared to go home to Raytown and his uncle.

Others, however, besides Webster were interested in him, among them an Adam L. Alexander, who had been one of the dead teacher's best friends, and who now came and told the boy that he knew of all that had been planned for him, and pledged himself to see the plans fulfilled. Several other gentlemen of the town, all members of the Presbyterian church, said the same. The world, it seemed, would not easily let him go: each time he supposed he was drowning at last, the fingers grasping his hair renewed their clutch. After a little hesitation, he decided to go on. From October 1827 to June 1828 he boarded, first with Alexan-

19 Webster's age was furnished by Dr. Robert G. Stephens, Washington, Ga.

der, then with one after another of the men who had under-
taken to patronize him. Less than a year after he had walked
into Webster's house he was adjudged ready for college.

On a brief visit to his uncle's in April 1828 he was fitted
out for the journey to Athens. John A. Campbell, one of
his sponsors, was to have taken him up, but he having died
toward the end of July, the son of another sponsor, Andrew
G. Semmes, accompanied him. Together they made the
trip, traveling by stage and arriving on August 1, at five in
the afternoon. For the first few days Alexander did nothing but acclimate himself, walking the streets of the little
hilltop town, and making himself at home in the house
of Professor Alonzo Church, where for the time being he
was to board. Saturday the 2nd was the date for the entrance examinations; and, writing home afterward, he casually noted: "After all my pains in reviewing at home, I
was not examined on a single thing I had reviewed, but as
good luck would have it I missed none, and was admitted
to the Freshman class."

There was a little more to it than that. The examinations
were to be held in the college chapel at ten in the morning. Alexander, not knowing he had the privilege of being
privately examined, nor thinking to question anyone about
it, took his Virgil and Greek Testament and went, his
knowledge of Virgil good, of the Testament fair, of Cicero
rather sketchy. In the chapel a large group of boys had
already assembled by the time he arrived; he sat down at
the foot of the class, "feeling foolish enough, and looking,
I suspect, just as foolish as I felt." Presently Dr. Moses
Waddell, the president of Franklin College, entered, accompanied by Professor Church, who, Alexander thought,
looked a trifle surprised at seeing him. The examination
commenced—with Cicero. "Despair seized me. I thought
I was ruined. I should be rejected!" Borrowing a Cicero
from another boy, he leafed hastily through it, but gave

up, more despairing than ever. He thought of walking out, but "that would never do," and he concluded to stand his ground and see what would happen. Upon being called to recite he would frankly admit he had read only the four orations against Catiline and had reviewed none of them.

While he sweated under this agony the examination moved on. The orations against Catiline were reached and three gone over before it came his turn. He was growing wilder with every line recited, and with reason, for if he were called on to give what he did not know, he might well be rejected. The clerk's stool was very close.

"Next," said Dr. Waddell in a deep guttural voice. Next was Alexander, who stood up. "On the next page," the doctor went on. "Beginning with the words *video duas adhuc*."

This to Alexander always seemed like a divine intervention. Of all the Cicero he had read, this passage, dealing with the problem of capital punishment, had stuck with him best. He had been deeply interested in the views expressed, and so "perfectly understood every word of the paragraph." He read without hesitation. Everybody looked. Waddell pushed up his spectacles to see who the clever boy was. Though he probably recognized him, he showed no cognizance, but said merely: "Parse *vita*," and when the boy had done this clearly and quickly: "Parse *punctum*." At the end he muttered something about Alexander's having read very well, and passed on.[20]

That afternoon, at the second half of the examination, Alexander was again fortunate in having to recite a verse of the Greek Testament that he also remembered perfectly. And that was all. In the evening, at dinner, Professor Church smilingly asked whether he had been scared. "I said yes, and told him just how the matter stood with me . . . but, to the best of my remembrance . . . I did not tell him that I happened to get the only passage in the

[20] *J&B*, 52, 55–6; *Recollections*, 9.

book that I could read in that style": concealing his good luck out of the prudent thought that if he told the whole truth the bright edge might be taken off his reputation.

When he came to Athens, Franklin College—as the University of Georgia was then known—founded in 1801, was twenty-six years old. Its first building was erected in 1802, its first class graduated in 1804. After prospering for a few years, it began to flicker out and was on the point of extinction when Moses Waddell became its president.[21] By any standard he was a character. Born in North Carolina, he moved to Greene County in Georgia in 1788, where he taught school and went through a terrifying religious conversion, being at one time so full of loathing for his own sinfulness that he considered himself "undeserving of the smallest natural comfort," and refused to drink water even when painfully thirsty. After his conversion he studied theology, and for some years preached at various churches in South Carolina, where he also taught. Among his pupils there were John C. Calhoun, whose sister he married, and William H. Crawford. Until 1818 he remained in South Carolina, returning to Georgia just before being elected president of Franklin College. Here he remained until 1829, and his reign was memorable for all who attended. He was an impressive man, a little corpulent, with an inordinately large head, a mop of dark hair, and bushy eyebrows, very pious and very strict, but much loved all the same. His students called him "Old Pewt" and not infrequently serenaded him late at night, but they were sorry when he left, turning the presidency over to Professor Church.

The college, when Alexander entered it, consisted of a number of buildings scattered over the slope of a hill along the bottom of which the Oconee wandered southward. There were two large brick buildings, known as the

21 Ellis M. Coulter: *College Life in the Old South* (New York, 1928), 32.

Old and New Colleges; there was another brick building
for the chemical and "philosophical" apparatus; there was
a chapel, a steward's hall or refectory, and a library hous-
ing about two thousand volumes. The town of Athens had
grown from a gristmill in a wilderness to a pleasant village
spread out on the hill, equipped with a reasonable number
of the conveniences of civilization, including a Society for
the Improvement of Sacred Music, a Vocal Music School,
and several "elegant" hotels. Its women refused to go anywhere on foot; its preachers were models of gentility, for
they said: "On thy stomach shalt thou go," instead of "On
thy belly." [22]

The college faculty consisted of seven members—the
president, a professor of mathematics and astronomy, a
professor of chemistry and mineralogy, a professor of
rhetoric and moral philosophy, a professor of natural
philosophy and botany, and two tutors. And here, in this
college and town, Alexander Stephens spent, as he afterward insisted, the happiest years of his life.

It was not a bad life, though strictly regulated. Freshman
and sophomores were required to attend three classes daily,
one of which met before breakfast; juniors and seniors had
but two. Examinations were held at the close of the first
and second quarters, with a comprehensive examination at
the end of the year. Seniors before graduating had to pass
an examination covering anything they might have learned
during their four years.

The student's life was closely ruled. After breakfast the
boys were supposed to study until noon and then have dinner. More studying followed until five o'clock; then came
chapel and supper and still more studying from seven to
nine thirty, which was bedtime. Breakfast was coffee or
tea, corn and wheat bread, butter, bacon and beef. Dinner was corn bread, bacon, vegetables, lamb, shoat, or

[22] Sherwood, op. cit., 24; Coulter, op. cit., 270f.

poultry. Soup was supposed to be served at least twice a week. Tuition was eight dollars a quarter, rooms one dollar.

By this pattern Alexander lived from 1828 until 1832. In studies he was consistently at the head of his class, but he was no bookworm. He was liked, and liked by more people than ever before in his life—by all sorts of people, boys his own age and older, boys with tempers similar to his own, and boys as far from him as Patagonia. Years later the recollection of his popularity in college aroused in him a kind of pride. "The most dissipated young men in college would come to my room, and there meet the most ascetically pious" [23]—a conjunction which fifty years later was to have its analogue at his funeral. Somehow he drew people to him, and in his presence they forgot their mutual dislikes. There was more good humor in his room than anywhere else in college. But no cards, no whisky, no dirty jokes. Though in afterlife he partook of all three in moderation, just now he was too deeply under a quasi-religious spell to tolerate them. Refreshment was therefore limited to fruits in season, spiced with conversation. And because he was the most highly regarded student in the college, and the most trusted, no faculty member ever came to investigate when loud laughter sounded in his room—an unusual immunity, for amusement at Franklin College was circumscribed by laws. No swearing, no fighting, no billiards, no cards, no blasphemy, no forgery, no fornication, no stealing, no dueling, no associating with "vile, idle or dissolute persons"—not even fiddling or flute-playing on Sundays or during study hours. These injunctions were enforced by professors patrolling the dormitory halls "at frequent and irregular intervals"; but sometimes the strain became too great, as when during Alexander's senior year the boys broke out at half past ten one night, smashed

23 *J&B*, 56–7.

every window and door in sight, and ended by tearing down the chapel steps.

But one could spend one's time more quietly, for instance in debating. This was an extremely popular sport all over the United States; at Franklin College there were two societies, the Phi Kappa, to which Alexander belonged, and the Demosthenian, which would meet and jointly declaim upon a vast variety of subjects, such as immortality, carrying the mails on Sunday, women (in general), novel-reading, whether a man must marry the girl he has seduced, prohibition, which they eschewed, and slavery, which they supported. Or if you did not always care to debate, you could join the state militia and go parading up and down the campus in white trousers, blue coats, and high caps, the envy of every small boy in town; or you could go strolling through the fashionable quarters from sundown to nine o'clock, serenading the girls.[24]

Alexander's poor health and his integrity kept him out of the militia and the rowdyism, and perhaps out of the serenading too. He read and thought and made his friends and kept thinking about the decision he would finally have to make. Long ago, before he had even taken his entrance examinations, he had gone to Dr. Waddell and explained to him the terms upon which he had been sent to college, and exactly what he himself felt about the scheme, making it as clear as possible that he did not honestly know whether he would want to go on to seminary. Waddell had then assured him that none of this made any difference, either to him or to the society that was furnishing the money. Now in 1830 he found himself unable to go on without definitely choosing. He wrote to his uncle, saying he would announce his decision not to study for the ministry, and would, in accordance with his pledge to Mills in 1827, repay the society whatever he had thus far cost it. Since he was still

---

[24] These details of college life are recorded in Coulter, op. cit.

under age, Aaron Grier had custody of his money, and
his consent was required before the society could be notified. The uncle readily agreed; and with what was left of
his $444, and a little he borrowed from his brother, Alexan-
der paid principal and interest. From then on he lived independently, which was what he really wanted.

The four years passed with the briefness of all happy
years; and as the time came on for study, talk, and laughter
to cease and the habits he had learned and the friendships
he had formed to be canceled, his melancholy deepened.
Walking about the campus those last few weeks, remembering the time old man Hopkins—who taught rhetoric
and moral philosophy, and wore a long white queue—was
hearing a class recite *Blair's Lectures,* and some bright boys
outside squeezed the door open a crack and shoved in a
mangy little pig, whose tail they had decorated so that it
looked like Hopkins' queue, and the pig went snuffing
and grunting around the room, every once in a while shaking its queue, while Hopkins stood there patiently waiting
for the roars to subside—or tutor Shannon, a wild Irishman who hated whistling with all his soul, and the time a
boy came innocently down the hall outside the lecture
room, whistling as loud as he could, and Shannon grabbed
a book and raced to the door, but was foiled by the boy's
too quick legs, only to be again thrown into a boiling rage
a few minutes later when the boy came back and bleated
like a goat and then locked the door of the room from the
outside, leaving poor Shannon foaming from within—or
the year everybody in college cultivated the growth of a
mustache—or the long conversations on sunny afternoons,
ranging as far as fancy willed—the vacations and the saying good-by for a few months, and the return—walking
the campus or the streets of the town, he was troubled and
sad. He had made arrangements to begin teaching and
was therefore not wholly rootless in the world, but the fu-

ture, "uncertain and impenetrable," perpetually goaded him. He would have to leave the pleasant gardens of the mind and "become dependent on my own exertions for success in a selfish world." The halcyon days were over; and for the first time his poverty appalled him. In school it had not mattered; no one had noticed, for merit ruled and he was meritorious; but where he was going now merit did not always rule. And he was doubtful of himself —though there was no particular reason to be. He graduated first in his class on August 1, 1832. The following day he left for Madison, where he was to teach, allowing himself no pause in which to let go, miserable because he had a future but could not know what it would be. There was an energy in him, restless, seeking release, an energy of ambition, at the moment baffled and confined, eating and burrowing and refusing to let him live a little life in peace.

III

While Alexander Stephens was growing up on the farm near Crawfordville, and studying at Franklin College, there were, not far away, growlings and grumblings in the land which he need not have put his ear to the ground to hear, because they were loud and unmistakable. The Union was not getting on well. This was not new: it had rarely got on well as a Union since it was made. Somebody was forever quarreling with someone else. It was an enormous country, and afforded even men of intelligence like Calhoun many opportunities for confusing particular with general welfare, not to mention the hosts of small-minded politicians who could not see beyond their county's, state's, or section's boundaries. With so many interests to please, with such a rapidly augmenting divergence in social and economic structures north and south and west, it was no wonder that the general government often ran afoul of states and sections, especially since the Constitution as written left the problem of the precise nature and limits of the powers of the government just ambiguous enough to give, until those powers were at length defined in blood, any state or section a weapon with which to terrorize the Union. The Virginia and Kentucky Resolutions of 1798, the behavior of Massachusetts between 1804 and 1814, the language employed during the debates on the admission of Missouri in 1819–21, all couched in terms like "disunion" and "civil war," and expressive of an acute sensitivity to the "unconstitutional" and "oppressive" encroachments, real or fancied, of the Federal government upon the states, were merely instances of a deeply rooted maladjustment. And the maladjustment in the course of time became rationalized into a theory of the nature of the American government and the relations between the states and the general authority. The theory had as its conscious and ostensible purpose the securing of the right of local government, but in its application was more often turned into a doctrine of social anarchy and blind particularism.

Like a cocked pistol in the center of the table the theory lay during the antebellum years; whoever wished could pick it up and present it to his colleagues' heads. Geography did not determine its use. With profound sincerity most of the time, with poisonous motives some of the time, there were everywhere in the Union men who held it to be purely an expedient arrangement, susceptible of dissolution whenever expediency so argued. And when such men were at the heads of state governments, or powerful in state affairs, the theory was invoked, the pistol grasped. Georgia, by 1832, had a long record of disputation and threat.

Her character was reflected in that of her governors, who were picturesque creations. There was James Jackson, who once bit off a man's finger in a rough-and-tumble fight; there was John Clarke, a hard-drinking North Carolinian who mutilated—how is not reported—a portrait of Washington hanging on a post in front of a tavern, and one day cowhided an old man in the street in cold sobriety; there was George Mathews, who wore a three-cornered hat all his life and spelled *coffee* "Kaughphy," and *revenge* "ravange"; and there was George M. Troup, a man of terrible temper, under whose administration the state came into heated collision with the Federal government over the Indian problem. The government had supposedly taken over the duty of extinguishing the Indian title to public lands within the state, but had not solved it as quickly as land-hungry Georgians desired: and when by a series of misunderstandings two treaties with the Creeks were made, one evicting them on September 1, 1826, the other leaving them in possession until January 1, 1827, Troup, who had sent surveyors into the Indian territory before the land had actually passed into the hands of the state, stuck by the first treaty and ordered the surveyors to proceed. When the Federal government, which had negotiated the treaties, protested, Troup announced that Georgia was "sovereign on her own soil," and served a practical declaration of war on President Adams. Luckily the affair went no further than that.[25] The Creeks surrendered and moved out. But Troup was in deadly earnest in saying that he would resist with all his power any Federal act designed to force his state to do what it did not freely want to do.

Some time later, while Alexander was at college, another such affair occurred, this time in South Carolina, which, feeling itself touched by the tariff of 1828 in that tenderest spot, the pocketbook, took up the pistol and told the Union: "Do as I say or die." And, Andrew Jackson not-

---

[25] Lucian L. Knight: *Georgia's Landmarks, Memorials and Legends* (Atlanta, 1913–14), II, 14–16, 139; J. E. D. Shipp: *Giant Days, or, The Life and Times of William H. Crawford* (Americus, Ga., 1909), 75; and George R. Gilmer: *Sketches of Some of the First Settlers of Upper Georgia* (New York, 1855), 62–5, contain these tidbits.

withstanding, the Union did. As South Carolina went through the motions of nullification, the rest of the South stood by, sympathetic and curious, but with no burning desire to join her. Georgia liked the tariff as little as South Carolina did, but was reluctant to apply so radical a remedy for such a disease. Fellow-feeling, however, was strong. At Franklin College the students proposed to the trustees in 1828 that every college man should wear a frock coat of gray homespun and trousers to match; and harried the board until the proposal was made into a regulation. And in 1832 on commencement day, when the exercises were over, a placard was posted inviting "the friends of Gen. Jackson and those opposed to the Protective system and opposed to a redress of Tariff grievances by Nullification" to meet in the chapel the following day. This was the opposite of fellow-feeling; but when the meeting assembled the nullifiers burst in, took charge, and called for a convention to meet at Milledgeville, the state capital, in November; and that convention when it met denounced the tariff and advocated resistance to its enforcement.[26]

What Alexander Stephens thought about all this nobody knows. In a letter written to his brother upon his arrival at Athens in 1828 he says merely: "The Tariff is carried to a high degree here. It is sufficient for me to say that some of the people are so incensed . . . that they wear their broadcloth every day and their homespun Sunday. . . ."[27] Possibly he paid the subject but little attention. That was not important. The important thing for him was that while he was still young and sensitive to outward influences the air about him was filled with talk about the nature of the government under which the American people—or were they indeed one people?—lived; and the

26 Ulrich B. Phillips: *Georgia and State Rights* (Washington, 1902) (cited hereafter as *Phillips*), 129–30.
27 *Recollections*, 9.

fact that where he was, conservative ideas prevailed may have had much to do with the character of the attitudes he was in later years to hold. Till now he had lived almost exclusively among conservative people, propertied, sober people whose sobriety suited well with his own temperament. Had one of them, at that commencement in 1832, been gifted with second sight, he would have glimpsed in the frail, pallid young man, darkly clothed, earnest of mien, with the face of a child and the spirit of a suffering old man, one of their advocates-to-be, for whom the rights under law which they venerated would be the firmest principle of political faith, and who would not even in the midst of ruinous civil war abandon their defense.

CHAPTER TWO

Apprenticeship (1832–43)

IN August of 1832 early risers in Madison, a pleasant coun·
try town of about a thousand people, twenty-seven miles
below Athens, could have seen a slender, pale young man
walking past the closed shop fronts toward the Athens
road at sunrise. He would walk a mile, perhaps two, along
that road, and then turn back. There probably was not
much traffic on the road, except on market mornings, but
the occasional farmers passing by might sometimes have
turned and looked back at him from their wagon seats, and
if they had sharp eyes they would have seen him crying. In
the cool morning air, with a long grotesque shadow to
ape his gestures, he would walk at the side of the red road,
along pastures and woodland and open fields, crying and
talking to himself.[1]

It was the effect of the impersonal world, which hurt
because it was impersonal. Till now he had moved always
with guides, if not one, then another, with people whose
interest in him was genuine. But here were a thousand
people who knew nothing of him and cared perhaps less.
Had he been large and beefy and substantial it might not
have mattered; but he was slight and sick and frightened.

There was an academy in Madison; and had anyone
recognized the miserable young man at dawn on the Athens
road it would have been as Mr. Stephens, the assistant to

1 A.H.S. to R. M. Johnston, in *J&B*, 67.

Leander A. Lewis, who had charge of the academy. The two men boarded together in a little office annex to the house of a lawyer named Wittich; and "in that little office," said the assistant, "I spent some most miserable days." Why? He tried to guess the reasons, supposing that maybe, like a newborn child, he had been translated from a warm, comfortable world into one that was rough, jostling, and indifferent. "The whole world and everything I came into contact with gave me pain." This was plausible, but his other guess was probably as good: he was learning the meaning of money. If he had had money he would not be here.

Teaching did not fret him. Though he was never enthusiastic about it as a profession, he took it as it came and buried himself in it so that he could regain his self-control. The Madison academy was similar to the others he had seen: there were about fifty students, of both sexes and various ages, in all possible stages of academic advancement, some studying Greek and some the alphabet. He and Lewis divided them and taught all together in one room, enduring the usual pandemonium attendant upon such arrangements from eight in the morning until half past five or six at night, with two hours out at noon. Under the circumstances it was a dispiriting existence for one who vaguely felt he had been born for better things. He bore it for four months. It was a strain on his nerves as well as on his patience, for the older pupils were at first disinclined to submit to the authority of so youthful and fragile a teacher, an attitude for which Lewis, by his lax administration, had well prepared the ground. On the first day the new teacher stood up before his class and announced that he expected his students to obey his discipline, laying down a few elementary rules of conduct. The older boys promptly challenged him, thinking he would not have the courage to carry out his program. But he did, and after that there was little insubordination.[2]

The efficiency he displayed caused the trustees of the school to wish to retain him after November, but he would not stay. He made arrangements with the father of William Le Conte, a boy with whom he had roomed in college, to teach in the former's private school in Liberty County the following year. And besides his impatience with the place and the attacks of severe headache which were coming with greater and greater frequency, there was another cause impelling him to leave Madison. He had fallen in love with one of his pupils. Who she was, what she thought, what she looked like, what he did, nobody knows. Apparently he did nothing. It was probably his first love. He was shy; he was poor; he had no future; he was chronically sick; and he kept silent. And on a night at the end of November he was called for in a buggy by his brother Aaron and driven home to Raytown, traveling all night over terrible roads, the buggy shaking, the springs squeaking, he and his brother always watching lest the horse make a misstep and ditch them miles from nowhere. He had a violent headache. . . .

The year that followed was uneventful and quiet, perhaps the quietest he ever spent. Immediately after quitting the school at Madison he went down into Liberty County, where he lived with Dr. Louis Le Conte, tutoring his children and those of a few neighbors, about thirteen in all. It was the fartherest he had yet been from home, and it was a different country, seacoast, low and level, damp and marshy. There were few people, few towns; and the pace of life was doubtless slower than any he had known, for the region lay out of the great lines of trade and traffic. The ruins of deserted villages, scattered here and there along the sea, attested to this stagnation. The atmosphere was cal-

2 Ibid., 68–9.

culated to soothe; so was the company. Such a year of re-laxation must have done Stephens good, though nothing, it seemed, could cure his periodic ill health. The Le Contes were people of cultivation, and the level of discourse in their circle was as high as that he had listened to in Washington, if not higher. What was more, he could now take part in it as an equal, and the stimulation did him good. The children were gentle and well-bred, Le Conte's two sons John and Joseph being the most promising, Joseph becoming eventually a noted geologist and John a professor of physics at the University of California.

In summer, when the dangers of malaria were acute in the rice-swamp country near the coast, the planters would move inland—the Le Contes to Bulltown in the south of the county. It was a gracious feudalistic existence, committed to the amassing of money, land, and slaves and the cultivation of a genteel sort of learning. It was interesting, but it was not enough. It was not what Stephens wanted—he had no desire to vegetate. Something else must come, but what?

Politics was catching his attention. In a letter written in December 1833 is to be found his first extant stand on a political question, and he is found precisely where he will always be,[3] with the middle-class conservatives. The gubernatorial election of that year was just over, and the candidate of the Union party, the party of North Carolinians and of the less well-to-do, had won, carrying even conservative Liberty County. Stephens, supporting the State Rights party candidate, was moved by this defeat to a burst of adolescent eloquence. "The genius of Yazooism," he wrote, "seems to have revived, and warmed by its genial influence men, who have, for years during the reign of sound wholesome principles, been as dormant and as torpid as reptiles, are beginning to move and crawl and show

[3] A.H.S. to A. W. Grier, December 2, 1833; Alexander H. Stephens MSS., Library of Congress (cited hereafter as *LC*).

their deformed images throughout the whole country." He deplored the advent of *"rank* Federalism," and concluded with a wagging of the head: "Alas! Alas! how are the mighty fallen!" The situation was not so bad as the rhetoric; but this was a common way of talking in antebellum America.

And while the mighty were falling, Stephens considered what to do next. His health was still bad, which excused his declining Dr. Le Conte's generous offer of a fifteen-hundred-dollar salary if he would stay on another year. Teaching was clearly not his profession. The energy in him was still seeking a proper channel, and so long as none was found, it went on tormenting him. Saying good-by to the new friends he had made, he left Woodmanston, the Le Conte plantation, about December 19, planning to return to Raytown by way of Savannah and Augusta. "Where I shall settle I have not yet determined—I have a strong notion of Washington," he wrote to his uncle. His debts were paid; he was twenty-two, and free to do whatever he wished.

Some time shortly afterward he came to a decision. He would study law. In many respects it was a logical choice, for teaching and the ministry had been eliminated and medicine probably did not attract him. Law was all that was left. He did not begin studying until May 1834, but spent the early part of the year with his uncle at Raytown, resting and taking a horseback trip into the west of the state, though he had an offer from a prominent Warren County lawyer that would have enabled him to read law under the latter's guidance for nothing. But rest was more important. Early in May he went over to Crawfordville, having heard that Swepston Jeffries, the local lawyer, was moving out. Stephens wanted to get Jeffries' books and his office. Most of the former had already been sold, but he picked up Starkie's *Evidence,* Maddox's *Chancery,* Comyn's

Digest, and Chitty's *Pleadings,* all for twenty-five dollars. Jeffries' office had been that in the courthouse belonging to the county sheriff, as rental for the use of which Jeffries had given the sheriff legal advice. Stephens moved in with the condition that this arrangement be continued, and set himself to read. He boarded across the hill from the courthouse, with a Methodist minister, Williamson Bird, a brother-in-law of his stepmother.

The next court term was set to begin in July. He determined to be by then prepared to take the bar examination, partly out of the desire to do something brilliant, and partly out of simple necessity. He knew there were people who thought well enough of him to be willing to finance him while he studied at a more leisurely pace, but he was done with borrowing. There were at most ten weeks in which to work. Almost alone, with no one but Quinea O'Neal, the county Ordinary, to guide him, he worked his way through the books Jeffries had sold and others he had recommended—Blackstone, the Georgia Statutes—reading and rereading and remembering, bent over the books in the upper room of the courthouse through all those warm quiet summer days.[4]

He was not alone; he knew a good many people in the village; yet he was lonely. There was no one to confide in. Therefore he kept a journal, telling himself that if it proved otherwise useless it might at least serve, should he ever in the future be miserable, to remind him that he had been so before and had survived. He conversed with the book and told it everything that happened, everything he thought. From it we learn that he was by now a passionate reader of newspapers. We learn other things too, some not so pleasant. "My soul is bent upon success in my profession, and the most trivial circumstance is frequently sufficient to damp my whole ardor and drive me to despair."

4 *Recollections,* 362.

This comment was occasioned by the incident, now well known, of his passing the Crawfordville shoe factory one morning, going up the hill at a brisk pace toward the courthouse, and hearing the superintendent of the factory ask one of his workmen: "Who is that little fellow that walks so fast by here every day?" and the man's amused reply: "Why, that's a *lawyer!*" The incident was trivial, but it cut deeper than he liked.

Under the intense stress of the work he had set himself it was natural that his changes of mood should be more frequent and fierce than usual. The entries in the journal for these two months display nothing so well as his ambition. He was bounded by a nutshell and he had bad dreams. "I believe I shall never be worth anything, and the thought is death to my soul. . . . I was made to figure in a storm. . . . Discussion and argument are my delight. . . . Crawfordville is too dull." But it was not Crawfordville alone: the whole world was detestable. "Sometimes I almost have a contempt for the whole human race—the whole appearing like a degenerate herd. . . . Sensuality is the moving principle of mankind, and the most brutish are the most honored." Nature had prohibited him from engaging in most sensual activity, and this was probably his unconscious protest against having been cheated. Dancing at this moment was to him the hopping about of apes, and sexual intercourse the wallowing of hogs in the mire. And if all this was so, what in the world was truly valuable and worth coveting? He wanted fame, and yet "A burning genius bursts forth in the darkness of surrounding ignorance, and shines afar, but soon expires, and sinks to nought, leaving darkness in his train." [5] What could stand up before incessant time?

This melancholy, this *Weltschmerz*, bordering at moments, it would seem, on hysteria, was made the more in-

5 *J&B,* 63–83 *passim.*

tense because there was no one to talk to, no close friend who would listen and understand. He read on and on, turned in upon himself, while the pressure within him mounted. It could not continue to mount indefinitely. A collapse was inevitable; and on June 20 he was visited by Dr. Thomas Foster, who had been watching him, and who now stepped forward with the suggestion that he make, by way of diversion, a political speech for the Fourth of July. The prescription was good, and he went immediately to work, rewriting his speech three times and finishing it on the 3rd. The controversy over Jackson's impetuous withdrawal of the public deposits from the Bank of the United States was just then at its height. Stephens had approved the withdrawal and was concerned over Henry Clay's "vile attempts" to oppose and condemn the President, an opinion which was not that of his party, which denounced the Administration as vicious and corrupt.[6] He read his speech at the celebration on the Fourth. It is interesting chiefly as an exposition of his views while still quite young. He denied the right of nullification, but insisted upon the doctrine of moderate state sovereignty and asserted the right of any state to secede from the Union if the "compact" —as Southern politicians never tired of calling the Constitution—were violated by the others: which was sound, orthodox, conservative Southern doctrine, and which, indeed, pretty well epitomized his constitutional thinking throughout life.

His political debut made, he went back to reading law, for there were only two weeks left before the examinations. On the night of the 21st he sat up until near daybreak, reviewing and digesting what he had learned. Remembering his college entrance examination, he had no particular wish to trust to luck again. He was supposed to appear in the courtroom at eight on the morning of the

6 Ibid., 75; *Phillips*, 138.

22nd, and he was there, having had at most an hour's sleep, facing four of the best lawyers in the state, William H. Crawford, then an old man, who had been Senator, Secretary of the Treasury, and unsuccessful candidate for the Presidency; Joseph Henry Lumpkin, brother of Wilson Lumpkin, who had been Union party Governor since 1831, a handsome and well-trained attorney; William Dawson, a graduate of the famous law school at Litchfield, Connecticut, who had just compiled the Statutes of Georgia; and Daniel Chandler. Before this array of talent Stephens was agitated and quite confident he would know nothing he ought to know. He stood before the bar, hoping against hope he could win the prize he coveted so—for if he were to fail, what then?—while, Crawford presiding, each of the other three examined him in turn on common, criminal, and statute law. Each, when he was done, turned to Crawford and said he was perfectly satisfied; and at the end the old judge himself looked pleased and said: "Take an order for the admission, Mr. Solicitor, and have the oath administered. I, too, am perfectly satisfied." This was the last examination he ever held, for the following week he died.

Stephens was welcomed into the profession by a little group of lawyers who had come to hear the examination. Jeffries was there, and immediately invited him to become his partner at Columbus—the other end of the state—at a guaranteed salary of fifteen hundred dollars a year.[7] Stephens asked what Jeffries thought he could make if he were to stay in Crawfordville. The other smiled indulgently and said: "Well, I can guarantee you a hundred dollars a year at any rate." Stephens nodded and quietly declined Jeffries' offer. He preferred to risk his chances among his friends and in a locality he knew rather than go elsewhere, even for fifteen hundred dollars a year. A crowd of those friends had gathered in the courtroom this morning, come

<hr>

7 *J&B*, 90; *Cleveland*, 43.

to listen to his examination; and perhaps their solicitude had made him forget that a month ago he had damned Crawfordville as a dull place. Besides, this countryside was peopled with memories for him; it was his home; and, his impatience to the contrary, he loved it.

The legal environment into which he found himself now thrown was comfortable rather than efficient. There were at that time in Georgia ten circuits, each administered by a superior court composed of a single judge. The inferior courts had five judges each. Until 1845 there was no supreme court, and a reasonable degree of uniformity in interpretation and decision was preserved by the judges of the superior courts, who met semiannually in convention from 1830 to 1845. Court sessions were held at the county seats of each circuit, one after the other. Judges and lawyers rode from town to town and put up at taverns and hotels. This was the practice throughout the country, and it bred a considerable amount of good fellowship and friendship among the travelers. And it was on his first trip through the northern circuit, which included Wilkes, Columbia, Oglethorpe, Elbert, Franklin, and Greene counties,[8] that Stephens met the man who, one or two others excepted, was to be his closest friend.

The week after his admission to the bar he went to Washington. He had no horse and no money to buy one. He could walk, but it was eighteen miles, and by the time he arrived he would be dead tired. The problem was finally solved by his walking to his uncle's at Raytown, with saddlebags slung over his shoulders, staying overnight, and going on next morning, riding a borrowed horse. Just outside Washington he dismounted, tied the horse, and went into the bushes to take off the coarse-made dusty suit he had started in and change to clean white cotton.

He had not enough money to stay at court more than

8 Pleasant A. Stovall: *Robert Toombs* (New York, 1892), 15–16.

one day. Nothing much happened, except that one of the lawyers became friendly with him—more friendly, that is, than any of the others; and Stephens immediately reciprocated the feeling. This young man, everything Stephens was not, strong, healthy, full of large emotions violently expressed, quick-tongued, a red-faced, substantial animal with a great shock of hair, was two years older than Stephens, had been born in Wilkes County in 1810, the fifth son of a well-to-do planter, had been thrown out of Franklin College for defying the authorities, had gone north and graduated from Union College in Schenectady, returned home in 1828, been admitted to the bar in 1830, had married the same year, and was now busily making as much money as he could. Stephens felt himself at once drawn to this handsome swaggerer, whose name was Robert Toombs; and the two quickly became intimate friends.[9]

Next day Stephens went home, his legal career commenced. For a while business languished, and at times Jeffries' prophecy of one hundred a year seemed optimistic. He sat in the little office over the courthouse, waiting for something to come; but nothing came until September 10. A man named Uriah Battle had married a woman with the equally nonsensical name of Amanda Askew, had had a daughter by her, and died. Battle's father had thereupon taken out letters of guardianship over the baby. A little later Amanda married a habitual drunkard named Hilsman, whose name was anathema to old Battle, who thereupon demanded possession of the child. Amanda refused to give it up, and Battle hired a man to go to Hilsman's house and kidnap it. This having been done, the mother could only appeal to the courts. Hilsman came to Stephens and engaged him to recover the little girl from her grandfather's custody.

[9] *J&B*, 89.

Most of the people in the region sympathized with the grandfather, and when the case came up in court Stephens had to face a large and hostile audience. The Battles, moreover, had as their counsel none other than Swepston Jeffries. Teacher and pupil faced the five judges of the inferior court. When it came his turn to present his argument, Stephens stood up, pale and trembling, and plunged into a rhapsody on motherhood. The only way he could get the child returned was to have the letters set aside, and the only way he could do that was to make the judges forget that Hilsman was a good-for-nothing bum, and the only way to make them forget was to enlist their sympathies with a mother violently separated from her child. So he harped upon this theme until most of the courtroom, including the judges, was in tears—or so tradition says—and as a result the letters were revoked and the girl returned.

This speech gave him publicity, and he soon found his practice spreading into other parts of the state. It was the customary kind of practice, involving a great deal of routine in collecting notes and paying debts; and it kept him busy. It could be more than routine, too, for the lack of any real uniform system of interpretation had led, in Georgia practice, to the cultivation of the art of oratory as a means of obtaining decisions; and at this art Stephens was quite adept, knowing how to appeal to a judge's sympathies, how to be passionate and how to be cool, and when to be either. Once, it is told, he and Joseph Lumpkin were engaged on opposite sides in a very minor piece of litigation in Wilkes court. Lumpkin was highly excited, and as he argued grew more excited still. Stephens sat by, listening, quiet as a mouse, and when it came time for him to sum up his case, he did so in a gentle, rational, conversational manner, and won, saying afterward that if he had allowed himself to become heated, Lumpkin would have got an-grier still and have had little trouble in tearing Stephens' case to shreds.[10] Work like this taught self-control and the subtleties of acting, of saying one thing and meaning another, subtleties that would be useful to a politician.

During the next two years he waited and matured, learning to know more and more people, and often at the points where people are most vulnerable, in the ordinary, dull monotone of their daily lives. He had stayed in Crawfordville, this dusty little village, mainly because he wanted to buy back his father's land. It was a dangerous step, for he might easily stick here the rest of his days, lost in the obscurity he so much dreaded. That he took the risk is a measure of his attachment to the place and to the memory of Andrew Stephens, the anniversary of whose death he still observed in his journal, and whose grave he often visited.

In 1835 his restlessness led him to take several trips, one, in March, into the west of the state and across the Alabama border; the other, in May, to visit an uncle in Pennsylvania. He paused on the way in Washington to see the sights, and even had the good luck to spend an hour in conversation with President Jackson about Indian affairs in Georgia. At his uncle's he was received with delight, until the old man asked what business he was in. "I am a lawyer," he replied, whereupon Uncle James laid down his fork and looked at him with great sorrow. "A lawyer?" he said. "Alexander, don't you have to tell lies?" The young attorney, full of pride in his profession, said no, and launched into an encomium: "The business of the lawyer is neither to tell lies nor defend lies, but to protect and maintain right, truth and justice. . . . [It] is the highest and noblest of any on earth. . . ." [11]

By July 4 he was back in Crawfordville, where he read

10 Richard M. Johnston: *Autobiography* (Washington, 1890), 103–6.
11 *J&B*, 104–5.

the Declaration of Independence at the usual celebration, and at the barbecue that followed toasted nominating conventions as dangerous things,[12] a sentiment with which few present agreed. He was leaning toward politics, was acquainted with a good many politicians, was popular in his town and county. About this time he became friendly with Dr. Thomas Foster, a local practitioner, who, having taken an interest in the young lawyer and thinking he worked too hard for his own good, would stop in at his office and take him along wherever he went on calls, sometimes fifteen miles out of town. Foster was stuffed with a mass of heterogeneous learning, and on those rides the two managed to converse upon hundreds of subjects; but the important thing was that the doctor had ideas, perhaps purely benevolent, perhaps tinged with self-interest, about Stephens' future. He had said one day that he expected him to get to Congress within ten years. It is quite likely that he took every opportunity to talk Stephens into actively entering local affairs. Judging by the sequel, there may have been something of a bargain in it, for Foster had a project and wanted an advocate. In the summer of 1836 Stephens announced that he was a candidate for the state House of Representatives. His brother Aaron, with whom he spent much time, roaming over the old homestead and taking long walks, was surprised at his having consented to run, and cautioned him to "take no particular interest in the Election." [13]

II

The political situation, state and local, into which Stephens entered that summer had a long history and was excessively complicated and confusing. The parties of the 1820's and '30's traced themselves back to the 1790's, when

12 Ibid.
13 A. G. Stephens to A.H.S., July 16, 1836; MS. in office of Clerk of the Superior Court, Taliaferro County, Crawfordville, Ga.

Georgia was largely Republican, with a dying remnant of incorrigible Federalists. A venomous controversy over the great Yazoo land fraud (by means of which several land companies, with the connivance of members of the .state legislature, were able to purchase for a song vast tracts of public land in the west of the state) split voters and politicians into two camps, one, the larger, led by Senator James Jackson, who took so prominent a part in the repeal of the Yazoo grants that the parties became known as the Jackson and anti-Jackson parties. Now those implicated in the deal were largely Federalists; those opposed, mostly Republicans. Also, Jackson came of a Virginia family, while his most powerful antagonist, John Clarke, was of North Carolina stock. The result of this was that during the succeeding thirty years the two predominant political parties were divided along certain broad social and geographic lines. Under varying leaders, the Jackson party, lineal descendants of the old Republicans, but no longer known by that name, ruled along the seacoast and throughout middle Georgia, where Virginians had settled; while the Clarke party, heirs of the Federalists, controlled the barrens and the frontier country to the north and west.

So far as national affairs were concerned, there was no clear distinction between the parties for a long while. Both were anti-tariff, both were anti-internal-improvement, both supported Andrew Jackson. Even during the first years of the South Carolina nullification dispute, they remained united in their advocacy of a moderate doctrine of state sovereignty. There were extremists, but they belonged to both groups. The distinction between parties was almost exclusively social and personal. In 1832 Henry Clay received scarcely a vote from either party, so singly did the partisans of each support Jackson—mainly because of his championship of Georgia's claims against the Cherokee

Indians. In 1833, however, with the passage of the force bill, the split came.

Already the Jackson party had dropped its personal sobriquet for the more interesting one of "State Rights party," and the Clarkeites had likewise turned to ideas, calling themselves "Union" men—though with little justification. Now the State Rights party, numbering among its adherents more out-and-out Calhounites and nullifiers than the Union party could count, began attacking Andrew Jackson, and in 1834 completely broke with him. The Clarke Unionists, being a shade more moderate and caring perhaps a little less about the tariff, stuck with the Administration. The State Rights party, in 1836, refused to support Van Buren for the Presidency, and carried the state for Hugh L. White of Tennessee. Since 1831 the Unionists had held political power in the state; and this sudden swing to the other side may partly have been because there were voters who would go with Jackson so far and no further and would not swallow his own personal candidate for the succession. As affairs stood when Stephens entered politics in 1836, the Union party was pretty clearly aligned with the national Democracy, while the State Rights men were friendly toward Clay and on the point of joining the newly formed coalition against Jackson and Van Buren calling itself Whig.[14]

Party organization was tight, with small cliques of politicians determining, in secret caucus, the course of party opinion and the nature of party measures, and conducting, through the party newspapers, vigorous propaganda campaigns in support of their own policies. Because newspaper consumption was limited and the population widely scattered, the chief method of getting out the vote was stump speaking to mass meetings of farmers and their families,

14 Cf. *Phillips*, chs. iv and v.

usually brought together at the county seats. Such meetings, in which opposing candidates often debated together in gamecock style, could be exciting events even to those who understood little of the issues being aired. The exact mental level of the average Georgia small farmer is a dubious matter, classically illustrated in the story of the upcountry man and his son who, traveling to town, came upon one of the early railroad lines just as a train was passing. The boy: "Dad, what is that ar thing?" Dad: "I dunno, son, but I 'spect hit ar the tariff." Not all Georgia farmers were that naïve, but many were, and they, of course, were always more easily convinced by oratory than by argument.

Prominent in the leadership of the State Rights party at the time Stephens entered politics were John Mac-Pherson Berrien, one-time United States Senator and Attorney-General in Jackson's Cabinet, a man of impeccable manners and considerable eloquence, whose home was in Savannah; George Michael Troup, who also had served in the Senate, and eight years in the House as well, and was a man of great wealth, owning six plantations scattered over the state; and George Rockingham Gilmer, of Virginian ancestry, a pupil of Moses Waddell, who had served in Congress prior to his election to the governorship in 1829. All three were in their late forties or early fifties, and soon to leave politics.

Stephens' own locality, through the years of his childhood and youth, had consistently gone for the State Rights party; and he, in being an ardent State Rights supporter as early as 1833, was only following a general trend, responding to a local attitude. But Taliaferro County, which had been carved out of Wilkes and Greene about ten years previously, and of which Crawfordville was county seat, had its own rivalries, two families, one named Brown, the other Janes, competing for control of the local machine,[15]

15 *J&B*, 125.

though both belonged to the same party. Stephens, perhaps through Foster, became a Brown partisan and waged his campaign as a Brown man.

It was as bitter a campaign as one based on local animosities could be; and Stephens was pressed hard all summer, especially because the Janes faction had until now been dominant. Besides this, he had taken up a position in regard to antislavery literature which was susceptible of easy misinterpretation in the slaveholding South. The abolitionist societies in the North had, during the past few years, been flooding the South with propaganda, against which a tacit censorship had arisen. Several Georgia counties, feeling a need for stronger measures, organized vigilante committees in 1835 and 1836, which were given power to take and punish persons suspected of circulating antislavery publications. When such a movement was begun in Taliaferro County, and a public meeting was held for the purpose of establishing such a committee, Stephens almost alone stood up and spoke against the idea. He characteristically took the ground that such a procedure was contrary to law, and if these persons were to be chastised, it must be by the legally constituted authority and not by an unauthorized mob. There was a sharp clash over the matter, but in the end he took the people with him and defeated the proposed committee. The opposition, however, carried the issue into the campaign and fought him on it there.

Now, just when he needed to be in good health, he was taken with a violent fever, which lasted from the middle of August to near the end of September. A few weeks before he was stricken, he had gone to a class reunion at Athens, and there he and a few classmates had weighed themselves to see how life was treating them. He weighed ninety-six pounds, and was surprised, for it was more than he had ever weighed before. But here he was in bed. The election was to be held in the first part of October, and it was imperative that he take the stump and explain himself to be not an abolitionist but a lover of justice. And so, scarcely able to walk, let alone talk, he dragged himself out of the Bird house into the village, attending meetings and barbecues, standing on benches and boxes, angular, awkward, and white, his black eyes unnaturally bright with fever. On election day itself he went down to the new brick courthouse—it had been erected only the year before—and made a speech to the voters as they came in. It was his first chance, and he was perhaps haunted by the fear that if he missed it he would not get another. But he did not miss it, for he beat his nearest opponent two to one.

At the beginning of November he went to Milledgeville to attend his first legislative session in the grim and rather dilapidated stone state house, which looked more like an embattled fortress than the legislative hall of a sovereign American state. The job for which, presumably, he had been coached confronted him almost immediately, and it was an important one.

The first railroad in Georgia had been incorporated only three years before, but there were men who sensed the possibilities of steam locomotion in a region where transportation was so uncertain and uncomfortable. Such men existed in South Carolina as well as in Georgia; and the question the Georgians were asking themselves—Shall the state construct and own a railroad?—was linked with the additional question: Which is to be the great Southern Atlantic port, Charleston or Savannah? Now, the answer to this last conundrum depended largely upon which city managed to tie itself most firmly and efficiently to the hinterland, the whole interior basin of Georgia, South Carolina, Tennessee, perhaps even Kentucky. Savannah had a considerable natural advantage in the Savannah River, which, more than two hundred miles long, and navigable for at least a hun-

dred and thirty, lay like an extended finger thrust into the
hill country, almost tickling the foot of Tennessee. As a
matter of fact, Savannah already had a comfortable lead
over Charleston in the matter of trade; but she wanted
more. If Augusta could be connected with the Tennessee
River where it grazed the edge of Georgia, it was thought,
the tide of commerce from the northwest would be slowly
but inevitably turned through Augusta to Savannah. So
argued Georgia railroad enthusiasts; and at a great convention held at Macon in November 1836, at which Dr.
Thomas Foster represented Taliaferro County, plans were
made to introduce a bill into the state legislature providing for the construction of a road from the Tennessee
to the Chattahoochee.[16] This was the plan that Foster had
drilled into Stephens on their ten-mile rides, and it was
this that the young Representative was supposed to fight
for.

Soon after the opening of the session the bill was introduced by a Democratic member of the House. Absalom H.
Chappell and Herschel V. Johnson, its chief proponents,
were also Democrats, but the struggle that developed was
not based on party alignments, but rather on simple preju-
dices against railroads or against the state's spending
money on internal improvement projects of this kind. It
was argued that the road would cost a fortune to build and
would bankrupt the state; that there was nothing in northwest Georgia worth building a railroad for; that if there
was, the terrain was far too difficult. Having been referred
to, in speech after speech, as "the main trunk," those who
were weary of the subject mocked the railroad as "the great
snout," and did their best to ridicule it out of the legislature. Debate dragged; it looked as though stupidity were
winning. Then, one day, a shrill voice spoke out from

16 Ulrich B. Phillips: *A History of Transportation in the Eastern Cotton Belt to 1860* (New York, 1908), 308.

under the gallery: "Mr. Speaker!" it said. The voice had scarcely been heard till now, and the session was a month old. There was a craning of necks, and a thin young man with a cadaverous face and feverish eyes stood up.[17] Few in the hall knew him; still fewer knew that he had got up from a sickbed, where he had been confined with pneumonia, to deliver the speech he was about to make. He spoke for half an hour, and when he sat down, there was a spontaneous burst of applause.

It was his first major political speech, and he had prepared with painstaking thoroughness. Its burden, fortified with as conclusive an array of statistics as he could muster, was that the road, at a cost as then estimated of $4,000,000, would enhance the aggregate wealth of the state by at least $15,000,000 and would bring in, after it was in full operation, not less than $300,000 a year to the state, far more than the amount of interest to be paid off. These were large figures, but the future proved Stephens to have been not far wrong in calculation.[18]

His precise and confident defense galvanized a House that was falling asleep, and on December 10 the bill passed by a decisive vote of 100 to 54. Rewards for services were not long in coming. At this first session he had been included on no committees because he was a nobody; but in 1837—when he was unanimously re-elected to his seat —he was put on the Judiciary Committee, and in 1838 was simultaneously a member of the Committee on the State of the Republic, the Judiciary Committee, and the Finance Committee.[18a] Here in the House, as he learned what legislative routine was, and how to handle constituents,

---

17 *J&B,* 126–7; *Cleveland,* 609.

18 *Cleveland,* 610. After just getting by for twenty years, the Western & Atlantic (as it was named), began paying well, netting the state $1,200,000 between 1859 and 1861. Phillips: *History of Transportation,* 320.

18a Georgia, House of Representatives, *Journal,* 1837, p. 56; 1838, pp. 36, 66.

and how to distinguish important from insignificant problems, and how to deal with fellow politicians, he became acquainted with several men who were to be prominent in state politics during the next quarter of a century—men such as Charles J. Jenkins of Augusta, who was to sit in the lower house from 1836 to 1850, and who, too, was a Waddell product; and George W. Crawford, who came into the House in 1837 and was later Governor of the state for two terms. These men were State Rights partisans, but there were Democrats of importance as well, such as Herschel V. Johnson of Jefferson County, with whom Stephens would be friend and enemy and friend again, who also was a future Governor of the state. Antipathies and likings founded in these years could have much to do with later behavior which would be otherwise inexplicable, curious, irrational.

In Taliaferro County there was a steady current of opposition to Stephens, led by a physician named Lawrence and a gentleman named Simpson Fouche, who taught at the local academy. Fouche was a Wilkes County man in origin, who had been educated at the University of Virginia, and who practiced law as well as teaching. Politics was his bottle, and he hugged it tightly. The sound of his voice pleased him, and so he went in for campaign oratory; but since he was a very hot-tempered man and often said what he really did not want to say, he was generally at a disadvantage in debate. In 1839 he and Stephens became involved in a dispute over the latter's allegedly having called him a Van Buren and Union man, and Stephens in the end gave him up as a man of incredible littleness of soul. A majority of citizens must have thought so too, for at the polls they returned Stephens to his seat by 307 to Fouche's 160. But this was purely personal wrangling and apparently had little political meaning. In 1840 he was re-elected yet again, beating Dr. Lawrence (between whom and Dr. Foster there may conceivably have existed a professional rivalry) by 362 to 68.[19] When in the following year, therefore, he refused to run, it was not because he was afraid of losing, but because his legal affairs had got quite out of hand and badly needed all the time he could spare them.

In the autumn of 1837 a boy came to Crawfordville from Culloden, a quiet village in Monroe County, and was entered in the following year as a pupil at the academy, his tuition being paid by Alexander Stephens. He was fourteen years old, a mild, easily handled, hard-working youngster, almost, it would seem, too virtuous for one his age. His name was Linton Stephens; and he was Alexander's half-brother. Until now he had been under the guardianship of John W. Lindsay, his maternal uncle, and had been going, somewhat irregularly, to school. Why the guardianship was transferred at this particular moment is unclear; but during the eleven years between the scattering of the family in 1826 and Linton's coming to Crawfordville, Alexander had occasionally seen his brother and felt now, it may be, that he could do more for him than the uncle was able to do.

With Linton's entrance into the academy a correspondence was initiated that was to persist for thirty-four years. There was no more need for a diary. Stephens had found that "bosom confidant" with whom he dreamed he could "live and learn and be happy." Had he ever married, he might still have been as intimate with Linton as he was; but he did not marry; and Linton was his wife.[20] No

[19] R. M. Johnston: *Autobiography,* 25–6; *MC,* August 19, September 12, October 7, 1839, October 5, 1840.

[20] There is, in the passionate devotion of these brothers, and especially on Alexander's side, an unmistakably pathological tone. His love for Linton was highly complex in nature and origin; he loved him both as the son he could not have, and as the brother who most resembled their father (for whom he retained through life a profound veneration). And at the same time there was in his love a distinct, unconscious sensual bias,

other person who knew him was so close. Yet it was an asymmetric friendship, for the disparity in age gave it from the beginning at least partly the character of a father-son relationship, which, once set in motion, persisted side by side with a strangely passionate fraternal attachment, and did not die even when the difference of age no longer mattered.

Probably because of the troubles he had himself experienced, Alexander intended Linton to receive an adequate education without having to consider the source from which it came. Therefore the year of preparation at the academy, where the boy studied under Simpson Fouche and apparently did not get on well with him. Fouche was a harsh disciplinarian, and Stephens advised Linton, in case the two should clash, to "quit instanter." "I do not intend that you shall be abused or trod over by any mortal," he added.[21] This fierce announcement was the precursor of a flood of letters written during the next four or five years, crammed with all sorts of advice, with admonitions and warnings, anxiety and solicitude, so explicit at times as to reach the limits of endurance.

And while Linton attended the academy and in August 1839 went up to Athens to enter Franklin College as a freshman, Stephens wrestled with the sickness of his body. He had never been well, but from 1836 on he was continually at the mercy of one disease or another. The flesh did all that malignancy could devise to confine and cripple the mind: he was an intellectual in spite of himself. In the spring of 1837, just after recovering from pneumonia, he was again in bed for several months, his nerves having completely given way, leaving him so weak that he had

which caused him to treat and address his brother with that tenderness and that kind of affection which men ordinarily feel for women. Linton was the substitute-object for the woman he could never have. All this is clearly evident in the letters in *MC*.

21 *MC*, June 4, 1838.

to be carried from one part of the house to another. He spent the summer journeying by buggy through the west of the state with his brother Aaron. Rambling in this leisurely fashion did him good, for he was able to attend the legislature when it met in the fall; but by the spring of 1838 he was once more incapable of any work. He was compelled to lay aside his practice and take another trip. Toombs generously offered to attend to his more urgent cases while he was away.

He went north by packet ship to Boston, passing Fort Warren in the harbor on May 25. From Boston he moved on by rail to Lowell and Concord, then by stage to Montpelier and Keene, New Hampshire. The New England countryside interested him, for it was not like that he had known. "Land very poor and full of rocks," he noted, but he found traveling "cheap and expeditious," [22] which it was not in the South. From Keene he went over to Saratoga Springs and on down into Pennsylvania, stopping at Carlisle. In August he spent some weeks at White Sulphur Springs, Virginia, where he found some easing of his pain. All during the trip he kept writing and thinking of Linton, giving him advice about what to read, which indicates something of what he himself admired. "Get your philosophy from Locke, Bacon, Brown & Franklin," he urged, "and train your imagination by the standard of Milton & Shakespear—adopting with the latter only his sound maxims—repudiating his vulgar obscenity." Virgil, Horace, Livy, Cicero, Cervantes, Burns, and Paley he unreservedly recommended; but as if he feared Linton would do nothing but stick to books like a bur to clothes, he concluded: "Cultivate female society—it tends wonderfully to refine the coarser feelings" [23]—showing that his notions of what

22 Ibid.
23 Ibid., June 30, 1838.

women were made for were the most conventional of his time.

At the end of August he returned to Crawfordville, strong enough to pick up his practice where he had dropped it, and to attend the legislature in November. In the spring of 1839 he was considered prominent enough to be chosen as a delegate to a commercial convention meeting at Charleston. The commercial convention, the first of which had been held at Athens in 1837, was one sign of the growing anger felt by many Southerners over the economic slavery into which they thought they had fallen to the North. By this time cotton was the overwhelming export item of Southern agriculture; and all but an insignificant fraction of the South's cotton was being sold to England by Northern commission merchants and cotton brokers, passing to Europe by way of New York. In return for the cotton they sold, Southerners bought from Northern merchants the vast majority of the things they needed to live, at prices they considered extortionate, since the Northern merchant added his profit to the normal price. If, it was argued by those Southerners who felt this arrangement an insult to themselves, the South could sell cotton directly to Europe and buy back directly from Europe its necessities and luxuries, and if it could also, by means of improved transportation, seduce the Northwest away from the East as a market, the tables would be turned. The conventions of 1837 and 1839 were among the first efforts to propagandize the direct trade movement. As efforts they proved insignificant; the convention Stephens attended, after much to-do, arrived at the obvious conclusion that direct trade was possible—and let it go at that. Stephens himself made a speech at the convention in defense of the better right of Savannah as against Charleston to initiate direct trade with Europe; which was to be

expected from one who had just fought to establish a railroad in Georgia supposed in the end to bring the whole
West to Savannah. The speech was well received, and it
was good he had made it, for it brought him to the attention of men from every state in the lower South but
Louisiana. They were not great men, but they were important merchants, and it was worth while to cultivate
them. His physical appearance doubtless helped them remember him. On his arrival at Charleston, being fatigued
from the trip, he lay down on a sofa in the lobby of the
hotel to which his two companions, Georgia merchants,
had taken him. The proprietor of the hotel, seeing this boy
comfortably and coolly stretched out with a group of
middle-aged gentlemen standing round him, came fussing
up and said: "Here, boy, don't take up the whole lounge
—let these gentlemen sit down." The boy got up, his presence was explained, and everybody laughed. He was beginning to accustom himself to being called "Sonny,"
though it hurt. There was nothing he could do about it—
except perhaps by demonstrating that he had a mind.

III

"Trust too much to no man," Alexander warned Linton
with a terseness surprising in him. All through 1838 and
1839, because, for one reason and another, he could not
see his brother often, he bombarded him with letters. "Be
courteous to all—I mean by *courteous* that kind of intercourse which is becoming considering the character of the
parties—If I go into the Penitentiary I may demean myself
properly and *cautiously* towards the convicts—without giving them any occasion of insult. . . ." Again: "I would
not say be *irrespective* of the opinions of others—but ob-
serve them only as you would beacons or light houses in
order more correctly *to know your own position*." And
again: "Always look up; think of nothing but objects of

the highest ambition . . . but never forget your dependence and mortality." The emphasis, nervous and intense, in these letters is always upon independence, moral and intellectual. "I like to see," he averred, "a man possessed of a proud independent unyielding spirit," and he was straining every fiber to make Linton such a man. The mass of mankind, he told the boy, must be kept at a distance; and this distance he compared to the lever "in mechanicks," calling it "the great engine by which mankind can be governed—Its successful use and application always bespeaks the popular man." [24] This jealous concern to see Linton aloof and free, a man who leaned upon nothing but himself, paralleled in his own mind by an extravagant admiration of men like Alexander Hamilton and Napoleon, perhaps arose out of his forced dependence upon others, natural as well as accidental, and may have expressed itself so powerfully about this time because he had succeeded in liberating himself from most, if not all, of those old chains.

His profession was the chief agent of liberation, for he was now pretty well released from the fear of poverty that had made his early years so painful. The average income of a Georgia lawyer at that time was about three thousand dollars a year; [25] and Stephens must have been earning at least that, if not more. The volume of business he had to work through was extremely heavy, especially when his physical capacities are considered. In March 1840 he bought himself a buggy, which was no luxury, for the courts traveled fast and the lawyers had to keep pace, often visiting as many as five county seats in five weeks. When the buggy was lost in a muddy swamp, he promptly bought another for three hundred and five dollars. About this

---

24 Ibid., June 30, 1838; October 13, 21, 1839; February 13, 1840; *J&B*, 129–30.
25 R. M. Johnston: *Autobiography,* 102.

time, too, he became an owner of slaves, though for the moment he was still boarding at Williamson Bird's house. In February 1841 he purchased a Negro from his uncle Aaron Grier for six hundred dollars, and a year later, for the same sum, but from another source, he bought a Negro woman and two children. At the same time he was buying parcels of land in various counties and financing his less fortunate relatives into the bargain. All this argues a comfortable income. He had come a long distance since those first wretched days of 1832.[26]

These years of early political service, at the same time that he was establishing his place in the society of his state, saw him slowly, almost unconsciously, drift into a political position from which he was not to swerve for the next fifteen years. When the State Rights party broke with Andrew Jackson in 1833 and 1834, because its leaders and a good many of its members felt that the force bill threatened the theory of state sovereignty, it dallied for several years without committing itself to any other major party. It could not join the Democrats, for it was the Democrats it had just fled; but the obvious alternative was one before which State Rights men drew up short and deeply pondered. The opposition to Jackson, by 1835, was consolidated into what liked to call itself a party, but was actually a conglomeration of contradictions united only in dislike of the old soldier in the White House. To trick the country into calling Democrats Tories, it took the name Whig, and kept it, though the trick failed.

The basis of Whig politics was expediency and not program—a difficulty that weakened the party from the start. Its Northern wing was nationalist, antislavery, pro-tariff; its Southern wing was anti-tariff, state-rightish, and rather proslavery. This difference caused many Southerners who

[26] MC, March 29, 1840; February 22, March 25, 1841; March 6, 1842; May 28, 1843.

did not wish to be Democrats considerable anguish before they finally decided to go with the Whigs. The State Rights party in Georgia hesitated until 1840, when the Whigs, to defeat Martin Van Buren in his campaign for re-election, laid Henry Clay, their titular leader, aside in favor of old William Henry Harrison, whose military past was a godsend. On the question of endorsing Harrison's nomination the State Rights men divided. Stephens did not like him because he was ignorant of politics and so could easily fall under the influence of the wrong kind of advisers, especially the old "Federalists"; [27] and until August 1840 Stephens, with a substantial segment of State Rightists, maintained an independent position, favoring George M. Troup for the Presidency. In a speech on the Fourth of July 1839 he had excoriated the Van Buren Administration as a pack of "Judas-like traitors" who had sold out the old Jeffersonian Republicans, but he had thought equally little of Clay, saying the patriot should support neither man. Now in 1840 he feared that Clay would dominate Harrison. It was not until the pressure of the bawling Log Cabin and Hard Cider campaign had become psychologically irresistible that on August 13 the Georgia Whigs met in convention and endorsed Harrison's nomination. Stephens did not like this, but there was nothing he could do. He got on the bandwagon, supported the Gallant Old Soldier of Tippecanoe; and when, the following April, one month after his inauguration, the sixty-eight-year-old warrior, who had vanquished Indians, died of office-seekers, he felt he had to mourn the loss, writing to Linton: "Harrison had the confidence of the people of all sections of the Union," [28] and he was gloomy about the future, predicting "feuds, dissensions and division"—which swiftly came in clouds.

27 *J&B*, 140.
28 Ibid., 136–7; *Niles' Register*, LVIII, 408; *MC*, April 11, 1841.

The year 1841 was a comparatively quiet one, with Linton away most of the time at college, and Stephens himself for a brief moment out of the main stream of politics. At the Bird house, where he still lived, was quite a group of boarders, a convivial society of teachers, lawyers, and one physician, almost the whole professional population of town under one roof. Stephens loved diversion, loved company, enjoyed nothing better than good conversation, preferably with women; but even now there was an opposite, contradictory streak in him which every now and then cropped out, an inclination toward solitude and melancholy introspection. It had always been noticeable, but in earlier years seemed to be caused from without, by the pressures of the careless world. Now it increasingly became something to be cultivated for its own sake, a state of mind no longer set in motion necessarily by outward situations, but self-sufficient, independent; in a word, a habit. And since Linton was most intimate, these moods invariably found their way into the letters he wrote to Linton. "The light is growing feeble," he wrote one winter Sunday in 1840. "And if you have ever been sensible of any peculiar feelings when the dim & shadowy & melancholy twilight of a lonesome Sunday evening has been gathering fast around, and the shrill tones of the village church bells . . . summoning its few . . . worshippers to the performance of their *vesper vows* you know something of the feelings, musings & reflections that crowd & press heavily upon my brain just now. . . ." Under the influence of such moods he would keep to himself, "like a mad-dog in a fit," walking alone up and down the gentle hills in back of town, following creeks and branches for miles on end, "devoid of thought—the sea of mind . . . at its lowest ebb-state and motionless the tide flows neither way. . . ." [29] Ill health had little or no connection with

29 *MC*, January 26, September 27, 1840.

depressive feeling: he could be cheerful in sickness and miserable in health. In 1842 he spent six weeks in bed with an abscessed liver, coughing, sweating, drinking extract of liverwort, blistering his breast with tartar emetic, eating nothing, being cupped several times, but losing not much blood: and he had thoughts of death being near, yet he was not gloomy. "We have all got to die," he told Linton quietly. "Then why should we suffer any uneasiness from any indication of the immediate approach of death?" and he commanded his brother: "Be therefore not disturbed—because in the first place I think there is no immediate cause . . . and secondly it is wrong in principle." [30] By September he was tolerably recovered and able to go out stumping the county for himself. He was running this time for the state Senate, against one Felix Moon, a gentleman who had a few months previously got drunk and cursed him up and down, threatening to have his friends haul Stephens over to the grocery so that Moon could cowhide him—for what reason Stephens could not fathom. The affair blew over, but the people apparently thought Stephens better qualified for the job, and voted him in by 295 to 102.[31]

During his single term in the Senate he labored mainly to defeat a strong movement aiming at the extension of the charter of the Central Bank of Georgia, which had been organized in 1828 and empowered to issue notes equal to the aggregate of the bills and specie of the state's other chartered banks, plus the bills of the Bank of the United States in its vaults. On this basis it operated well until the panic of 1837, at which time its supporters, who were mostly Democrats, demanded that its note-issuing powers be liberalized so that it could relieve the distress of the other banks. In 1839, with Democratic domination

30 Ibid., August 14, 1841.
31 Ibid., October 3, 1842.

of the legislature, this was done. Stephens and Toombs, among other Whigs, had then protested, for they believed the bank's whole structure to be financially unsound, pointing for evidence to the fact that it could include as part of its capital nearly $200,000 worth of "ancient bonds," obligations due the state, "that has been for many years suspended in their collection." They contended that "the direction and management of the fiscal affairs of the state, should be plainly ascertained, and cautiously guarded. Power . . . should be restrained by abundant and appropriate checks." [32] This was sound doctrine, but the majority had thought otherwise; and by 1841 the bank had issued almost $3,000,000 in notes, which underwent a steady depreciation. It had then been enjoined from any further issues. Now, at the 1842 session, its friends sought again to pump blood into its rotten veins; but because of the Whig opposition, led by Stephens and Toombs, it never again resumed operations. As always, the debtor classes, most of whom at this time were Democrats, welcomed cheap paper money, whereas the creditors, largely Whig, opposed. And Stephens, by now, in his moderate way, was more closely bound to the latter. When Crawfordville citizens went bankrupt, it was he who served attachments upon their property. Once he had known poverty, and the memory of those bitter years would always keep him from indifference and callousness toward those who could not, like himself, climb out of economic bogs; and yet his thinking could not but be colored by his new environment.

To be a Whig, though, was not easy. The party had split into two factions, one headed by the President, John Tyler, the other by Henry Clay. To join the Tyler faction

---

[32] Thomas P. Govan: "Banking and the Credit System in Georgia, 1810–1860," in *Journal of Southern History*, IV, ii, 164–84; Georgia, House of Representatives, *Journal*, 1839, 410–12.

would be to commit political suicide; while to stick with Clay was to swallow a party program with which a Southerner found it hard to sympathize, including as it did a national bank and a high tariff. But apparently anything was better than being a Democrat; and when the Georgia legislature severely censured Senator Berrien (who had once been a Democrat) for favoring both bank and tariff, the Whig minority, Stephens leading, dissented and quite plainly announced the conversion of the Georgia Whigs to Clay's "American system." The elections of 1843 demonstrated that this conversion was endorsed by most Whig voters, and that there were more Whigs than Democrats for the time being: for after two years of Democratic rule, George W. Crawford, a close friend of Stephens, was elected Governor by a majority of three thousand votes, and Stephens himself was sent to Congress.

His opportunity came in this wise: Mark A. Cooper, an ex-Whig who had bolted to the Democrats in 1840, had been elected to Congress in 1841, but in the summer of 1843 resigned in order to run against Crawford. To fill the vacancy the Democrats nominated a man named Stark; the Whigs, Stephens. He knew nothing of the nomination until it had been made, and at first declined—a tactic which was to become habitual with him. But it was his chance, and to let it go would have been foolish. He accepted.

To win did not look easy. The year before, the Democrats had elected their Congressmen by an average majority of two thousand. He would have to stump the state aggressively to whittle down that edge, and, because the legislature in 1842 had refused to divide the state into Congressional districts, he would have to stump the whole state. By August he was in the swing of things and hugely enjoying himself. Only a few months before, he had been depressed and irritable, rhapsodizing about the history of the mind: "a strange mixture of pleasure and pain, joy and sorrow, hope and despair, life and death! A mystery deep, dark, and unfathomable! To live today—to be warm—to move, and think—and tomorrow to be Silent—and cold and dead—devoid of mind and sense—fast mouldering to dust—only fit food for worms. . . ." But now this spirit was notably absent. "I am in perfect fine spirits," he said, telling of a speech he had made at Cassville, against William H. Stiles, a new Democratic Congressman. In his own opinion he had beat Stiles hollow. "I never had an antagonist," he crowed, "who exposed himself to such broadside sallies." [33]

He did not spare himself, riding from one town to the next, speaking an hour here, two there, meeting with local leaders and party chiefs, buttonholing people at Campbellton, Marietta, Rome, Dahlonega, Canton, Newnan, and Jackson, among other places. Once he scored a mild sensation. At Newnan, late in September, when his lungs were paining him because of his protracted speaking, he met Walter T. Colquitt, a Senator and an extremely popular man. Newnan was in Colquitt's own county, Coweta, and Stephens' friends sought to dissuade him from the debate, supposing it would be but wasted breath. Stephens went ahead anyhow, for he liked to strike dangerously. Colquitt spoke first, quoting from the journals of the state House to show that Stephens had voted against bills providing pensions for Georgia soldiers who had fought the Indians. This was intended to do moral damage; and Stephens, when he got up, admitted he had voted against the bills, but it had been, he said, because Congress had already made provision for those soldiers, and he had voted against an unnecessary duplication. Moreover, he added, picking up a state Senate journal that he had asked for while Colquitt was speaking, "Whether my vote was right

[33] *Phillips*, 147; *Cleveland*, 58–60; *MC*, May 19, August 16, 1843.

"A YOUTH IN DELICATE HEALTH . . ."
STEPHENS, PHOTOGRAPHED AT AUGUSTA,
PERHAPS IN THE EARLY 1840's.

(Liberty Hall collection, Crawfordville)

ROBERT TOOMBS. HE AND STEPHENS WERE
CALLED THE DAMON AND PYTHIAS
OF SOUTHERN POLITICS.

(*National Archives, Photographic Records Office*)

or wrong, it was just as Senator Colquitt's had been on the same resolution." To this there was obviously no reply. And despite his friends' pessimism and his own uncertainty, he beat Stark by 38,051 to 35,001. Since it was a general-ticket election, and many voters doubtless marked a whole ballot for one or the other party, the returns indicated little as to his relative strength. But the largest Whig vote came from the eastern middle and extreme southern counties, showing that the old division still prevailed.[34]

As he packed and prepared, in late November, for his trip to Washington, there was much for him to think about. Ten years ago he had been a frightened, uncertain young teacher without a perceptible future; now he was a Congressman-elect with six years of political experience behind him. What he had was not much, but it was a good beginning. He was well known in his state; he was well situated and in no apparent danger of forced retreat; it was possible he might achieve still more. Suffering still hounded him; yet in some subtle fashion it may have had an effect on his success, and without its pressure he may have lived a perfectly anonymous life. A question that must always have been in his mind was the one of how much longer he would live. The answer and its implications would doubtless then have astonished anyone who knew him, and especially himself. As, accompanied by his body servant, Bob, he traveled out of Georgia in the crisp winter, by stage to Charleston and then on by coastal steamer, walking the decks, wrapped in shawls, his thin face peering at the sea, he moved into a future more ironic than he dreamed.

[34] Colquitt incident in *Cleveland*, 63–4. All election figures in the text, unless otherwise cited, are quoted from the *Tribune Almanac* for the appropriate years.

CHAPTER THREE

Congress (1843–59)

On the left hand, gray November hills; on the right hand, gray November hills; between them the Potomac, spacious and somber in a November dusk; ahead, an indistinct mass of walls and roofs, over which, pale in the evening, a gleaming low dome, the Capitol. In the river, swinging in toward shore, a coastal steamer; behind her, slowly widening, turbid water and bursting bubbles, a long trail across the silent surface; on her deck, Alexander Stephens, muffled against the cold, watching the East Branch and Greenleaf Point slide past, and the buildings of the Navy Yard. Ahead, a thin line stretched over the gray river, Long Bridge. Behind, along the far shore to the south, in the mud flats, pinpoint figures walking, bending; crabbers. Rhythmic to-and-fro of torso and arms, forward, back, forward, back, a skiff gliding silently by across the steamer's bows, and momentarily a face upturned, wide-eyed, tensed. Sudden rush of wings, flapping loudly over the deck, gulls curving down, then up, then away. The steamer nears the wharf, scrapes, is brought to rest by squealing hawsers. Stephens, amid pandemonium of escaping steam and cursing sailors, comes down the plank, one of a crowd, accompanied by one or two colleagues, and is surrounded by yelling hackmen. He gets into a hack and is driven inland through uneven, unlit streets lined with spasmodic clumps of wooden houses. In the twilight the city is very large, almost lonely. The hack jerks to a stop in front of a boardinghouse not far from the Capitol; and Stephens enters, to be greeted by Mrs. Rumney, the keeper of this dusty den for the nation's hopefuls. Here, on the right as you enter, is the drawing-room, furnished with dingy plush chairs, tables, lamps, and a fireplace. Down the hall is the dining-room, with a long table that is kept constantly laid, the dinner plates being put on (upside down) as soon as breakfast is over. Up the stairs, and there is the bedroom, whose contents can be rapidly inventoried: a four-poster, a large table for business purposes, a few chairs, a wash-basin and ewer, a spittoon, a fireplace. These boarding-houses are called messes, and most members of Congress, being too poor to rent whole houses, resort to them when they are in Washington, paying ten or twelve dollars a week for the privilege.[1]

For the first week of the session, perhaps because of the sudden change in climate, Stephens was in bed, taking doses of nitric acid under the supervision of a doctor. But on December 11, accompanied by another Georgia Representative, Absalom Chappell, he went over to the Capitol, which stood quite alone atop its hill, surrounded by lawn and trees, the grounds being enclosed all round by a low stone wall. Up the great staircase, into the impressive and lavishly decorated rotunda, down a corridor, and he entered the hall of the House of Representatives, a large semicircular room sixty feet high, lined with columns of dark blue puddingstone capped with white marble Corinthian capitals. The members' seats were in semicircular rows, each row a foot above the one in front; and because the House was a large body, the members had to share desks, each having a compartment of drawers for his papers and paraphernalia. A huge chandelier swung from the ceiling; and over the Speaker's head on the wall was

[1] James S. Buckingham: *America, Historical, Statistic and Descriptive* (London, 1841), I, 319, 347–50; *MC*, December 2, 1844.

a clock. The floor was well carpeted with rugs and tobacco-juice; the hall being difficult to keep warm, nobody stared to see Representatives legislating with their coats and hats on. Downstairs in the inside of the building was an eating-counter, which was especially useful on those not infrequent occasions when the House remained deadlocked in an all-night session—though there were always a good many members whose heavy eyes could not be held open by so mild a stimulant as coffee, and for whose convenience there were not far from the Capitol quiet little "holes in the wall" where they could get their Bourbon.[2] The worst thing about the House chamber was the acoustics, which were abominable.

A few moments after the session's beginning on December 11 Stephens was sworn in and took his seat as a member of the House he was not to leave for sixteen years, and then only by resignation. The chronicle of political events in America during those sixteen years has been told and retold, and is, in its great outlines, generally known; and since Stephens was not a Douglas, nor a Seward, nor a Jefferson Davis, in the depth of the influence he wielded upon history, no significant purpose could be served by telling once more, in all its ramifications and complexities, a tale that cannot now be given a new twist. What is important is not Stephens' political power, which was locally far greater than nationally, but his behavior as a man and as a Southerner, in times of crisis and struggle. His part in the origins of the Civil War, save at brief moments, was not one of power. The war, if the statement means anything, would have come had he been what he was or not. But he was part of the society that precipitated the war upon itself, and situated with a peculiar advantage

2 Eudora R. Richardson: *Little Aleck, A Life of Alexander H. Stephens* (Indianapolis, 1932) (cited hereafter as *Richardson*), 86; the Capitol is described in Henry Tudor: *Narrative of a Tour in North America* (London, 1834), I, 59–63; Buckingham, op. cit., I, 305.

because, like all politicians, he was both public and private, governor and citizen. And for this reason, if for no other, to study his course and to attempt to ferret out his motivations is to study the South in little, and to gain some insights into the dim borderland between individual character and social determination.

He entered Congress a Whig and left it a Democrat, and the central problem of his career is that of why and when the change occurred. As a turnabout it was far from odd or novel; indeed, perhaps its main meaning lies in the fact that so many Southerners did the same thing. It argues an alteration in national circumstances between 1840 and 1860; it is an obvious and outward reflection of that underlying crystallization of the American people about the two opposing poles of North and South which found its final expression in the existence of two distinct governments where only one had been before. Southerners like Stephens first looked for what they wanted in the party components of the American political structure, and when they could no longer hope to find it there, they turned to independence. The crucial question for them was when they could truthfully say that what they wanted was not to be found in either traditional party. At the bottom, far below the tricky surfaces of political dogmatics, they all, conservatives and radicals, instinctively wanted the same things, and differed only upon degree and mode.

II

The period in which Stephens could with accuracy be called a Southern Whig extends at most from his entry into Congress in 1843 to the territorial crisis of 1850. Doubts of his orthodoxy may arise even earlier, but 1850 marks a definite stopping-place on the Whiggish road beyond which he did not travel farther.

Except for two occasions he held himself, in his first

session, fairly inconspicuous. The first occasion came on February 9, 1844, when he delivered a long speech attacking his own right to hold the seat he occupied. In disregard of an act of Congress ordering that every state elect its Congressmen by districts, Georgia had elected them by general ticket. The act was stigmatized as unconstitutional, and a movement for its repeal was under way. Of the seven Georgia Representatives involved, six expressed themselves as upholding the right of their state to elect by whatever method it chose, and opposing the act of 1842. Only one argued that his election was illegal. That was Stephens. He had fought for a districting law in the Georgia legislature, believed Congress' right to govern the regulations of the states in regard to elections included the right to require districting, and believed too that the House had the absolute power to qualify or disqualify those members who had been elected by general ticket. This was sensible and moderate, unlike the strict-constructionist frothings of his colleagues; and the House, next day, agreed with him, confirming the credentials of every member whose admission was in doubt.

His other moment came on May 7, when he came out in emphatic support of a protective tariff, and "piled it down upon them for an hour." His commitment was bald enough: "Mr. Stephens said he came from a section of the country which had been said to be robbed by the protective system. . . . He would . . . show that it had no such effect. . . . He was prepared to show that so far from the constitution being for the establishment of free trade, one of its main objects was the protection of the industry of the country." [3] This was—or appeared to be—more than

---

[3] *Congressional Globe,* 28th Cong., 1st sess., 249, 270–2, 582. The February 9 speech is in *Cleveland,* 259–79, and 28 *CG,* I, App., 196–201. (The *Globe* will henceforth be cited in the following form: number of Congress, *CG,* number of session, page reference.) *MC,* May 8, 1844, for his comment on the tariff speech.

Southern Whiggism: it was National Whiggism, Clay Whiggism of the most unequivocal variety. The reason for it was not hard to find. 1844 was a Presidential year, and strict party unity was necessary if the Whigs were to capture the election. And only a few days before this speech Stephens had gone to Baltimore to see Henry Clay nominated in a burst of wild enthusiasm. Clay's popularity, especially in the South, was temporarily enormous, and George W. Crawford was writing Stephens that Georgia would go for Clay by five or ten thousand votes.[4] If the Southern Whigs were ever to gain control of the national party they would have to concede some points to the dominant elements, and the tariff was a concession not too difficult to make.

Late in June, Stephens returned to Georgia to throw himself into two campaigns, Clay's for the Presidency, and his own for re-election. Despite his earlier dislike of Clay, he was now committed to him so far that he had been one of those in Washington who had been shown the draft of Clay's Raleigh letter opposing the immediate annexation of Texas—a letter that Stephens thought "very full, clear, and satisfactory," especially after he had heard from Clay's own mouth that he might favor annexation if war with Mexico could be avoided.[5] With the nomination by the Democrats of James K. Polk, an ardent expansionist, the whole question of Texas annexation was referred to the Presidential election. According to the Whigs, annexation now would mean disunion, if not war; and the Whigs of Georgia, who probably wanted Texas as badly as anyone, shuddered so far before these possibilities as to pass, in June, resolutions drawn up by Stephens, favoring the

---

[4] *LC*, G. W. Crawford to A.H.S., March 6 and 10, 1844.

[5] *J&B*, 179; Arthur C. Cole: *The Whig Party in the South* (Washington, 1913), 109–10. In *Recollections*, 17–18, Stephens in 1872 remembered himself as having opposed publication of the Raleigh letter—which ought to warn anyone to question everything he "remembers" in his old age.

postponement of annexation to a more auspicious time.

In company with Toombs and other leaders Stephens stumped the state, attended Clay Club dinners, mass meetings, debates, barbecues, several times traveling out of Georgia to speak elsewhere. Clay's constant hedging on the annexation issue—for he wished to lose neither Northern anti-annexation nor Southern pro-annexation votes—made it extremely difficult to win any votes at all. At one Alabama meeting Henry W. Hilliard, a future Congressional associate, spoke with Stephens and wrote afterward of how he looked at thirty-two, "pale, with piercing dark eyes, an intellectual cast of features, slender, he might have been mistaken for a youth in delicate health"—as at this time he was—"just emerged from college. . . ." His voice, said Hilliard, "was shrill but musical, and while not flexible, singularly pleasing. He attracted great attention," and made, in Hilliard's opinion, a brilliant speech.[6]

And while he fought Clay's battle he also fought his own. In January he had received from certain of his constituents a testimonial approving his stand on the districting question and assuring him that he was "the most prominent man the Whigs now have, or ever had . . . the most popular man in Georgia"; but there were others who disagreed, and against them he won a clear but close victory in October by a margin of 944 out of a total of 7,448 votes. Clay was not so lucky, his indecisive utterances having cost him many supporters. He lost Georgia and the country to Polk,[7] and it looked as though the Whigs were finished.

Stephens had been a member of a majority party in Congress for merely a brief few months (and even its

[6] Henry W. Hilliard: *Politics and Pen Pictures at Home and Abroad* (New York, 1892), 112, 119; *MC*, August 9, 1844.

[7] *LC*, 47 signers to A.H.S., January 29, 1844; *Phillips*, 150.

majority was questionable); for the next four years he was to be in opposition to practically everything the government was to do. The prospect was not particularly cheering in December 1844; and he returned to Washington in a sulky, sullen mood, taking up quarters at Mrs. Carter's on Capitol Hill, paying twelve dollars a week for the privilege of living with Chief Justice Taney and Associate Justices Story and McLean of the Supreme Court. "I am once more in this great sewer of political filth," he wrote Linton, who was now studying law at the University of Virginia, adding: "It is almost as impossible to resist the wind . . . as to count upon the devastations of time—I mean its blasting and destroying effects upon man's prospects, hopes, and ambition." Not even the Yankee yarns of Representative Collamer of Vermont and old Judge Story's enormous capacity for roaring laughter were able to bring him out of this depression. Everything disgusted him; his dislike of President Tyler was even greater than usual, and that strange hatred of Polk which he was to carry with him almost to his death was already manifesting itself. Even trivial things reminded him of his political position. A man stopped him on the street one December day, saying: "Howdye Captain—will you stop a moment— you look like a gentleman and I am in want—will you give me a little change to get me some cheeze and crackers?" "How much?" queried Stephens, pulling out a purse. "Give me a quarter sir if you please . . . I have given a many one in my time." "That is the reason," Stephens remarked, "perhaps you have got none now," but gave him the quarter. "Thank you Sir," the man said, "You look like a gentleman—and may be you are a Whig —but I is a Polk man." To this Stephens added a mournful comment: "Was it not too bad?" [8]

[8] *MC*, December 2, 14, 24, 1844.

Polk had been elected on a platform of immediate annexation; and the Tyler Administration, which, though
Whig, had steadily been working toward the same end,
now determined to get Texas before it went out of office.
Between December 12, 1844 and January 25, 1845 there
was a rash of bills and resolutions in Congress on the
subject, differing each from each largely in the ways in
which they tried to solve the problem of slavery in Texas.
On January 13 Milton Brown, a Whig Representative
from Tennessee, submitted a joint resolution admitting
Texas as a state, with the provision that new states might
be formed out of her territory, and those lying south of
the Missouri Compromise line of 36° 30′ be permitted to
enter the Union either with or without slavery, as their
inhabitants desired. This resolution, Stephens afterward
claimed, was written by Brown in consultation with him.
All Stephens wanted in any annexation bill was a specific
guarantee of "the right of all states that might be formed
out of the territory South of 36.30 . . . to come into the
Union with slavery. . . ." As to Texas itself, he did not
much care, and was criticized in the South, especially by
Democrats, as being more violently opposed to annexation
than John Quincy Adams himself—as he certainly was not.
His point of view came out on January 25, when, on the
last day of annexation debate, he shook off the boredom
that had been gripping him and made a speech in favor of
Brown's resolution. He liked it, he said, because it clearly
settled the slavery issue; and he remarked that he wanted to
see Texas annexed because the Texans were Americans,
not bcause of any supposed economic advantages to the
South, since those would really accrue to the North and
West. He closed with a curious apologia: "I am no defender of slavery in the abstract," he said, and explained
that "stern necessity" only persuaded him to accept it in
the concrete. "If the annexation of Texas were for the

sole purpose of extending slavery . . . I should oppose it." [9]

"I spoke and made one of the best speeches I ever made. Everybody nearly said it was the best speech made—You never heard me make *half* such a speech," he wrote Linton in an outburst of boyish exultation. Toombs, though he disagreed with its content, thought the speech good; old John Quincy Adams called it "sophistical." Which it was, in the sense that it appealed to extremists on neither side. Like most Southerners, Stephens wanted Texas; and the concessions as to slavery that he asked for were an irreducible minimum beyond which he would never go.[10]

Within a month from the time of his speech Brown's resolutions were passed by both Houses; on March 3 Tyler sent them off to Texas; the following day James Knox Polk became President, and Stephens' career of opposition began. Political action and opinion for the next five years centered mainly on the war with Mexico which was the sequel to annexation, and on the rivalry between Northern and Southern power groups over the disposition of the vast territories that were acquired as a result of that war. Stephens had welcomed annexation, but he opposed the Mexican War with a bitterness and an intensity so extreme as to seem to derive from some other source than a simple hatred of unjust and aggressive warfare. That source was probably his hatred of Polk, for which no reasonable explanation exists. It was more than political; it was personal; and so far as can now be guessed, it had no particular

[9] A.H.S. to R. B. Burch, June 15, 1854, in *American Historical Review*, VIII, 91–7. *Recollections*, 18, speaks with as much inaccuracy as egotism about A.H.S.'s part in annexation. Speech in 28 *CG*, II, App., 309–14; criticism in Milledgeville *Federal Union*, undated clipping in *MC*.

[10] *MC*, January 25, 1845; John Quincy Adams: *Memoirs*, XII, 153; *The Correspondence of Robert Toombs, Alexander H. Stephens, and Howell Cobb*, ed. U. B. Phillips (Washington, 1911) (cited hereafter as *TSC*), 64. A Crawfordville friend assured him that local Whigs applauded his act, notwithstanding Democratic taunts that he had gone for a Democratic measure. *LC*, D. S. Anderson to A.H.S., February 11, 1845.

motivation. No cause appears. There may have been a cause—a word, a gesture, an act—but if there was, it has disappeared. All that can be said is that Stephens hated Polk and everything he did.

His hatred showed early in 1846, when he voted against a resolution terminating the convention between the United States and Britain under which both countries had been occupying the Oregon territory pending final settlement of a boundary between Canada and the United States. The negotiations had gone badly, and Polk was trying to bluff Britain from her position. "I am for our rights," Stephens wrote, "as far as they are clear"—which was ambiguous—"and in maintaining them thus far I should not suffer myself to be unfluenced by any consider-ations growing out of a fear . . . of war. Nor do I con-ceive that the questions of peace or war are at all involved in terminating the joint occupancy. . . ." If he thought this, and yet voted against the resolution, it is hard not to suppose that he did so largely because he did not like Polk.[11]

Perhaps, too, he was in a rebellious mood. His Texas speech had drawn sharp criticism. Democrats called him an abolitionist, to which charge he had an answer: "Bah!" And there were Whigs who had been disappointed at his favoring annexation.[11a] The year had been melancholy; at its opening his life had seemed to him a waste, "just as we gaze upon the surface of water we have crossed, filled with a consciousness of the transit, with but few traces or points to mark the path of our passage." He and Linton were most of the time still separated, and would continue to be so, for he had persuaded his brother to leave the University of Virginia for Harvard Law School. The summer, which

---

[11] *TSC*, 71–2; 29 *CG*, I, 349. "England has got rights in Oregon," he wrote the day before he voted. *MC*, February 8, 1846.
[11a] *Ibid*, W. M. Reece to A.H.S., February 18, 1845.

he had spent at home, had been marked by one event, his purchase from the estate of Williamson Bird, who had died, of the house where he had for several years been living. It was now his own house, and he at once had it repapered and reshingled and added a portico. Guests began coming in numbers; one day he had seven for dinner, but was too sick to attend to them, and so lay in bed sleeping while they amused themselves on the back porch. In the same year he bought a seven-acre tract of land in La-Grange. Things were going well; yet he was unhappy. All year thoughts of the dead oppressed him; he indulged often in solitary walks and dark musings; loathing and detestation of the human race filled his mind—"the baseness, meanness & brutality that abound everywhere"—and he even came to wonder how it was that man could fall so low as to "turn upon his own species . . . and make beasts of burden of them. . . ." When he went back to Washington at the end of November, he left his dog—whose illness in August he had treated with galvanic shocks and shower baths, for all the world as if he were a man—with the thought: "I do not know that I shall ever see him again." This profound gloom lasted into 1846, and while the country watched the Oregon squabble and looked for war with Mexico, he read Herodotus and other writers on ancient Egypt, Greece, and Mesopotamia, brooded upon the past, and kept much to himself.[12] His excitement over ancient history was for a time at a high pitch; he wrote Linton twelve- and sixteen-page letters crammed with information and read every book he could discover. What so fascinated him was mainly time, the mood of Shakespeare's sonnets of the "Devouring Time, blunt thou the lion's paw," brand, time the toppler of monuments, sower of grass in the deserted streets of populous cities. The

12 *MC*, January 5, February 28, March 1, 23, July 2, August 13, 15, 24, November 20, 1845; January 9, February 1, 1846.

vastness of history impressed him; and he was an American, citizen of a nation whose cities were growing faster than any had ever done before, and which was just now reaching out to snatch up into its empire yet more cities and more land. Perhaps he was thinking of a day in the future when America too would have fallen under the hand of time.

He still boarded at Mrs. Carter's in 1846–7, had a seat in the House in the third row, directly in front of the Speaker, and habitually dressed in black French cloth suits costing fifty dollars. His regimen was rather taxing; he lived, as he said, "completely by the clock," rising at half past eight, dressing in twenty minutes, spending ten more leafing through the morning papers. Breakfast was at nine promptly, after which he sat in his big armchair and smoked a cigar or two, meditating the while, finished the papers, took a walk alone where he could enjoy that "seclusion and loneliness" which he coveted, and then went to the House. After the day's session, which generally lasted until three or four in the afternoon, he returned and took dinner. Then he attacked his correspondence, writing steadily until about seven. His evening closed with reading or conversation until nearly midnight. At this moment his most constant companions were two young Representatives from his own state, an urbane and well-polished lawyer named Howell Cobb, aged twenty-seven, married, scion of one of Georgia's better families, serving his first term in the House; and John H. Lumpkin, nephew of old Governor Wilson Lumpkin, a few months younger than Stephens and very probably a friend of college days, since both had attended in the same years, though not members of the same class. With these two he lounged in his rooms at night, smoking and talking politics and life.[13]

13 *MC,* December 3, 5, 1845; December 20, 1844.

All through the spring of 1846 American relations with Mexico worsened. On January 13, the same day Stephens declined a dinner invitation from Polk, American troops were ordered to move to the Rio Grande, across territory claimed by Mexico. This they did, arriving late in March. Mexico protested, but the troops, under General Zachary Taylor, remained where they were. Under such circumstances an incident was inevitable, and on April 25 it occurred. The news took some time to reach Washington, but Polk, whose stiff Presbyterian mind was outraged by Latin indecisions and evasiveness, and who, besides, sensed that America would sooner or later take Mexico's vast California territories and perhaps felt himself the appointed instrument of the spirit of manifest destiny, had already decided to recommend war to Congress, and the news from the Rio Grande only hastened his plan. On May 11, a Monday morning, he sent a message to Congress, recommending war. The Mexicans, he said, "have at last invaded our territory and shed the blood of our fellow-citizens on our own soil." The House quickly found itself cheering this and other sentiments of similar purport, and responded to the President's appeal to arms by drawing up, reporting, and passing a declaration of war in a few hours by a vote of 174 to 14. Stephens abstained from voting, but both Toombs—who had just been elected to his first term in Congress, and whom Stephens was coaching with a solicitous eye—and Cobb voted aye, though each, not long before, had deprecated war. In the Senate there was more delay, the opposition of Calhoun and Benton contending that negotiations had not yet broken down and that until they did no declaration of war should be served. But the majority went ahead and announced that war existed by act of Mexico. Stephens was much pleased by Calhoun's stand, writing: "He said just what I should have said in substance if I could have gŏt a *chance*. . . . The whole catalogue of evils is properly and justly chargeable upon Mr. Polk. . . ." [14]

Whig opposition to and condemnation of the war was most bitter and vocal in its early months, before it had become painfully obvious that the mass of the people boisterously welcomed the war and gave not a tinker's damn for morality. The opposition had, in fact, only a lame leg to stand on. California was there: unless Britain got it, America would have to get it eventually; Mexico would not voluntarily give it up; therefore the only way to get it and save face was to provoke Mexico into war and claim it as an indemnity. The dispute between Mexico and America over the Texan boundary was the perfect *casus belli*: Mexico was weak and America strong. And therefore America's taking what she wanted was as natural as a cat's killing a bird. Stephens, who could see only that Polk had tricked the Mexicans, could never understand this point of view; and his condemnation of the war did not relax even when his party's clamor died, but persisted for years after the affair was ended.

He put himself on record on June 16, barely a month after hostilities had been commenced, speaking in approval of remarks made the previous day by Culver of New York, one of the fourteen who had voted against the declaration of war. Rising in his seat, dark eyes burning, black hair rumpled over his eyes, thin, awkward, pale, he began by denying that he was always opposed to war, but supported it only when he thought it just. Then he attacked the justice of the present war, ascribing its cause to Polk's ordering Taylor to march to the Rio Grande, an order he stigmatized as illegal and unwarranted, since the territory in dispute was empty and claimed by Mexico. The power to negotiate or act in respect to it lay solely

[14] *TSC*, 74, 76; *MC*, May 13, 1846.

in Congress. But since the war existed, he said, he would not hinder its speedy termination. What worried him was Polk's ultimate aim in waging it. If it was to be a simple war for conquest, he would have no part of it. America was destined to extend from ocean to ocean, but he deprecated a destiny realized by the sword. That would be a downward progress leading only to violence and licentiousness.

"It is to progress in *these* essential attributes of national greatness I would look: the improvement of mind; 'the increase and diffusion of knowledge amongst men'; the erection of schools, colleges, and temples of learning; the progress of intellect over matter; the triumph of the mind over the animal propensities; the advancement of kind feelings and good will amongst the nations of the earth; the cultivation of virtue and the pursuits of industry; the bringing into subjection and subserviency to the use of man of all the elements of nature about and around us; in a word, the progress of civilization and every thing that elevates, ennobles, and dignifies man. This, Mr. Chairman, is not to be done by wars, whether foreign or domestic. Fields of blood and carnage may make men brave and heroic, but seldom tend to make nations either good, virtuous or great." [15]

He had been reading ancient history, had seen the degradation and sodden decadence that came to empire after empire when they had swallowed all they could digest, and had grown old and bloated, their energies dissipated, their centers disintegrating, waiting for death. And he feared the same would happen to America. Granted the nature of man, the same course would necessarily produce the same result. His view of man was intensely conscious of sin and imperfection: "What is man," he had written, "but an animal—and one of the worst kind?" He saw it in

[15] *Cleveland*, 32, for his appearance while speaking; speech in 29 *CG*, I, App., 946–50.

history and he saw it everywhere in his world, and saw it
perhaps most profoundly in himself. Man, for him, was an
unmitigatedly evil thing. In his human contacts throughout life he never behaved as though he believed this; he
behaved, indeed, as though he supposed men to be the
purest idealists; and he firmly believed in progress of the
most orthodox nineteenth-century kind, as this speech on
the Mexican War shows. Despite his convictions about the
nature and possibilities of his race, he believed in telegraphs, in sanitation, and in railways. He shared in the
common romantic fallacy, so persistent even in our day,
that material and moral improvement would walk hand
in hand like lovers, that telegraphs and sanitation and railways would make men automatically virtuous instead of
becoming simply instruments by which men would ex-
ploit one another, instruments that would not eradicate
evil but merely give evil greater power to hurt. Of the con-
tradiction implied in his two notions of human baseness
and human progress he seemed never to be aware. They
were two poles of thought and feeling round which, on
one level at least, his personality was ordered.

His suspicions of Polk's intentions grew with the President's every act. Late in the summer Polk sent a special
message to Congress, requesting an appropriation of money
to be used in negotiating peace with Mexico. Money could
be only used to purchase territory, since Mexico, as Polk
remarked, could not possibly indemnify us with anything
else. But the acquisition of new territory like a magnet
pulled up once again the ancient slavery problem. As soon
as the special message was read on August 8, David Wilmot, a Pennsylvania Democrat, submitted an amendment
to the bill appropriating the money for which Polk asked,
the amendment providing that in any territory acquired
in consequence of the appropriation slavery should be
forever prohibited. The amendment passed in the House

without debate, Stephens, Toombs, and Cobb all voting against it, but it was killed in the Senate. At the moment almost no one realized what possibilities for trouble lay in this little sentence.

Stephens, going home late in the summer to campaign for re-election, did not mention the Wilmot Proviso; he had his hands full defending his speech on the war. Calhoun had so far approved it as to ask him to call so that he could tell him so in person; Justice McLean, who was angling for the 1848 Presidential nomination, had written a congratulatory letter; and the speech had won praise from many of his constituents. But in the Milledgeville *Federal Union* of July 21 there had appeared an article signed "Baldwin," flaying him for his attitude toward the war. He soon discovered that "Baldwin" was his old friend Herschel V. Johnson. This was unfortunate, but it did not deter him from serving notice upon Johnson that he wanted to fight a duel. Johnson, perhaps out of good nature, perhaps out of indifference, declined the challenge, and for nearly a decade the two men were not on speaking terms. Johnson being one of the Democratic leaders of middle Georgia, his attacks were those of his party; but Stephens, whose personal popularity in his own section was still climbing, defeated his opponent, a man named Turner, by a margin substantially greater than that of 1844,[16] and so could feel free when he returned to Washington to amplify his hatred both of Polk and of the war.

The war stumbled on through 1847 and into 1848, the Americans winning almost in spite of themselves; and while the armies marched into Mexico the politicians wrestled over the spoils. Polk delivered a steady stream of critical remarks about those, mostly Whigs, who disap-

16 *Recollections*, 18, recalls the wrong date for the Calhoun interview, which could not have occurred in May. *MC*, J. McLean to A.H.S., July 15, 1846; *LC*, T. Foster to A.H.S., August 29, 1846; L. Pendleton: *Alexander H. Stephens*, 85.

proved of the war, accusing them of giving aid and comfort to the enemy; and again requested a special appropriation for negotiation with Mexico. A bill to that effect,
with the Wilmot Proviso attached, was debated and defeated in the House—the same House that had five months
before passed the Proviso without debate. Then Polk had
a bill introduced providing for an augmentation of the
army, the result of his decision not to wait upon negotiations, but to push an aggressive war into the heart of Mexico. This bill was the signal for a flood of rhetoric, pro-
war, anti-war, pro-Polk, anti-Polk, proslavery, antislavery.
By January 5, 1847, Stephens was beginning to feel that
the government was about to go to pieces. "Quite a storm
is brewing about the slave question," he wrote to Linton.
"The North is going to stick Wilmots amendment to
every appropriation—and then all the South will vote
against every measure thus clogged . . . and perhaps Polk,
in starting one war, may find half a dozen on his hands.
. . ." 17

He himself was angry enough to start one of the half-
dozen. On January 22 he asked leave of the House to offer
a preamble and resolutions. The preamble stated the desire of the country to be to terminate the existing war as
soon as "honorable peace can be obtained," and noted
that some confusion existed as to the ultimate aims for
which it should be fought. The resolutions maintained
that the "present war with Mexico 'is not waged with a
view to conquest,' or the dismemberment of that republic
by the acquisition of any portion of her territory"; and
that the United States was willing to negotiate whenever
Mexico signified her readiness to do so. Immediate ob-
jection was made to the reception of the resolutions; and
Stephens moved to suspend the rules so that he might introduce them anyhow. The vote on this motion was al-

17 *MC,* January 5, 1847.

most a strict party division: the Whigs, aided by 9 Democrats and 5 members of the Native American party, voted to suspend, while the mass of Democrats, except for 16 Southern and 5 Northern members, who refused to vote at all, voted against suspension, defeating it by 88 to 76.[18]

In introducing these resolutions Stephens had acted independently and against the advice of the Whig leadership; yet when the moment came, the Whigs voted yea. They probably did so because they felt that the resolutions, ostensibly aggressive, were fundamentally defensive, implying as they did that if the territorial question were to prove so troublesome, the most expedient way to solve it was not to demand any territory. Whigs knew very well that the American people, by and large, wanted more territory rather than less or none at all, and that this evasion was therefore only a temporary expedient; but they knew too that party unity was of great importance and that on the basis of these resolutions some measure of unity might be preserved.[19]

Stephens' part all through these years was one of a minority critic, and his remarks on February 12 more than underlined his position. On that day he delivered a savage castigation of the President. According to him, Polk was the sole beginner of the war; he was a megalomaniac who considered himself a king whose ukases were not to be questioned but mutely obeyed; he was insolent, ambitious, unscrupulous, arrogant, dictatorial, "a self-constituted lordling," and he was warned to study the history of Charles I. He was fraudulently elevated to power; he was wicked; he was mischievous. As for his war, it was unnecessarily and unconstitutionally begun and waged solely for conquest and the President's self-aggrandizement. Finally, glancing

[18] 29 *CG*, II, 240.

[19] Berrien introduced similar resolutions in the Senate, probably in co-operation with Stephens. The Senate dealt likewise with them. 29 *CG*, II, 310, 545.

at the Wilmot Proviso, which Wilmot was threatening to introduce again come what might, Stephens accused the North of harboring a "fixed determination . . . that, if territory is acquired, the institutions of the South shall be forever excluded from its limits." He pointed out that the North would not yield and the South would resist; and wondered how, unless the acquisition of new territory were abandoned, the nation could resist civil war. If this was rancorous and intemperate talk on Stephens' part, it was only typical of the tone of debate, which terminated on February 15 in a snarl of bitter voting, when the Proviso was attached to the special appropriation bill by a close margin. Eventually the Proviso was removed and the bill repassed without it, but by then Stephens had gone home.[20]

At the end of 1847 Polk sent a commissioner to accompany Winfield Scott's army on its march to Mexico City, with powers to negotiate a treaty of peace whenever the opportunity offered itself. Early in 1848 it came; and on February 22 Polk submitted the treaty to the Senate. Until then Stephens said and did little, but so did Congress. On December 22, during a debate on the war, he had his resolutions reread, just in case anyone had forgotten them; and on January 3 Ashmun of Massachusetts moved to add to a resolution of thanks to General Taylor the statement that the war had been unnecessarily and unconstitutionally begun by the President. This sniping amendment, which Stephens claimed Ashmun introduced at his request, passed the House by 85 to 81. On February 2 Stephens fired another round in his verbal vendetta against Polk, an hour's speech interesting now only because it moved Abraham Lincoln, then a representative from Illinois, to pick up his pen and write his partner Herndon that "Mr. Stephens of Georgia, a little, slim, pale-faced consumptive

20 Speech in 29 *CG*, II, App., 351-4.

man, with a voice like Logan's, has just concluded the very best speech of an hour's length I ever heard. My old, withered, dry eyes are full of tears yet."

Lincoln's eyes, and Stephens' too, were full of tears for another reason on the 23rd of that month, when John Quincy Adams, diplomat, Senator, President, Secretary of State, and lastly Representative, died in the Capitol after suffering a stroke on the morning of the 21st. Stephens was moved with a more than public grief at his death, for the old man had been kind to him during his first years in the House, and in the summer of 1844 had written him a poem entitled "To Alexander H. Stephens, Esq., of Georgia," reading:

> Say, by what sympathetic charm,
>   What mystic magnet's secret sway
> Drawn by some unresisted arm
>   We come from regions far away.
>
> From North and South, from East and West,
>   Here in the People's Hall we meet,
> To execute their high behest
>   In council and communion sweet.
>
> We meet as strangers in this hall,
>   But when our task of duty's done,
> We blend the common good of all
>   And melt the multitude in one.
>
> As strangers in this hall we met,
>   But now with one united heart,
> Whate'er of life awaits us yet,
>   In cordial friendship let us part.[21]

It had been a plea from a lonely old man to a lonely young man, a plea for the salvation of America through mutual

21 *Richardson,* 87. This is a more wistful Adams than the one of the *Diary,* and an answer to those people who conceive of him as a walking iceberg with acetylene lips.

goodwill; and now Adams had died, having fought as hard as he could against the slaveholders of the South; had died at the beginning of a struggle between slaveholders and abolitionists and moderates beside which the worst he had seen looked like a wedding breakfast. By the treaty of Guadalupe Hidalgo the United States had gathered up New Mexico and California, and the slavery caldron began to bubble in deadly earnest.

III

In 1845 Stephens had professed to be no defender of slavery in principle; but from 1848 on, if he was not so hysterical a defender of it as men like William L. Yancey or Albert G. Brown, he at least did his best to apologize for its existence and explain away its more displeasing sides. His course was not unusual nor even hypocritical. Southern politicians who actively disliked slavery were becoming more and more scarce, and for two reasons. Firstly, they were for the most part either drawn from or allied with the handful of families that owned the majority of slaves and acres; secondly, the virulent onslaughts of abolitionists in the North upon not only their institutions but their whole society inevitably led them to defend themselves, and to defend the harbor the more viciously they were attacked. And therefore, though many Southerners, for various reasons, hated the society they lived in, their hatred did not find its way to the surface of political action.

As a society it was scarcely homogeneous, yet it had certain distinguishing characteristics, among which might be remarked its climate, generally warmer than that of the North; its most important staple crops, tobacco and cotton, around the cultivation-cycles of which a great deal of Southern society was built; and the presence (or absence) in it of the Negro. Details of life and custom varied from place to place, but always within the frame provided by these large conditionals; and the local culture in which Stephens lived, while it could not be typical, was as Southern as any other.

The belt of middle cotton counties, whose spokesman in Washington he was, had reached its highest prosperity during the 1830's and steadily thereafter lost ground. In the succeeding decades before the war the relatively untouched land in the southwest of the state received most attention; and not a few planters from the older region packed themselves off bag and baggage to Mississippi or Arkansas. In consequence, the population of Taliaferro County, the hardest hit, sank from roughly 5,000 in 1850 to roughly 4,200 in 1860. Between 1840 and 1850 it remained almost stationary. Of the twenty-two counties that at one time or another between 1840 and 1860 lay within Stephens' Congressional district, fourteen suffered a decline in population during the two decades.[22] At the same time the population of Georgia considerably increased.

The pace of life in middle Georgia—and this is true in some degree of the whole South—was slow and in some sections at a standstill. The Crawfordville of the 1840's was the Crawfordville of the 1850's, a very small and very provincial hamlet straddling the Augusta-Atlanta railroad line, lying in a slight trough between two rolling ridges, surrounded by gently undulating red country cultivated chiefly in cotton. In 1845 it was listed as having a brick courthouse (on the shoulder of the hill opposite Stephens' home, which he had named Liberty Hall), a jail, two "temperance" taverns (for there was a strong temperance movement during these years), an academy, a church, three stores, and four groceries. Its professional population counted four lawyers and five physicians, who served, not

22 This paragraph summarizes results obtained from studying the U. S. Census for 1860 (Population volume), and the *Compendium* of the 1850 Census issued by J. B. D. DeBow.

the needs of the town alone, for it had but 250 people, but those of the entire county.

It was profoundly rural, this region, as so much of the United States then was; and it measured time by seasons and rural rituals, by cotton-planting and cotton-picking, by hog-slaughtering and cornshucking, by wind and cloud —and railroad whistles. The railroad was its main connection with the large world, and people in the fields listened for the whistles coming west from Barnett and Thomson, east from Greensboro; and whenever the up or down train pulled in on the track of cast-iron rails spiked to rough-hewn ties, and stopped at the Crawfordville station to throw off bundles of mail and newspapers, there were groups of men and women, slaves and owners and yeomen, not waiting for anything particular, waiting merely to see the train.

There were likely, anywhere you looked, to be more slaves than white men in view. Taliaferro (they called it "Tollaver") lay in the black belt, where slaves outnumbered whites, sometimes seven to four. These slaves represented a great investment on the part of a comparatively few men, the planters, the men whose position the small independent farmers were striving to attain. Some of the planters were lawyers too, sometimes legislators—Stephens was both—but some were content to tend their acres and leave politics to the professional men. American government has always been government by lawyers, and it was especially so in the decades before the Civil War. And lawyers stand for the law and are possessed of a kind of legalistic *Weltanschauung*, and the law, in nineteenth-century America no less than anywhere else, was founded upon certain traditional conceptions of property and family; so that the lawyer's outlook was in general the outlook of the man of property, an outlook that distrusted change, admired stability, and loved the past.

The South at this time was sick. There was a routine of life, and a certain kind of prosperity, but something was wrong. Cotton was being grown in ever increasing quantities, but the planter found himself no richer. He had long ago suffered the Northern merchant to take care of the commercial end of his business: and now he could not free himself. The Northerner handled his crop, advanced him credit on it, shipped it for him, sold it for him, and in return kept the profits of the sale. The planter purchased most of his goods, imported or domestic, from the Northern merchant. And the price of cotton kept sagging—in the 1840's it dipped to seven cents a pound—and the price of slaves kept rising. When the price was high the planter planted feverishly, to realize a profit; but the result was overproduction and a fall in prices. And overproduction did not improve the quality of the soil, which, because the planter, with few exceptions, was ignorant of intensive methods of cultivation, wore out, cracked, and eroded without a pause year after year.

Population in the South increased, but that of the North increased much faster. Material wealth in the North multiplied at a dizzy rate; in the South it merely walked along. The greatest single item in the Southern balance sheet was two or three billion dollars' worth of human labor— and it was precisely this item that the abolitionists were seeking to destroy. It is no wonder that Southerners, though they felt something wrong, leaped to the defense and hysterically affirmed the beneficence of slavery. Nor is it a wonder that in their groping way they sought to render themselves independent of the radical and dangerous North, filled with European immigrants and refugees of 1848. They held conventions for direct trade and turned them into agitations for reopening the slave trade instead. They tried to organize their own factory system, and miserably failed. They tried—a very few—to reform their agricultural methods, but were not imitated. And they tried to keep control of the Federal government.

The struggle in which Stephens was involved was basically the struggle of the holders of nominal power—political power—to retain possession of it against the growing holders of real power—economic and financial and demographic. But the holders of nominal power were disunited themselves as to their plan of defense; and their disunity became most obvious whenever new accretions of land were made by the nation. There were those among the slaveholding oligarchy who believed that the only way to preserve their society and themselves was to expand the area of the slave economy as far as possible, to keep it dynamic and growing. There were those who believed rather that it would be best to maintain slavery where it now existed and not to extend it unless the North made a free gift of additional slave territory. There were also those who insisted upon an equal division of any new territory between North and South, and Stephens was one of these. At the moment, and until late in the 1850's, few Southerners believed in any independent political action. The parties as they existed were good enough for their purposes. Some favored the Whigs, some the Democrats: but whichever it was, their end was, by hook or crook, by logrolling, and backscratching all the Northerners they could, to keep themselves in power. Their lives depended on it, or so they thought—and considering their constant fear of slave uprisings, inspired or spontaneous, and the complicated system of patrols and passes and legal legerdemain they had erected, that they should think so was not surprising.

In such an atmosphere Stephens lived. The Georgia he loved, and the region in Georgia he loved yet more, for personal and psychological reasons, was stationary or decaying. He walked streets where commercial activity was slow; he traveled roads that were the worst in the country, past gullying fields belonging to men whose production costs were climbing and whose debts were increasing; he read and wrote by kerosene-oil lights; he washed himself with home-made soap; he studied ancient history, preferred Bulwer-Lytton to Sir Walter Scott, delighted in *Manfred* and the *Essay on Man,* planted corn and peas and snapbeans and tomatoes with his own hands in the garden behind his house, rode often to his plantation two miles off, where he grew cotton and wheat; he rode from county seat to county seat, arguing with clients and lawyers and judges; he dined on beeksteak, biscuits, waffles, and coffee, with vegetables in season; he attended marriages and funerals and parties—lived, in short, the ordinary round of life, and intensely loved it. He knew everybody in the county, and everybody called him "Ellick." And from 1846 on, his attachment to this town, these hills and creeks he knew by heart, became if anything yet greater; for Linton had come home from Harvard and hung out his shingle as a lawyer.[23]

He was, then, profoundly Southern; and when the wrestling began over the new lands that Mr. Polk had won from Mexico, his basic loyalties revealed themselves more sharply than they had yet done. In the spring of 1848, at the same time that New Mexico and California thrust themselves on Congress, there was trouble over Oregon. Southerners who did not know whether the North would agree to give them more room in which to extend slavery were reluctant to help the North extend freedom; and a bill for the territorial organization of Oregon languished

23 Crawfordville statistics from George White: *Statistics of the State of Georgia* (Savannah, 1849), 531–4. Description of middle Georgia partly from Arthur F. Raper: *Tenants of the Almighty* (New York, 1943), 40ff, and partly from observation, since the Crawfordville of 1945 differs from that of 1845 mostly in having a concrete highway, a movie theater, and several other degradations that may be lumped under the name of progress.

for some time, until Polk sharply reminded Congress that
the people in the region had a right to be protected from
the Indians. Then the bill was taken up in Senate. Now
the people of Oregon had prohibited slavery; and in
the bill was a section affirming the validity of all laws
passed by the provisional legislature of Oregon, including this one. The more violent Southerners refused to
stomach such an affirmation, for they feared that if Congress approved a territorial act forbidding slavery it would
create a bad precedent; and in any case they held with
Calhoun that nobody could prohibit slavery in a territory
until the territory was about to become a state. They
therefore fought bitterly to eliminate the sanction by
Congress of the antislavery clause in the Oregon laws.
Moderate Northerners suggested that the line of the Missouri Compromise be extended to the Pacific, thus solv-
ing the whole question; but the Southern radicals could
not be appeased by such compromises. The Wilmot Proviso had made them too suspicious of Northerners. Calhoun accused the North of trying to monopolize the territories—the accusation of a paranoiac, perhaps, and it
was impossible to reason with a paranoiac.

Reason, nevertheless, was tried. A select committee,
headed by Clayton of Delaware, was appointed in Senate
to adjust the Oregon dispute and to make some sort of
settlement for New Mexico and California. Stephens, in
the meantime, suddenly offered resolutions asking the
President, on July 10, what the boundaries of New Mexico
were. According to the Texans, Santa Fe belonged to
them; but the provisional New Mexican government had
taken up residence there and was daring Texas to come
and get it. In noticing this germ of possible trouble, Stephens was probably more actuated by an urge to embarrass Polk than anything else.

The compromise bill reported by Clayton, and passed

by the Senate on July 27, rendered valid all laws passed by the provisional Oregon legislature, unless they were incompatible with the Constitution. This meant, according to Clayton, that the question of slavery in Oregon would be referred to the Supreme Court. At the same time the bill provided for the territorial organization of California and New Mexico, but restrained their legislatures from enacting any laws respecting slavery, all disputes upon the subject to be likewise referred to the Court. This "compromise" was a simple evasion. When it came up for debate in the House on July 28, Stephens moved to lay it on the table; and after much angry bickering the motion was sustained, 112–97.

Those who supposed that at last the slavery question was solved were chagrined and disgusted. A long howl went up from Southerners, Whig and Democrat, who could not see why Stephens had behaved as he had. His reason was a legalistic one: he believed that if the question of the status of a slave in California or New Mexico were to come up before the Supreme Court, the Court would be bound to uphold the validity of the old Mexican law abolishing slavery in those regions—at least until they were ready for statehood. His critics were equally certain that the moment the United States acquired the territory, Mexican law ceased to operate and the Constitution, under which they claimed slavery could not be excluded from a territory, was automatically extended to cover it. The point was obscure; but Stephens' opinion caused him to vote, on his motion, with abolitionists like Horace Mann and Joshua Giddings, and against his own friends Cobb and Toombs, though he was fighting abolitionism as hard as they.[24] Clayton's bill was rejected, but Oregon was organized as a territory under the Northwest Ordinance of

24 *Cf.* Savannah *Georgian*, August 2, 1848, for a sample howl. Stephens' argument in *American Historical Review*, VIII, 94–5.

1787. At that the session closed, with everything in the air.

1848 was the Whigs' year of opportunity. Having chafed under the Polk collar for four years, they could, if they nominated the right man, tear it off. The right man, Stephens thought all through 1847, was Zachary Taylor, who had won enough battles in the late war to be eminently eligible for the Presidency. Taylor, who had never voted in his life, and was neither Whig nor Democrat, had sense enough to see that if he kept quiet both parties would scramble in the dust for the privilege of nominating him. And as it happened, the Whigs were a little quicker about it.

The subtle New York leader Thurlow Weed had been thinking of Taylor since 1846; but after the general's victory at Buena Vista in February 1847 other Whigs, especially those who did not want to see Clay capture the nomination again, took up the Taylor flag. Stephens at the time was messing with Senator John Jordan Crittenden of Kentucky, once Clay's friend but now no longer; and it was to Crittenden that Taylor wrote expressing his interest in the notion of becoming President. And Stephens, though he still admired Clay, so far approved of Taylor as to get the Georgia Whig convention in July 1847 to endorse Taylor's candidacy. He heard, during the fall, that Clay had approved his "no-territory" resolutions, but as soon as Congress met he got together with Lincoln, Toombs, and Truman Smith of Connecticut to form a club called the "Young Indians," for the purpose of propagandizing Taylor. Clay was coming to Washington to try to mend his broken fences, and to hold him back would be not easy.[25]

Until April 22, 1848 nobody knew whether Taylor would actually run or not. Two things forced his hand. One was Clay's announcement that he would seek the

[25] Thurlow Weed: *Autobiography* (New York, 1883), II, 571; *MC*, January 11, 1848.

AMBIGUOUS FRIEND AND CLEVER POLITICIAN:
HOWELL COBB.

(*National Archives, Photographic Records Office*)

LIBERTY HALL BEFORE IT WAS ENLARGED IN 1876.

(*From an engraving in Cleveland's A. H. Stephens*)

nomination; the other had to do with Stephens, Toombs, and Crittenden, who this year were living together at the Rush House. As soon as Clay had made his statement, the three sat down and drafted a letter for publication over Taylor's signature that was sent off to him at his sugar plantation in Louisiana, putting him on record as being a Whig, but desirous of becoming more than a mere party President, and as being opposed to the use of the veto power unless the Constitution were clearly imperiled. This letter arrived just in time to stop Taylor from sending a rather bald communication to the editor of the Richmond *Whig* declaring he would take a Whig nomination only if no pledges—such as one to veto the Wilmot Proviso should it pass in a bill—were required of him.

And when the Whig convention met at Philadelphia on June 7, the Southern delegates were met by Taylor managers who talked them from the station to their hotels and from dinner to bed if necessary to convince them that Clay was out and Taylor in. Their persistence was well rewarded, for on the first ballot Taylor received all the votes of Georgia, Alabama, Mississippi, Louisiana, Arkansas, and Missouri and majorities from Virginia, North Carolina, and Kentucky. Clay had only 14 votes in the South. Taylor was nominated on the fourth ballot without a platform —a deliberate omission. The Whigs were too hopelessly motley a party to elect a President except by concentrating their campaign upon him as a personality, avoiding national issues as much as possible. Taylor was boomed as a Fine Old Southern Gentleman and a brilliant soldier, and the Democrats to oppose him had only Lewis Cass, who held some very unsound opinions, such as that the people of a territory could exclude slavery if they wished. The men who pushed Clay out and Taylor in did so with a purpose. Clay was a trained politician, headstrong and impulsive, nationalist in his views, and it would be hard for a small clique to manage him. Management was vital to the Southerners, who were beginning to be outnumbered everywhere they turned. They needed a President they could handle; and they thought Taylor would prove such a man. He was a planter: which would win votes in the South; he was a soldier: which would win them in the North. And being a planter, he was one of them; his interests were theirs.[26]

The election of 1848 was, in a sense, the test of the Whigs as a party in the South. They could still count most of the aristocracy of land and professions in their ranks; but for how much longer depended upon what a Taylor Administration would do when put in office. Stephens went home that summer to campaign for Taylor, but spent most of his time defending his action on the Clayton bill. His district was fairly well under control: in the gubernatorial elections of 1845 and 1847 it had gone for the Whig nominees with room to spare; but in the latter year a Democrat named Towns had become Governor, and Towns was a radical. Stephens was the target of great abuse. The Milledgeville *Federal Union* propounded him a series of questions to which on August 30 he made careful answer, and among which were these: "Do you believe that Congress has the right under the Constitution to prohibit slavery in the territories?" This he denied in orthodox fashion. "Do you believe that the Constitution guarantees the slaveholder the right to carry his property into any part of the Union?" Yes: into any part where slavery is not prohibited by law. Then: "If you believe slavery to be excluded in California and New Mexico, how can you say the Clayton bill yields Southern rights, if no rights exist?" This was pertinent; and Stephens could only reply that since the South had given blood and treasure to make the con-

26 *J&B*, 226; George R. Poage: *Henry Clay and the Whig Party* (Chapel Hill, 1936), 175–80.

quest, she had a moral right to enjoy its fruits as well as the North. These were good answers, but many politicians were unsatisfied by them. Old Wilson Lumpkin pointed a finger of scorn: "Look at our little *pigmy* Stephens," accusing him of seeking "the distinction of infamy"; and even Berrien, who had voted for the Clayton bill, joined in the attack. "How," wrote a Kentuckian to Cobb in September, "does Stephens prosper under his motion and vote to lay the Compromise Bill on the Table?" [27]

Among the Georgia delegates to the Democratic convention was a judge of the northern circuit named Francis Cone, a capable lawyer who had ridden the circuit with Stephens in the early days. When Stephens came back from Washington in the middle of August, he was told that Cone had spoken in extremely bitter terms of his tabling the compromise—had called him a traitor. Stephens at first discredited these rumors, but decided to ask the judge whether they were true; and when the two met late in the month at a Whig rally out in the open, he did. The judge, a portly, dignified man weighing about three hundred pounds, said no, he had not called Mr. Stephens a traitor. This should have ended it, but Stephens thereupon explained to Cone that, had the rumor been true, he would have slapped the judge's face. Only a few weeks earlier he had again challenged Herschel Johnson for remarks the latter had made about him, and Johnson had again refused, saying, some told, that he had a soul to save and a family to support, while Stephens had neither.

Cone took the remark with good nature, and all might yet have gone off well had not the episode become a matter of public gossip. People asked the judge whether he had been slapped yet and whether he needed help to defend himself. This was tantamount to an accusation of

[27] Catechism in *TSC*, 117–24, 126; Richard H. Shryock: *Georgia and the Union in 1850* (Philadelphia, 1926), 166.

cowardice; and in the antebellum South to be called a coward was the unpardonable insult. So the judge sat down and wrote Stephens an angry letter demanding his retraction of the slap-in-the-face remark, to which Stephens calmly replied that the remark had merely been contingent.[28]

On September 3, before Cone had received this reply, the two men met accidentally on the piazza of the Atlanta Hotel. Cone demanded a retraction. Stephens quickly replied in his sharp, shrill voice that he had written a note and had nothing further to say. Cone called him a traitor. The teacher had raised the birch, and now the boy picked up the stone. Stephens, who never walked without a cane, raised the thin one he was carrying and struck the judge across the face. Cone, momentarily insane with rage, pulled a knife from his pocket and lunged at Stephens, who, dropping the cane, wrenched an umbrella from the judge's other hand and tried to parry the thrusts of the blade. Time after time the knife cut into his arms and torso; finally the judge flung his entire weight upon the slight pale gasping Stephens; the umbrella broke; Stephens fell backward to the floor with Cone on top of him, waving the knife in the air. "Retract," yelled the judge, pushing Stephens' head against the boards, "or I'll cut your damned throat!"

"Never! Cut!" The knife came down; he caught it in his right hand; the blade sliced through skin and flesh; the judge twisted it violently and pulled it away. Both men got to their feet; and now the judge was pinioned by several bystanders, while Stephens, breathless, his hair disheveled, his clothes torn and bloodstained, was carried into the hotel. One stab had come so close to the heart it was a miracle it had not penetrated. Dr. Eve of the Georgia

28 *Cleveland*, 97; *J&B*, 232; *Richardson*, 119.

Medical College thought at first he would not live, he was so weak and had lost so much blood. At Crawfordville that night crowds of people waited for the Atlanta train, to learn the worst. But by that time he was judged to be out of danger.

The assault put him out of the campaign. He stayed at home while his wounds slowly healed, writing letters of advice and persuasion with his left hand in a painful and laborious scrawl. The Whig leaders tried to use him as a political martyr who had come close to death in defense of his convictions, but with relatively little effect. Crittenden, looking on from Kentucky, was somewhat alarmed because with Stephens inactive the whole burden of the campaign in Georgia was thrown on Toombs, who could not do everything and be everywhere at once.[29] But there was no real need for alarm; in the Congressional elections, held in October, Whigs and Democrats broke even, each party electing four Representatives; and on November 10 Taylor received a generous majority, with hundreds of Democrats going to the polls to vote for him.

Once again—and for the last time—the Whigs had triumphed. The moment the election was over, Democrats began accusing them of having excuses prepared for Taylor, should he refuse to veto the Wilmot Proviso. Though the charge was not true, it did rather pointedly needle the Whigs' most tender spot. And events gave the Whigs no respite. They had asked for power: now what? The short session of Congress of 1848–9 accomplished nothing, as such sessions rarely did; but problems went on rising none the less. Polk, afraid lest the Californians grow weary of waiting, prodded Congress to provide some sort of government for the new territories; but when Stephen A. Douglas introduced a bill admitting California as a state

[29] *TSC*, 127; *LC*, J. J. Crittenden to A.H.S., October 6, 1848.

and New Mexico as a territory, it was laid aside and quietly forgotten. The most the expiring Congress was willing to do—and it was done only after much sordid and stupid quibbling—was to extend the Federal revenue laws over both California and New Mexico. In the course of debate upon this measure Stephens got up one day and irritably remarked that he opposed it, because he was not nearly so anxious as some might suppose to see governments established in the new territories: he did not care, in fact, whether they had governments this year, next year, or ever. And his angry indifference shocked James Buchanan, the Secretary of State, when Stephens told him that he was against the United States' keeping New Mexico and California. Having wanted no territory in the first place, his attitude was quite consistent. He was, in point of fact, thoroughly disgusted with the whole situation, South and North; and when Calhoun, concluding that the time for patience was over, called a meeting of all Southern Congressmen on December 22, 1848, Stephens at first refused to have anything to do with it, but then attended, and upon the presentation of a set of fiery resolutions moved to refer them to a select committee which was to report by January 15. This was the same caution that had prompted him to write Crittenden that he hoped the South would leave the territorial question alone until the territories were ready for statehood; and it was a caution shared by numerous Southern Whigs, who did their best to keep the tone of Calhoun's caucus moderate. They could not stop the rabid Democrats from signing and publishing a declaration of grievances, which met with approval in Mississippi—which issued a call for a Southern convention to meet at Jackson and consider Northern outrages—Alabama, and Missouri. But in Georgia there was strong resentment; even Cobb, good Democrat though he was, wished Calhoun would die and rid the world of a great nuisance.[30]

Taylor, meanwhile, was jogging toward Washington, stopping at Lexington to try to persuade Crittenden to become his Secretary of State. Crittenden declined, recommending Clayton of the Compromise. Stephens, hearing this, frantically wrote the Kentuckian to accept the post, saying in italics: "You must not refuse." But Crittenden did refuse, and the most Stephens could do was to persuade Taylor to make George W. Crawford his Secretary of War, and William Preston of Virginia Secretary of the Navy.[31]

The new President, a blunt and honest-looking man, but hardly handsome—his soldiers thought he looked like a toad on horseback—delivered a pleasantly brief inaugural on the 4th of March, and settled down in the White House with two influences at work upon him, one at either ear—Stephens and Toombs, and William Henry Seward. Seward, who had recently remarked: "There are two antagonistical elements of society in America—freedom and slavery," came down from New York, cigar in mouth, and spent the spring and summer trying to seduce the President away from the slavery element. Stephens was soon aware of this, and began suspecting Preston of becoming friendly with Seward—for some personal purpose. But until the beginning of December there was an ostensible breathing-space, while radical fires, North and South, smoldered, waiting for the wind that would puff them into open flame. In Georgia, Towns the radical was re-elected Governor. In Mississippi radicals were calling a Southern convention to meet at Nashville the following June. . . .

Stephens spent the summer attending to court business,

---

[30] James K. Polk: *Diary* (Chicago, 1910), IV, 249, 252-3, 300-1; Poage: *Henry Clay*, 193; A. C. Cole: *Whig Party*, 140; 30 *CG*, II, 348-9.
[31] Poage: *Henry Clay*, 183-4; *TSC*, 146; *Recollections*, 24-5.

except for July, when a severe attack of diarrhea drove him
to Warm Springs for relief. It was a dismal interlude, for
there were few more depressing things than the spas of the
nineteenth century. It rained incessantly; there were goats
wandering on the piazzas of the buildings; the cabins were
dirty, with broken mirrors, uneven-legged chairs, and beds
full of insects; but he played chess, read Carlyle, and got
to sleep at midnight every night.[32] From here one could
take a view of the world and of one's place in it. He
still brooded far too frequently upon such subjects, in
his dark and sometimes melodramatic fashion, and was
still intensely unsatisfied with what he had done. "How
intimately connected is mind with matter," he had once
exclaimed; and cursed the fate that made him puny, continually at the mercy of disease, and never able to meet
stronger men on their own ground. And because he could
not be physically equal, he more and more tended toward
the belief, perhaps largely unconscious, that he was mor-
ally superior. "Of right, truth, justice and moral excel-
lence, which is real greatness," he told Linton, "I have
my own notion, and in my way may not be without ambition, but I am conscious that there is little or no con-
geniality of spirit, views or desires between me and those
who are considered models in those respects in our own
day. . . ." And this consciousness of difference took long
to be reconciled to: he was as yet too acutely aware of it
to be happy. It must have contributed to his depressive
states, perhaps in considerable measure. Those moods
came and went, and he felt himself utterly helpless: he
spoke of melancholy as "that mental night-mare that seizes
upon and enervates every faculty of the soul—Who has
not felt its stealthy approach—and yet who has ever been
able to resist its power?" [33] The influence that melancholy

32 *MC*, July 23, 1849.
33 Ibid., December 12, 1847.

exerted upon his political opinions can only be guessed at; yet it must have been incalculable.

The period of Stephens' Whiggism was by this time nearly ended, though he probably did not yet suspect it. How should he, having only a year ago been instrumental in the election of the last Whig President? How could he have supposed that within another year the Whig party would be caught in a fatal disintegration? The signs looked bad in December 1849, and they grew progressively worse; but the full realization of his position did not come for some time.

The events of 1849–50, and the achievement and meaning of the Compromise of 1850, have been intensively studied again and again and are matters of common knowledge. Stephens' part in them was one of defense and protest, rather than of positive action—it may, indeed, have been a sense of the ineffectuality of the position he held so long as he remained with so unstable a party as the Whigs, especially during this year, that spurred him eventually to sever his connections with them. The Congress he returned to in December 1849 had 112 Democrats, 13 Free-Soilers, and only 105 Whigs—and the Whigs were supposed to be in power. In preliminary caucus the Southern wing of the party, led by Stephens and Toombs, demanded pledges from the Northern wing that it would oppose the Wilmot Proviso and the abolition of the slave trade in the District of Columbia; but the Northerners refused. They were growing restive, growing tired of deferring to Southern sensitivity; and upon their flat refusal to do so any longer Stephens "quit the meeting, as did Toombs, Cabel, Merton, Hilliard, Owen and some others. I told them distinctly and positively that I should hold no connection with a party that did not disconnect itself from these aggressive abolition movements. . . . My Southern blood and feeling is up and I feel as if I am pre-

pared to fight at all hazzards and to the last extremity." [34]
This was an abrupt flash of temper, but it lasted; and all
through the prolonged contest for the speakership, fought
out between Robert Winthrop, the Whig candidate and
a Massachusetts man, and Howell Cobb, the Democratic
candidate, Stephens and his friends refused to vote for
either man. Both he and Toombs let themselves go in an
orgy of fire-eating, he warning the House on December
13 that "the day in which aggression is consummated upon
any section of the country . . . the Union is dissolved,"
adding: "If gentlemen suppose that by singing pæans to
the Union it is to be preserved, they will find themselves
mistaken. The Union was founded upon justice—immu-
table justice—and right." He questioned: "Would you have
us of the South to be an appendage to the Union?" and
replied: "I tell you for one . . . before that God who
rules the universe, I would rather that the southern country should perish. . . ." [35] Even conservatives were getting
angry. To Linton, who had been elected to the Georgia
legislature, he wrote: "If the South intends really to resist
the abolition of Slavery in this District . . . it is time they
were making the necessary preparations of men and money
arms and munitions. . . . No step should be taken unless
we intend to stick to the Union at any hazzard. . . ." This
was confused; for if steps were taken, there would be no
Union to stick to. "I shall yield nothing to the aggressor,"
he said, but ended with an admission no fire-eater would
make: "I believe the agitations at the South for several
years have done more to effect it [i.e., the present crisis]
than all others united." [36] The reasons for his alarm were
genuine: the California and New Mexico controversy had
not been settled, and if settled favorably to the North, they

[34] *Ibid.*, December 2, 1849.
[35] 31 *CG*, I, 29.
[36] *MC*, December 3, 4, 1849.

constituted together with Oregon three additional states thrown against the South; and the sudden movement for the abolition of the slave trade—and possibly even slavery —in the District of Columbia might be an entering wedge for a general legislative campaign to strangle slavery everywhere in the South.

He had still one hope: the President, whom he visited on December 5, coming away satisfied that Taylor would in his message take a general position similar to his own. When the message was read, it merely noted that the people of California had written a state constitution and would petition Congress for admission into the Union. This petition Taylor recommended should be favorably acted upon: a view with which Stephens disagreed. He— and many other Southerners—persistently refused to let California come in as a free state without some reciprocal concession being made to the South.

And so it took from February to September to work out, with pain and sweat, a plan of compromise. The California constitution was sent in to Congress by Taylor on February 13, with a strong plea for approval; but several weeks before that the ominous state of affairs in both parties had given Henry Clay the excuse to appear for the last time before the American people in his role of the great Compromiser. After all, men were carrying bowie-knives and revolvers to the Capitol, and talk was growing loud. Southerners stood firm; Free-Soilers and their Whig allies were ready to fight to the end to stop appeasement to the South. It was worse than 1820; worse than 1833. Perhaps Clay could do something. Of his speech, delivered on February 5 and 6, and his eight resolutions, supposed to be known by every schoolboy, Stephens thought very highly; yet Clay's action did not lift his own gloom. He feared that the North, growing triumphantly powerful, would "carry abolition wherever by the Constitution [it] can"; and he could not see that there would ever be "harmony and peace between the two great sections of the Union. . . . A dismemberment of this Republic," he went on, talking his thoughts out to Linton, "is not amongst the improbabilities of a few years to me—In all my acts here I shall look to that event—I shall do nothing to favour it or hasten it but I now consider it as almost inevitable." [37]

With one significant exception, though, Stephens stood passively by during the juggling and adjustments out of which the Compromise came. The House, most of the time, discussed other matters, leaving the arrangements to the Senate; it was only on February 18, when a man named Doty from Wisconsin moved a resolution instructing the Committee on Territories to prepare a bill for the admission of California, that the House exploded. On his resolution Doty moved the previous question. The Southerners, desperately anxious to prevent anything being done about California without some concessions to themselves, organized to defeat Doty's motion. Stephens went the rounds of the House to see that the forty-one members who constituted one fifth of the membership would demand the yeas and nays on every motion. Then, until midnight, the chamber was a bedlam, with incessant motions to adjourn and incessant demands that the roll be called. So well did the forty-one members hang together that nothing was accomplished until midnight, when the Speaker—Cobb—ruled Doty's motion out of order.[38]

Stephen A. Douglas, chairman of the Senate Territorial Committee, growing annoyed at this filibustering, sent his lieutenant in the House, John A. McClernand of Illinois, to see Stephens and Toombs that evening, to find out what they wanted. They told him they did not object to the admission of California as a free state (though less than a

37 Ibid., January 21, February 10, 1850.
38 *View*, II, 201–2. 31 *CG*, I, 375–85.

month before the admission of California had been made
a condition on which the Georgia legislature had resolved
to call a state convention) "if the Territorial question
could be first satisfactorily adjusted," meaning if the people of New Mexico and Utah were to be permitted to
admit as well as exclude slavery. McClernand thought a
compromise could be effected on this basis, and suggested
that Stephens and Toombs meet him next night at the
Speaker's house for a full discussion. On the 19th, then,
Stephens, Toombs, and Linn Boyd of Kentucky met at
Cobb's house with McClernand and Richardson of Illinois.
McClernand reported that Douglas was satisfied in substance with the Southern proposal; after some talk the
drafts of the bills dealing with New Mexico and Utah were
written out, and the little group separated.[39]

The job now was to make certain of the President's
support, and also to ensure his vetoing of the Wilmot
Proviso should it be attached to any of the bills. And on
the 23rd Stephens, Toombs, and Thomas Clingman of
North Carolina went to visit Taylor, whom Seward had
pretty well convinced that Congress was against him and
that he must save the Union. The interview was discon-
certing. When the three asked Taylor what he intended
to do, the President replied that he would approve any
constitutional bill—meaning he would not veto the Proviso. Stephens and Toombs protested angrily, and the
President replied in kind. Whether Stephens threatened
disunion and Taylor countered with a promise to hang
disunionists the instant they appeared is not certain, but
the exchange of opinions left all parties considerably
ruffled: Taylor, a few moments later, greeted Seward's associate Thurlow Weed with: "Did you meet those damned
traitors?" The "traitors," for their part, went to talk to
Webster, their account of what had happened startling

[39] *View,* II, 202–4; Shryock: *Georgia and the Union,* 217–32.

him into making a definite decision to address the Senate in favor of Clay's compromise resolutions.[40]

It looked therefore as if the settlement would meet with Taylor's opposition. There was friction, too, between Clay and Douglas, especially when, after several months of debate in the Senate, a select committee headed by Clay was appointed to study the whole involved tangle of disputes; and this committee reported as its compromise a long bill —the famous Omnibus—composed of territorial bills for New Mexico and Utah which had been introduced in March in both Houses by Douglas and McClernand as the fruit of the conference at Cobb's house on February 19; of a bill for the admission of California as a state; of a bill for the awarding of ten million dollars to Texas in return for her abandoning her territorial dispute with New Mexico; of a new fugitive-slave bill; and of other bills embodying all Clay's original compromise proposals. Douglas disliked Clay's amalgamation of all these bills into one, for he feared that Senators who would vote for certain parts of it if they were separated would vote against the Omnibus because it contained other parts they did not want passed.

The Omnibus was debated until July 31. Stephens looked on, as depressed as ever, going his daily rounds up and down the city, carrying his papers, like Lincoln, in his hat, attending to his constituents' business at the Land Office or the Pension Office or the Surgeon-General's Office. "The only hope I have for the future," he wrote, "is in the virtue of the great mass of the people . . . in resisting the temptations of those who would deceive, cheat, degrade

40 Weed: *Autobiography*, II, 176–8; Claude M. Fuess: *Daniel Webster* (Boston, 1930), II, 208. Weed said Stephens had threatened disunion unless Taylor complied with Southern demands; and in 1876 got into a public argument about it, Stephens categorically denying (New York *Herald*, August 8, 1876) that he had ever had a stormy interview with Taylor, or induced him "to veto any bill." But Stephens by this time was in no condition to be categorical about anything except the events of the current year.

and destroy them. . . ." At the same moment he learned that Preston and Clayton—the former his recommendation to Taylor—were urging the President to oppose the Omnibus. He learned too that Georgia papers were attacking him for first threatening disunion and then favoring Clay's compromise. His opinion of human nature sank almost below zero: "As to the Democrats . . . they are a poor ignorant deluded set of fools. . . . The same may be said of the great majority of all who bear the name of man— selfishness, cunning, baseness, intense ambition, ignorance and folly rule the world. . . . Oh the villiany the villiany of this world's meanness. . . ." His solicitude for Linton, as always at his more desperate moments, deepened past its usual intensity. "I have a great desire," he told him, "that you may succeed in attaining the brightest honors and distinctions in your day—I dont mean offices—they may come or not—But I mean that you may be able to command the respect regard and esteem of men. . . . All the hopes, objects, desires and ambition of my life are now centred in you. . . ." And he advised Linton to have nothing to do with the coming Southern convention at Nashville, declaring himself unequivocally opposed to disunion.[41] He watched and waited, spent his evenings playing euchre or walking with Toombs or writing Linton, or attending dinners and teas. At one of these teas a Virginian lady asked him a riddle: Why is love like a canal? He confided to Linton the answer he would have liked to give: Because it is certain evidence of a spirit for internal improvement. . . . But he reserved his outspokenness for politics.

His relations with Taylor became more and more strained just before the President's unexpected death on July 9. The people of New Mexico had drawn up a state

41 Shryock: *Georgia and the Union,* 247, 251; *MC,* February 10, March 19, April 12, 21, May 19, 1850.

constitution, prohibiting slavery, of which Taylor approved, while at the same time he revoked, over George W. Crawford's protest, orders to the commandant at Santa Fe instructing him to avoid collisions with Texan authorities. Crawford told Stephens and Toombs; and Stephens went on July 3 to see the President, but could not make him change his mind about New Mexico. Thereupon Stephens fetched Toombs and went to find Preston, whom he believed responsible for Taylor's attitude. They met Preston in front of the Treasury Building. Stephens told Preston what he thought, warning that if troops were sent to Santa Fe, or resistance offered to Texas, the President would be impeached. "Who," Preston demanded, "will impeach him?" "I will," Stephens answered, "if nobody else does." Preston turned away without a word. Next day Stephens announced in the *National Intelligencer* that if armed conflict should occur over Texan claims on Santa Fe, the cause of Texas would be the cause of the South.[42]

It might have been; but on the 9th Taylor died, and the whole complex changed color. Stephens, writing Linton, protested: "I had for him [Taylor] a high respect and sincere regard," and blamed Seward and Preston for their differences. It did not matter now. Debate on the Omnibus went on and on until the 31st, when, the vote being finally taken, section after section was stripped from it until nothing but the territorial bill for Utah was left. Stephens, utterly disgusted and convinced that "the people before long will find that this Government is a humbug," decided to go home, though on August 6, before he went, he made some remarks in the House. In private he spoke of the slave trade as "the infamous traffic," and speculated upon the "fate of the poor African," whose "condition as a

---

[42] *MC*, July 10, 1850; *Recollections*, 26; *TSC*, 192–3. Cf. *ante*, p. 110. The Texans still claimed Santa Fe.

slave is certainly not a good one"; but to the House, while affirming devotion to the Union, he made a blunt threat: "Whenever this Government is brought in hostile array against me and mine, I am for disunion—openly, boldly and fearlessly, for *revolution*. . . ." To the majority he said: "I am for conciliation, if it can be accomplished upon any reasonable and just principles. I am also for making a clean business of it. If we aim at peace, let us have no temporary truce, but permanent quiet and repose." He contemptuously repudiated the accusation that the South, out of petulance and ill grace, was trying to force the rest of the nation to accept its dictates: "When . . . did the South ever attempt to control the action of this Government for the promotion of her peculiar interests? . . . A public domain has been acquired by the common blood . . . of all, and the South . . . asks nothing but that the common territory . . . may be opened to the entry and settlement and equal enjoyment of all. . . . There must be concessions by the North as well as the South. Are you not prepared to make them?" If not, "the responsibility will rest upon your own heads." The responsibility would ultimately rest upon more than Northern heads. When he had spoken he went home, though the Compromise was not enacted into law under Douglas' guiding hand until the middle of September.[43]

The mass of the Southern people had paid very little attention to the Nashville convention: the elections for delegates in Georgia, for example, were a complete fizzle. But the moment the Compromise became law the radicals redoubled their efforts to bring on a general hysteria; and their efforts were most conspicuous in South Carolina, Georgia, and Mississippi. Governor Towns, in correspondence with the Governor of South Carolina, called a state

[43] Speech in 31 *CG*, I, App., 1080–4; *MC*, March 25, May 20, July 14, 16, 31, 1850.

convention to meet on December 10 to decide what Georgia would do about the settlement; and the Carolinian and
Mississippian radicals sat down to see what Georgia's response would be before calling similar conventions of
their own.

The elections for delegates were to be held on November
25, and Stephens, Toombs, and Cobb, all of whom were
back in the state by October, had until then to clinch the
Compromise with the people. Stephens was assured that
almost nobody was prepared for violent action; but the
disunionists, led by Henry L. Benning, who favored immediate secession, Walter T. Colquitt, and Charles Mc-
Donald, and aided by Towns—all of them Democrats—
thumped their tubs as noisily as they could, attacking the
North, the Union, and the Compromise. But the moment
had not yet arrived. To the small farmers and the small
planters, to townspeople and professional people, California and New Mexico were far away; and the South was
experiencing just then a prosperity it had not known in
nearly a decade. Stephens later calculated he had traveled
three thousand miles over Georgia that autumn, addressing mass meetings and barbecues, speaking from wagon
tops or courthouse steps or platforms to crowds of farmers
dressed in their Sunday clothes—had traveled over low-
land, hill country, piedmont, on rutted, leaf-dampened,
rain-filled roads, late cotton being picked, rows of corn-
shucks in the fields. And on November 25 the people went
to the polls and elected an overwhelmingly conservative
convention, the radicals winning in but ten of ninety-three
counties.[44]

On December 10 the convention met at Milledgeville,
elated, peaceably disposed, two hundred and sixty-four
strong, mainly composed of the well-to-do. The radical
minority was ruthlessly gagged, and on the 13th came

[44] Shryock: *Georgia and the Union*, 310 et sqq., 316, 319.

the report of a select committee on the state of the Union, posing the question: "May Georgia, *consistent with her honor,* abide by the general scheme of pacification?" Georgia, the committee replied, could and would abide; but it then issued a warning against further aggressions by the antislavery element in the North; and, saying that Georgia would remain in the Union only so long as the Union protected minority rights, it concluded that on the faithful execution of the new fugitive-slave law depended everything else. This report, to be famous for the next ten years as the Georgia Platform, was ratified next day by 237 to 19. Everywhere it was praised by moderate-minded men. Clay wrote: "It crushed the spirit of discord, disunion, and Civil War." [45] And yet—the contingencies expressed were as significant as the pledges. It did not say the South would not resist; it named the cases in which it would. It guaranteed no peace.

The Georgia political situation, that December, was unrecognizably confused. Union men, Whig or Democrat, and radicals, Whig or Democrat, acted together regardless of party lines. And on December 11 the Union men met in the state Capitol and formally organized as a political party, with Stephens, Toombs, and Cobb at the head. The Whigs were finished as a national party; they had been born in a spirit of coalition, and the pressure that had held them together had given way before another, far stronger pressure. Stephens understood this; and he conceived the notion of a great national party of which this Union group would be the nucleus, a party composed of men North and South who believed in conciliation and in the Union. The Whigs were gone; the Democrats were knaves. But perhaps no such party as the one he imagined

45 *Journal of the State Convention Held in Milledgeville in December, 1850* (Milledgeville, 1850), 11–19, 33; Shryock: *Georgia and the Union,* 337–9.

could exist in his America. The ignorant, the foolish, the malignant, were in a majority. The air was thick with false lights, and reason was neither common nor wanted.[46]

Stephens was now not quite thirty-nine, and already, at times, weary of ambition. "I am . . . sick of public life, public men, and public events." All his hopes, he said, were nailed to Linton, for "I feel as if my race is nearly over . . . I am inclined at an early day to retire from the public gaze." But he seemed always to think so, and yet kept on. "I am very much like some chronometer, I need a weight or something bearing down upon me to keep me in motion. . . . The greater the weight generally the greater the reaction." [47] And so he went on—in spite of himself. The years of minority criticism were drawing to a close. His tone had of late become rather more fiery than it had been at the outset; for though his love of the Union was real enough, and sincere, so was his fear that the South was in danger of becoming a Northern province; and out of this fear, augmented by his profound passion for justice and equality, came those somewhat strident words of warning about revolution.

Who those Southerners were who consistently championed disunionism was not determined by economics alone. Nothing ever is. Economic elements figured in the situation, as they inevitably do, but that which caused this man to be a Unionist and that one a disunionist was a complex of elements in which a decisive factor is often impossible to find. Speaking as broadly as possible, however, there are several facts which cannot be ignored: the fact that the small farmers and so-called "poor whites" of the barren regions and the mountain areas of east Tennessee, western Virginia, western North and South Carolina, northwest Georgia, and northeast Alabama—that

[46] Shryock, op. cit., 335.
[47] *MC*, December 22, 1847; March 6, April 21, 1850.

these people, who held few or no slaves, hated the Negro and disliked the planter, opposed disunionism with some consistency all through this period; the fact that in the main the planters—including all holding more than fifty slaves—while always on the alert against danger to their vested interests and social status, were not aggressively inclined, deprecated violence, hoped their interests might be maintained by astute political maneuvering and the winning of "collaborationist" Northern support, and tried to persuade the North that its own prosperity lay in "collaboration"; and the fact that the shrillest, most raucous disunion agitators were men whose convictions were not necessarily determined by their economic or social position. They might be upcountry poor-boys-turned-rich, like Albert Gallatin Brown; but they might just as easily be men whose fathers had achieved position and bequeathed it to them, like Howell Cobb. They were, in any event, the Sam Adamses of their time; and the planters, like the colonial merchants, hesitated to co-operate with them whenever it seemed as though they were going to precipitate violence. The planters and the yeomen farmers, who generally shared their viewpoints and aspirations, were willing enough to fight when they believed their existence, to be preserved, demanded fighting; but it took the agitators a long time—with the unwitting help of the abolitionists—to convince them: it took, in fact, until 1860.

Now, Stephens came of meager circumstances; but he was bred in a region of planters and yeomen farmers; for many years his contacts were mainly with people of these strata; and he shared their abhorrence of lawless violence. But if he loved the Union, he loved Georgia more, and through Georgia the South; and he would not hesitate to join the agitators, even though he spoke contemptuously of them, whenever he thought overt aggression was being committed against the South. In 1850 the oppression was

not yet overt; it was potential, not actual; something to
be averted, not resisted. And when Clay came forward with
his compromise, Stephens saw no reason for further opposition. The new fugitive-slave law and the law enabling
the people of New Mexico and Utah to admit or prohibit
slavery as they wished were concessions heavy enough in
his eyes to balance California. A settlement had been arrived at, and in the process he had discovered that Northern Whigs could not be relied on to "collaborate." He
therefore cast about for some new party whose Northern
members could be trusted. Why he so disliked the Democrats is hard to fathom. He was willing to co-operate with
individual Democrats, but could not stomach the party,
and suspected it—especially its Southern wing—of the
rankest venality and opportunism.[48] Perhaps his detestation of Polk had colored his whole view. At any rate, here
he stood, in December 1850, on the edge of five years of
indecision.

III

Until the winter of 1854 there was, in a political sense,
so far as he was concerned, comparative quiet. Psychologically, though, it was a time of intense conflict, a conflict
which he succeeded in concealing so well even from Linton that its causes can now only be guessed at. At the beginning of 1851 he wrote Linton a wild, Werther-like letter
running in part: "Man's life is but a dreary pilgrimage
through an inhospitable clime. . . . Sometimes I have
thought of all men I was most miserable—That I was particularly doomed to misfortune, to melancholy, to sorrow
and grief—That my pathway of life was not only over the
same mountains and heaths and deserts with others but
that an evil genius was . . . following at my side and forever mocking and grinning and making those places which

---

[48] *Cf. MC,* December 31, 1849: "The Southern Democrats are using the
slave question for nothing but political capital."

in the lives of others are most happy . . . most miserable."
Was he perhaps here thinking of marriage? As if he would
break off he scrawled: "No it is useless—" but went on, for
he could not help himself: "The misery—the deep agony
of spirit and soul I have suffered no mortal on earth
knows. . . . The torture of body is severe. . . . But all
these are slight when compared with the pangs of an
offended or wounded spirit. . . . I am tempted to tell you
a secret—It is the secret of my life. . . . The secret of my
life has been *revenge*. . . . Not revenge in the usual ac-
ceptation of that term—But a determination to war over
against fate—To meet the world in all its forces, to master
evil with good. . . . My greatest courage has been drawn
from the deepest despair! . . . I have often had my whole
soul instantly aroused with the fury of a lion and the ambition of a Cæsar by . . . as *slight* a thing as a *look!* Oh
what have I suffered from a look! What have I suffered
from the tone of a remark . . . from a supposed injury?
an intended injury? But each . . . such pang was the
friction that brought out the latent fires. . . ." [49]

Physical inferiority, apparently, still made him unhappy; he had not yet made peace with his body. All his
friends were healthy men, relatively untouched by the
agonies he was compelled to suffer—indeed, it would seem
as though he chose them for their virility. Cobb was a great
eater and a corporeally imposing person; Toombs boasted
he had not known the taste of medicine until he was
thirty-five or thereabouts. Even Linton, who was never in
the best of health, was larger and stronger than himself.
These men could do things he could not permit himself—
they could drink on a magnificent scale; they could eat

[49] *MC*, February 3, 1851, a trifle misquoted in *J&B*, 262-3. *J&B* did a
considerable amount of such misquoting. Perhaps they were trying to
patch the cracks in their hero's statue, for he read their proofs from the
sublime heights of seventy years, with the valley of the past somewhat
blurred by haze.

what they liked; they could have sexual intercourse. Most of them were married; but he had convinced himself long ago that marriage was for him out of the question. Leaving aside the problem of the woman who might feel, not only intellectual love, but physical desire for him, the pitiful inadequacies of his body probably would have precluded him from sexual activity. His nervous energy at all times was phenomenal, and its source a mystery—unless its manifestations in personal and political efforts be regarded as some kind of sublimation—and, he very likely thought, if he were to do all he intended to do he could not afford to spend that energy gratuitously. He had to be so careful, and even with all his care he was continually falling ill: either it was a cold, or it was the bowels, or it was neuralgia, or it was migraine, or it was the liver. . . . And therefore he was barred out, irrevocably barred, from a vast area of normal human action; and the fact infuriated him.

His consciousness of inferiority, and the constant strain it imposed upon his nervous system, led him often to be irritable and brusque and even overbearing in his dealings with others; for if he could not impress the world with his masculinity, he would impress it with his intellect and rectitude. Therefore even if he was wrong on some occasions, it was absolutely necessary to his pride that he be right. The structure of his defense was based upon infallibility. If once he were, in his own eyes, proved wrong, the whole house would come tumbling down. A delicate foundation; a top-heavy edifice; yet he somehow managed to keep it together.

If his inferiority made him proud, it also aggravated his natural inclination toward melancholy. He suspected this, attributing his moods once to "some physiological derangement." And yet they were not wholly due to physiological causes, as the last twenty years of his life would show. He knew in his heart that they were a weakness, not a trait to glory in, and made spasmodic efforts to cure himself. In 1847 he prematurely announced that he had done so by reading Burton's *Anatomy of Melancholy* and finding himself suddenly laughing at his foolish indulgences; but the sickness was deeper than that, and more difficult to reach. It could not, in the nature of things, disappear until he had learned to be content with himself as he was.

While he struggled with himself, letting never a hint of the struggle escape, maintaining a front of good nature and social poise, so that wherever he was, the conversation was lively and suffused with humor, politics was almost at a standstill. In January 1851 he signed, together with Clay and other Congressmen, a card pledging himself to oppose any candidate for office who did not support the principles of the Compromise.[50] He had immediate occasion to fulfill the pledge, for this year there was a gubernatorial election in Georgia. The Constitutional Union party, which he had helped to found, nominated Cobb in June; the radicals, uniting under the name of Southern Rights, nominated the secessionist Charles McDonald. Old party lines were deeply cut across; and Stephens was convinced by the end of the year, if he had any doubts, that the Whig party was dead.

He spent the summer assisting Cobb's campaign by mail, being too ill to travel. "Show," he urged Cobb, ". . . that the settlement is better than 14 slave states asked. . . . In reference to the calling out of the militia, etc., maintain the right of the President . . . to execute the law against all factious opposition. . . . Warn the good people of Georgia to beware of revolution. . . . The right of secession treat as an abstract question. It is but a right to

50 James F. Rhodes: *History of the United States from the Compromise of 1850* (New York, 1927–8), I, 207.

change the Govt., a right of revolution, and maintain that no just cause for the exercise of such right exists." [51] This was considerably cooler than what he had been saying a year ago; and yet it was not really inconsistent. His fundamental doctrine was that revolution is right whenever it is right to revolt: and it was no longer right.

Cobb in his evasive fashion subscribed to most of this; the opposition, typified by Herschel V. Johnson, sneered in almost Stephens' own words at "The Senseless Clamor of Union! This Glorious Union!" But the people were tired of quibbling. Cobb was swept into office by a large majority; and Stephens, who was running once more for Congress, experienced the greatest triumph of his antebellum career, receiving 70.8 per cent of the total vote cast in his district. Every county in it went for Cobb.[52]

When he returned to Washington he was still looking for a new party, or at least the purgation of an old one. "This is no time," he declared, "to conciliate the free soil vote by patching up old parties—If we do not purify the old ones we must make a new party." There was a brief flurry when a committee of a hundred New York businessmen sought to bring together Compromise supporters, North and South, Whig and Democrat; but some Democrats, notably Cobb—who considered himself too canny— refused to drop old party allegiances altogether, and the whole affair collapsed. Stephens told the House in January 1852: "I have no party." [53]

He did have two new things, though—a dog and a sister-in-law. The dog, whom he named Rio, was a large white poodle who came to him as a gift; and Rio was destined to be the most famous of all his dogs. His attachment to

51 *TSC*, 237–8.
52 Ibid., 238–41, 249–59; P. S. Flippin: *H. V. Johnson*, 39; *Phillips*, 166.
53 A.H.S. to N. Turner, December 19, 1851; Alexander H. Stephens MSS., Duke University; Philip S. Foner: *Business & Slavery* (Chapel Hill, 1941), 79–80; 32 *CG*, I, 405.

Stephens quickly became unshakable. He would be left with Linton when his master went to Washington, and on the evenings of his return the dog would be taken to the depot and would jump up into the train the moment it pulled in, and run through the cars until he found the man he sought. He always slept in Stephens' room, followed him all over the house and lot, and was happiest when doing something for him, fetching a hat or a cane.

The sister-in-law was a widow named Emmeline Bell, daughter of a wealthy planter and judge, James Thomas, whom Linton courted and married in late January, placing on her finger a wedding-ring sent as a gift from his brother in Washington. The couple soon moved from Crawfordville to Sparta, in Hancock County, where Linton set up a new practice. Though no hint escaped him, save in an oblique fashion, Stephens felt a difference now that his brother was married. A triangle had been created. Linton's love was divided, whereas his own could never be. And so he took to signing his letters "Alex," instead of the usual formal "Affectionately, Alexander H. Stephens"; and insisted upon his absolute dependence on Linton's affection—"You have perhaps no idea," he told him, "of how completely my feelings rise and fall with . . . your own." The most catastrophic thing that could happen to him would be the falling of a shadow between him and Linton; and with instinctive strength he fought to retain Linton's perfect confidence.

In 1852 there was a Presidental election; and Stephens, with no national party, found himself in a highly embarrassing predicament. He thought Webster would make a great President, and tried to persuade the Whigs to take him. The Democratic wing of the Constitutional Unionists declined to co-operate with the Whigs; and Stephens and Toombs declined to co-operate with the Democrats; and as a result the Constitutional Unionists broke apart after an existence of barely two years. Webster's possibilities dwindled rapidly after May, and Stephens was left high and dry, momentarily even dallying with the idea of supporting the Democratic nominee should he prove acceptable. But the Democrats nominated Franklin Pierce, a political nonentity; and when the Whigs nominated Winfield Scott, who was suspected of being a tool of the Free-Soilers, Stephens had nowhere to go. He, Toombs, and seven other Southern Whigs publicly announced their opposition to Scott on the ground that he was indifferent or even hostile to the Compromise. In the middle of August the Webster movement was revived and a ticket named, after Stephens had learned that a Webster campaign in Georgia would be echoed in Massachusetts. After Webster's death in October even this avenue appeared sealed off; yet so desperate were Stephens and 5,288 other Georgia Whigs that they voted for him anyhow; though Stephens' district gave Pierce a slight majority over Scott and a large one over Webster.[54]

It was a humiliating position to occupy; and a few days after Pierce's inauguration on March 4, 1853, Stephens went to call on him, coming away unexpectedly pleased; so much so that he decided tentatively to support the Administration, though jealously guarding his independence of all parties.[55]

Pierce was a handsome man, and an ingratiating one, but he lacked intelligence; and when the crisis which had been gathering for three years broke, he fumbled, hesitated, lost his nerve. During the summer, while Stephens lay at home in bed, recovering from a broken shoulder-blade which he had received when the train he was riding in was derailed near Macon, two groups of settlers in the

54 A.H.S.' admiration of Webster was always great; cf. *View*, I, 336. *LC*, G. T. Curtis to A.H.S., August 13, 1852, tells about the Massachusetts movement.
55 *MC*, March 8, 1853; *Richardson*, 140.

territory to the west of Missouri, and known as Kanzas, sent delegates to Congress praying for territorial recognition and organization. The movement to organize Kansas was connected with the movement to build a Pacific railroad, in which various groups, one of which was represented by Stephen A. Douglas, had interests. But there were complications: for some Missourians would not endure the organization of Kansas unless it were done so that slaves could be brought in, even though Kansas was wholly above the Missouri Compromise line. Therefore, when Senator Dodge of Iowa early in December introduced a bill for the organization of Kansas, Douglas was prepared for any eventuality; and when Dodge's bill came out of his Territorial Committee it contained a section abrogating, in veiled language, the Missouri Compromise by letting the people of the proposed territory exercise, whenever they should apply for admission as a state or states, the right to admit or exclude slavery as they desired. Apparently Douglas, believing that the central (Kansas) route for the Pacific railroad could not be adopted without Southern support, had decided to offer a bribe in exchange for that support. And so he tried to evade the Missouri Compromise and apply in the present case the same principles that had been successfully applied in 1850.

But veiled repeal of the Compromise was not enough for Southern hotheads; and the bill was twice revised until at last—after great pressure had been put upon Douglas by a few of the hotheads—it openly declared its intent to repeal the Compromise. In this form the bill received Pierce's support and became an Administration measure. Jefferson Davis, Pierce's Secretary of War, had persuaded his chief, who leaned heavily upon his judgment, to acquiesce. As soon as the revised bill was reported, the Free-Soilers pulled all the stops in a wild effort to scare the Northern people into a hysteria of opposition. And—

as the Free-Soilers might have guessed—the louder they shrieked, the more the moderate men of the South tended to act with the fire-eaters.

Stephens had nothing to do with these events; he spent all December and most of January in bed, feverous, attacked by spasms of nausea and by a bad cough. On January 18 he noted his pulse to be down to 55; he was eating very little and sleeping poorly, and hinted to his brother that he might not recover.[56] But by the end of January he was back in his seat. At first he dismissed the Southern agitators, calling them "a set of knaves"; but before long—when the abolitionist onslaught had reached its full fury—was aligning himself with those who "intended to carry out the principles of the compromise [of 1850] . . . which was based upon the idea of no congressional restriction against us in the territories with guaranty of right to come into the Union with or without slavery."

On February 15, the day the Senate passed the repeal amendment, he decided to deliver a speech in the House, where a Kansas bill similar to the Senate's was under consideration and receiving vicious treatment at Free-Soil hands. On the 17th, looking, according to some, like an animated corpse, very pale, his brilliant black eyes abnormally alive, he set his teeth and went through with it. The burden of his speech was a refutation of the idea that the Missouri Compromise was something sacred— which of course it was not. As a complement to this he placed on the North the responsibility for passing the Compromise, and on the South the credit for having sustained it since 1820. Apropos of the Compromise of 1850, he remarked: "The whole question of slavery or no slavery was to be left to the determination of the people of the territories, whether north or south of 36–30. . . . The

[56] *MC*, December 31, 1853; January 3, 18, 1854.

principle upon which that position rests lies at the very foundation of all our republican institutions; it is that the citizens of every . . . State should have the right to govern themselves in their domestic matters as they please"; and he accused the majority of Northerners of being opposed to such a principle. "I do not know," he concluded, "what you call me . . . whether whig or democrat . . . nor do I care. . . . I call myself a republican." [57]

Republican or no, as soon as the Senate's Kansas-Nebraska bill was passed, after long and acidulous debate, on March 4, 1854, with the guns at the navy yard firing a round in celebration, he joined Richardson of Illinois, chairman of the House Territorial Committee in working for its passage there. The Senate bill, when it came up in the House, was referred, not to Richardson's committee, but to the Committee of the Whole, to which the House Kansas bill had also been referred earlier. This was the result of a revolt on the part of some Northern Democrats, who, dissatisfied with Pierce's handling of patronage, joined antislavery men in strangling an Administration measure. This vote was considered a defeat, since fifty other bills on the calendar had precedence over the Senate bill, and twenty over the House bill; and the whole machinery of the Administration, led by Douglas, Richardson, and Pierce himself, was put to work to grind out the majority the bill must have in order to be considered and passed. By May 2 the backscratching campaign had achieved its purpose, for Richardson gave notice that the calendar would be cleared off on the 8th. On that day rollcall followed rollcall, one bill after another was laid aside, and at length the House Kansas bill was dug out. Next day anti-Kansas men absented themselves en masse

[57] Perhaps it was his habitual ghastliness of appearance that led the New York *Times* to call him the "Mephistopheles of Southern politics" (*Times*, August 24, 1858). Speech in 33 *CG*, I, App., 193–7.

from the House; and on the 11th Richardson moved to close debate on the 12th. Then followed a concerted effort by the opposition to badger, break down, and hound the Administration into giving it enough time to defeat the bill. All during the enactment of this comedy Stephens was furious: "Why, Mr. Chairman," he said peevishly on May 4, "we have been here for three or four months discussing this bill. Is that hot haste?" and on the 12th he remarked that "We have had questions of peace, and questions of war taken after less debate than has already been permitted on this measure." [58] Debate, however, did not close until the 20th.

Stephens, "getting insubordinate," and afraid the bill might yet be killed, hit upon an expedient for forcing an immediate vote. He discovered that under the 119th rule of the House a motion to strike out the enacting clause of a bill had the effect of cutting off all further action and compelling a vote strictly and at once upon that motion. If the Committee of the Whole were obliged to vote on such a motion, its action, whether for or against the striking out, would have to be reported to the House, and the bill would thereupon be in a position to be passed. Richardson, when Stephens explained this tactic, was unenthusiastic; but Stephens, on the morning of the 22nd, saying: "Why should we longer delay?" did just as he had planned. The motion to strike out was carried, 103–22; and after repeated motions to adjourn had been defeated, the House refused to concur in the Committee's vote, the Senate bill was substituted for the House bill and passed late in the evening, 113–100, with cheering in the galleries. Next morning an exultant Stephens wrote to Linton: "Nebraska is through the House—majority thirteen. . . . I took the reins in my hand, applied whip and spur, and brought the wagon out at eleven o'clock P.M. Glory enough for one

[58] 33 *CG,* I, 1093, 1183 and *passim.*

day." A little later he spoke of the "glorious news of the result of the Nebraska bill"; and wrote: "And when the signal guns upon Capitol Hill proclaimed the final passing of the Nebraska Bill I felt that the cup of my ambition was full." [59] A principle had triumphed; but at what cost? It forced settlers in the new territory to take an abnormal interest in a question that ordinarily would not much disturb them. It gave the Whig party its final knock on the head. It enormously aided the antislavery movement and gave the opponents of the further extension of slavery their excuse to create a sectional party, the Republicans. It was, in the last analysis, an announcement that the sectionalization of America was entering the last stage before war.

Stephens' *Gloria* did not last long. He went home from Washington tired and unhappy despite the triumph of justice he supposed he had achieved. Perhaps it was the aftereffect of the great strain he had undergone. The quiet unhurried rhythm of life in middle Georgia was especially soothing at such moments; it provided a perfect anodyne. There were many little things to be attended to, and he enjoyed it. He rose early, rode out a bit before breakfast, spent the morning reading and attending to his correspondence, went down to the plantation often to supervise the work and to ramble over the old homestead and visit the graves of his parents, rode out again in the evening, and after supper played whist or euchre with the guests who were always there. And there was his practice to be attended to, the circuit to be ridden; and his family connections were large, and there were always relatives to be visited and given advice and sometimes financial assistance. But he was cheerless enough this autumn, writing in October: "Everything seems stamped with the impress of

[59] *MC*, May 21, 23, 1854; 33 *CG*, I, 1241–54; *TSC*, 345; *American Historical Review*, VIII, 92.

decay and death," and a little later: "Oh! this world! this
world! how fallen! how sunken!" In December he reached
another nadir of gloom, saying bitterly: "Life to me is
desolate—For what object should I wish to live? . . . I
am litterally enveloped in gloom—Shades and shadows sur-
round me," and apostrophizing mankind: "The mass of
mankind are low, groveling, selfish and vulgar—Oh! the
world! the frivolous, gossipping world! how little they
know of me! And how long shall I be the object of their
inquisitive, vacant foolish gaze—A gaze held by me in
mingled pity and contempt?" [60] It was a sentimental custom with him always to write Linton a letter on the first
and last days of the year; and his 31st of December letters
habitually were cast in this kind of tone, the tone of one
who tried desperately to believe that the world was a
hideous mess and nothing really mattered. But it did matter, and he knew it.

In the spring of the following year he who had been no
defender of slavery in the abstract rose to its defense in
a long and rambling speech brought on by an anti-Nebraska attempt to introduce a bill prohibiting slavery in
Kansas and Nebraska. He so far defended the institution
as to assemble an elaborate table of statistics designed to
prove that slavery had made Georgia more prosperous
than freedom had Ohio; and boasted that the "negro population of the South are better off, better fed, better clothed,
better provided for, enjoy more happiness, and a higher
civilization, than the same race has ever enjoyed anywhere
on the face of the world," and concluded: "Away, then,
with this prating cry about slavery's paralyzing the energy
of a people. . . ." The statistics he quoted provoked Lewis
Campbell of Ohio to refute them and establish instead
the economic supremacy of his own state. But Stephens'
persistence was too much for him, and he was drowned in

a sea of figures covering everything from manufactures to churches and paupers, Georgia coming out the second time twice as far ahead as before, by half a million dollars a year. For Stephens this was a personal victory: he "utterly extinguished Campbell." His speeches caused something of a stir: when he spoke the second time there was a vast audience to hear him. So far as he was concerned he was absolutely correct. "I am never wrong," he peremptorily told Campbell, "upon a matter I have given as close attention as I have given this." [61]

This tone of proud confidence was not merely public; to Linton he was speaking of slavery as "the *granite* the foundation stone of a great structure of civilization." [62] Was he joining the fire-eaters at last? Such intricate apologetics as he was now indulging in sound curious in view of his earlier attitudes. These were years of prosperity for the South; and Georgia was certainly the most prosperous Southern state, with more railroads and manufactures than any other, her population steadily growing, her cotton production nearly doubling in the decade 1849–59, the number of her large plantations steadily increasing, and her more intelligent and farsighted planters learning every year new methods of soil rejuvenation: a precarious prosperity, resting as it did wholly on the price of cotton and the weather, but nevertheless a distinct improvement over the 1840's. The optimism generated by it may have affected Stephens' outlook—his cotton crop in 1855 brought him $564.67, a substantial sum. But there may have been subtler reasons.

In April 1855 he announced himself no longer a candidate for Congress. "I see that the old Whig Party is about to be sold out and out to the Know Nothings," he ex-

plained, "and I have determined to have nothing more to
do with public affairs. . . ." [63] The American, or Know-
Nothing, party had by this time begun to make serious
inroads into the old parties, especially in the South. Its
program, appealing to the electorate in terms of anti-
foreignism and anti-Catholicism, provided many anti-
Nebraska Democrats in the North, and many old Whigs
North and South, with a convenient way of side-stepping
the slavery issue. Georgia Whigs were being sucked into it
right and left, though some went in with the idea of making it into a proslavery party. Stephens was urged that it
would create divisions in the North over the irrelevant
issue of Catholic domination of American politics, and
should therefore be made use of. Yet though Stephens was
willing to co-operate with almost anybody to suppress
abolitionism, he drew a line when confronted with the
Know-Nothings. The decision to withdraw from politics
was based as much on expedient as on moral grounds, however, for the Know-Nothing clique in Augusta, the only
big town in his district, because he was agrarian in his attitudes and paid little attention to Augusta's wants ("There
is something pleasant in the country that I like," he had
once said; "Town scenery is monotonous"), had determined to wage an intensive campaign against him if he
ran.[64]

The news of his intention not to stand again spread
quickly through the state; there were those who could not
understand it. When Judge T. W. Thomas, a close friend,
wrote on May 5 asking his opinion of the Know-Nothings,
he replied in an open letter, arraigning the party's secrecy:
"No man is fit to represent a free people who has any
private or secret objects . . . who is not ready and willing

---

63 Ibid., April 20, 1855.
64 *LC,* W. W. Paine to A.H.S., February 23, 1855; *J&B,* 292; *MC,* March 6,
1842; R. M. Johnston: *Autobiography,* 138.

. . . candidly and *truthfully,* to proclaim to the assembled multitude . . . his views and sentiments upon all questions." He objected to the party's "looking not to *how* the country shall be governed, but *who* shall hold the offices." And he attacked the party's efforts to exclude foreigners and naturalized citizens from the exercise of the ballot.[65] The Know-Nothings countered this by hinting that he would not run because he was afraid of being beaten; whereupon he, always abnormally sensitive to the charge of cowardice, bearded the lions in their den, went straight to Augusta, and in a speech delivered to a great crowd there announced himself as an independent candidate, saying defiantly: "I am afraid of nothing on earth, or above the earth, or under the earth, except to do wrong." [66]

The campaign was one of the most intense in Georgia history. A governor was to be elected, and this time Stephens gave his support to Herschel V. Johnson, who was running on the Democratic ticket against the Know-Nothing Garnett Andrews. He pushed himself relentlessly, taking Harry, his body servant, and a satchelful of clothes, and riding from town to town in his buggy, stopping to speak for two or three hours, beginning quietly but soon working himself up to a pitch of passion, and upon the conclusion of his speech going into some private place where he could take off his underclothes, which were soaked with sweat, be rubbed down by Harry, and change to dry things, afterward getting into the buggy and driving on to repeat the performance in the next town. It was grueling work, and he began to fear he would not last long. "My God," one man who heard him is said to have exclaimed, "there is nothing about him but lungs and brains!" It was during this campaign that he first met his future biog-

65 *LC,* P. Clayton to A.H.S., May 11, 1855; A.H.S.' letter in *Cleveland,* 459–71.
66 *Cleveland,* 472–89.

rapher, Richard Malcolm Johnston, at Warrenton, where Johnston, who had studied law with Emmeline Stephens' father, James Thomas, consulted Stephens about accepting a circuit judgeship. Johnston, a tall, slender man who confessed to a high temper, was a Democrat. The two men quickly came to like each other—on Johnston's side it was frank admiration—and the friendship thus begun was never broken.[67]

At first Stephens was "perfectly prepared for defeat," but though to be officially associated with the Democrats might have enhanced his prospects, he resisted such efforts toward that end as were made; and in the final analysis did probably as well independently as he would have done otherwise. In his district Johnson lost three counties to Andrews, and Stephens himself lost Richmond, Augusta's county, while his percentage of the total vote cast fell to 65.3 per cent. But he had been re-elected, which was the important thing.

This election was a turning-point for him. The enmity of the Know-Nothings was an established fact; if he was to preserve himself as a political figure, he could not afford to stand alone. His own popularity, great as it was, unaided by a party machine, would not sustain him long. The decision was a hard one—it had taken him five years to make it—but there was no evading it now. He became a Democrat; and all the bitter words he had spoken about the Democrats would have to be forgotten.

IV

As he returned to Washington, one thing saddened him. Linton had run for Congress in the 7th district, but had been defeated by a very slim margin.[68] It would have been

[67] *J&B*, 298. His enemies would have mentioned merely the lungs. He seems indeed all his life to have been an incessant talker. R. M. Johnston: *Autobiography*, 140.

[68] *J&B*, 295, 297.

pleasant for the two to serve together; and his first few days in the capital were miserable ones. . . .

The state of the nation this year was bad again; for the fruits of the Kansas-Nebraska Act were dropping from the tree. Since the summer of 1854 Kansas had been settled by groups of both pro- and anti-slavery men, neither of which recognized the authority of the other; and by the close of 1855 two separate governments existed in the territory, one headed by a Presidentially appointed Governor, and dominated by the proslavery element; the other led by a small group of fanatical Free-Soilers, who in April 1856 submitted to Congress the draft of a state constitution, with a prayer to be admitted into the Union as a free state. Fraud and violence were charged by each faction against the other; both sides went armed; and the indifferent settlers who had come to Kansas merely to make homes for themselves became involved in a bitter struggle between extremists.

The Kansas "situation" had an analogue in Washington. The House, as Stephens found it on his return, was a confused collection of Administration Democrats, Anti-Nebraska Democrats, Whigs, and Know-Nothings, of which the first group was the one with which he immediately allied himself.

Trouble was foreshadowed by so complicated an alignment of parties, but the trouble quickly became a disease. No speaker was elected until February 2. The contest resolved itself after a few days into a triangular one, Nathaniel P. Banks receiving the vote of the anti-Nebraska, antislavery faction, Richardson those of the Administration and Douglas Democrats, and Henry M. Fuller, a Know-Nothing, those of the Southern Know-Nothings. Stephens, who could take neither Banks nor Fuller, voted for Richardson on ballot after ballot until on January 23, 1856 Richardson withdrew; and then he followed most of

Richardson's supporters over to James L. Orr of South
Carolina, who had little better luck in getting a majority.
The key to the deadlock lay with the Fuller men: if they
would unite with the Administration Democrats, Banks
could be defeated. On February 1 Stephens, thinking he
had a man who would be acceptable to both Democrats
and Know-Nothings, went the rounds, "carelessly" asking
whether William Aiken of South Carolina would do. The
response was encouraging, and Stephens began laying a
stratagem. Till now there had been repeated efforts made
to abolish the majority rule of election and substitute a
plurality rule instead; now if the majority rule could be
put aside, with the plurality rule to take effect after three
ballots should have been cast with no choice, Orr would
withdraw on the fourth ballot and Aiken would be substituted. This might have worked; but Cobb of Alabama
offered a resolution to make Aiken speaker before the
plurality rule had been adopted; and Stephens was furious,
for the resolution was defeated by 113 to 103. The end of
it all was that on February 2, on the 133rd ballot, Banks
was declared Speaker, having received 103 to Aiken's 100.
It was, Stephens bitterly wrote, *"purely a sectional election."* [69] Every vote cast for Banks came from the North.

And this was only the beginning. Since the proslavery
party in Kansas was also the Administration party, the
Free-Soil government was, in Pierce's eyes, pure treason;
and he stigmatized it as such, recommending to Congress
that the people of Kansas be authorized to hold a constitutional convention. But before this problem was taken
up another presented itself. Each of the factions in Kansas
had elected a territorial delegate to Congress; and on February 14 Andrew Reeder, the Free-Soil delegate, presented
his claims to the seat occupied by John Whitfield, the proslavery contestant. The dispute was referred to the Elec-

[69] *MC*, December 2, 1855; February 1, 4, 1856. 34 *CG*, I, 334-5, 337.

tions Committee, of which Stephens was a member. More was obviously at stake in this matter than the mere seating or unseating of a territorial delegate; for by officially recognizing one of the claimants the House admitted the legality of the government he represented. Therefore the case was worried about by the House until the beginning of August. When the majority of the committee, on February 19, asked the House for the power to send for persons and papers, Stephens, who was convinced of the legality of Whitfield's election, strenuously objected, and the power was not then granted. On March 5 the majority and minority reports of the committee were read, the majority again requesting power to conduct a full investigation; the minority, led by Stephens, who, outraged at the majority's point-blank refusal to let the minority see their report before drawing up its own, had stayed up till two A.M. that morning composing a protest, contending that the mere evidence of illegal voting was not enough to unseat a delegate; that a contestant must show that he received a majority of the legally cast votes; and that Reeder had failed to show any such thing. Stephens protested too Reeder's attempt to get the House to investigate the territorial law under which he had been a candidate—an assumption of a power of jurisdiction in the House that it did not possess. On March 11 he spoke at length in amplification of the minority report, to a House for which he felt "perfect indifference and contempt." [70]

The House, however, agreed with the majority report, and a special committee was sent to Kansas to investigate the situation. Its report, made on July 1, was sent to the Elections Committee, which on the 24th again divided into a majority and a minority, the former finding both contestants disqualified, but recommending Reeder's admis-

[70] 34 *CG*, I, 455 et sqq.; App., 179–83; *MC*, March 3, 11, 1856. The committee reports are printed as H. Rep. 3, 34th Cong., 1st sess.

sion on the ground that he had received more votes of bona
fide Kansas residents than Whitfield; the latter, again led
by Stephens, contending that Reeder's admission would
be an "open outrage upon both law and right." [71] The
House, choosing the easiest way out, finally ejected Whitfield and refused to admit Reeder, leaving Kansas with no
representative at all.

Meanwhile other things were going on. For three
months, until July 3, the House debated a bill admitting
Kansas as a state under the Free-Soil Topeka constitution.
At the same time the Senate had under consideration a
bill introduced by Toombs, providing for a government-
supervised census in Kansas, the election (under the
watchful eye of a commission of eminent citizens), on the
basis of that census, of a constitutional convention, and
the prompt admission of the state with whatever constitution, whether slave or free, it should then adopt. Such a
procedure would dispose of all Free-Soil claims that Missouri citizens had been illegally voting in Kansas elections
in order to pack them with proslavery ballots. When this
bill passed the Senate and came to the House, Stephens
gave it his support. On the 28th of June he had tried to
substitute it for the Topeka bill, claiming he wanted
"nothing but a fair expression of the will of the bona fide
residents of Kansas upon the subject," and denying that in
voting for the Kansas-Nebraska Act he had done so "for
the purpose of making it a slave State." But an amendment
restoring the Missouri Compromise had been tacked to
his substitute, and in this shape it was overwhelmingly defeated. On a pretty clear sectional division the Topeka
bill was passed on July 3, and House and Senate settled
down to a month of deadlock, neither deigning to touch
the other's bill. There was an attempt by the Free-Soilers
to forbid the President to use troops to aid in enforcing

[71] H. Rep. 275, 34th Cong., 1st sess., 7.

any laws passed by the proslavery Kansas legislature; and in the course of debate upon this proposition Stephens got up and said crisply: "It is not within the province of Congress to determine the question of the validity of the laws of the territory of Kansas." [72] And Congress, for one reason or another, agreed with him. The Free-Soil project was finally squashed, and all the Senators and Representatives put on their hats and picked up their bags and went home, having accomplished precisely nothing. And while they had been chattering, John Brown had done his avenging on Pottawatomie Creek; the Free-Soil capital of Lawrence, Kansas, had been sacked by a proslavery "army"; and Representative Preston Brooks of South Carolina had caned Senator Charles Sumner in the Senate chamber. The atmosphere this spring and summer of 1856 was ugly. It was becoming less and less easy for ordinary men and women to ignore the agitators North and South; it was growing more and more difficult to be sane and quiet and rational. Northerners in increasing numbers were feeling that in Kansas was being fought a noble battle for civilization; Southerners were equally persuaded that Kansas was an outpost of their society, and that if they were to lose it, their society would be under direct attack. Kansas was achieving the dignity of a symbol, and the sordid realities of land speculation and power-grabbing were painted inch-thick with bright shining words. Stephens was positive that the proslavery government was the legal government; and why? Because slavery was being attacked, and slavery was right, and therefore the regime that sanctioned slavery must be legal. And why was slavery right? Because it was being attacked. The entire fabric of Southern social and economic life was threaded by the Negro, both as Negro and as slave; and it was inconceivable that those most nearly affected by his presence should, under such

[72] 34 *CG*, I, 1790; App., 723–9.

relentless and bitter onslaughts as were coming from free-soilers and abolitionists, do anything but what they were doing—uniting in self-defense. A chain reaction had been set in motion whose end was an explosion.

There was a Presidential election this year. When the Democratic convention met on June 2, it had three possible candidates: Pierce, Douglas, and James Buchanan. Stephens and Toombs at first were friendly to Douglas, but soon veered toward Buchanan as a safer man. Pierce they detested; Stephens called him a "miserable little creature." Buchanan had been abroad for nearly three years, and so had nothing to be held against him; and after the customary bargaining he received the nomination.[73] The Republicans met soon after and nominated John C. Frémont on a platform of no slavery in the territories. The campaign, it was soon remarked, was sectional—the first in American history.

Stephens was at first in no mood for stump speaking, for on July 20 he heard that his brother John had died. For him, whose sense of family unity was so profound, it was an overwhelming loss. He was without control for weeks, brusque, nervous, unable to think of his brother without breaking down. As soon as he came home he went about the job of settling John's estate, which must have been cumbered with debt since he was himself constantly lending John money. An indication of the close ties that had existed between the brothers was in John's will, which put Alexander in absolute control of his estate and practically turned his widow and children over to Alexander's custody. One of Stephens' first acts upon returning home was to have John's family brought to Crawfordville, where he settled them and undertook to support them.[74]

[73] George F. Milton: *The Eve of Conflict: Stephen A. Douglas and the Needless War* (Boston, 1934), 222; *LC*, T. W. Thomas to A.H.S., May 20, 1856; *MC*, August 19, 1856.
[74] *MC*, July 20, 27, 1856; *Richardson*, 178.

After the initial shock had worn off, he plunged into the campaign, speaking in various states for Buchanan. He was fully satisfied with the Democratic platform, whose position on the territorial question was that the acceptance or rejection of slavery depended solely upon the will of the people by whom the territory was inhabited.[75] In Georgia the election was fought out between the remnant Know-Nothings and the Democrats. Benjamin H. Hill, then very young in politics, was almost singlehandedly carrying the Know-Nothing campaign. Brilliant and courageous, he rarely did things by halves; and in the course of the autumn he bearded both Toombs and Stephens in their lairs. On October 22 he and Stephens met in joint debate at Lexington, Oglethorpe County, an old Whig stronghold that might possibly fail to follow Stephens into the Democratic camp—for there were many old Whigs who would willingly vote for Stephens for any office, but who could not screw themselves up to the pitch of becoming Democrats. In the opinion of the audience Stephens was scalped by Hill, who harped on his conversion to Democracy and told him it ill behooved him to abuse those of his followers who had joined the Know-Nothings. Stephens was nettled by Hill's evident ability and therefore spoke with some asperity, as a result of which the two did not meet again during the campaign.[76] The election, considered both as a test of Stephens' power to take his constituency with him wherever he went and as a Democratic victory, went off very well. Only two counties in the 8th district—Richmond and Columbia—went for Fillmore; and in the state at large Buchanan won by 14,000 votes.[77]

Soon after the elections Stephens began hearing reports

[75] *TSC*, 367–72.

[76] Haywood J. Pearce: *Benjamin H. Hill, Secession and Reconstruction* (Chicago, 1928), 17.

[77] *Phillips*, 179.

of speeches Hill had made here and there, in which, alluding to the Lexington debate, he had said he had charged Stephens and Toombs with having out-Judased Judas in betraying the Whigs, for though Judas had sold his master, he had not abused him afterward. Stephens wrote to Hill on November 17 inquiring whether the reports were true; and an exchange of letters followed, in which Hill contended he had made the Judas remark but had not intended it to apply to Stephens. Stephens would not consider this a sufficient retraction, and from Washington, in the beginning of December, challenged Hill to a duel. Hill declined in a perfect and biting reply, saying he knew of nothing that would authorize or justify a duel. Stephens, confused and angry, could only vent his petulance by calling Hill a knave, a braggart, and a gasconader.[78] The estrangement thus begun was never completely smoothed over. Why Stephens challenged Hill in the first place is problematical; it may be that, sensing he had been worsted in an intellectual tourney—a field in which he could not allow himself to be defeated—he felt himself forced to descend to the physical in order to vindicate his superiority. The impression in this case is that he wanted very badly to fight Hill no matter what Hill said. And when Hill declined, he could not but suppose it was because of his, Stephens', physical inferiority—again. Hill had hurt him terribly, twice; had jolted him unforgivably; had pierced the armor that must not be pierced; and therefore remained an enemy who could not possibly be pardoned.

Try as he would to draw attention from it, his appearance was never forgotten. A casual visitor to the House in those years would never fail to come away without an impression of him similar to that recorded by one Southern

---

[78] *Benjamin H. Hill, His Letters, Speeches and Writings* (Atlanta, 1893), 20–30, contains the correspondence. See also Pearce: *Hill*, 18–19.

woman: "That vast crowd of listening faces were turned toward a shrunken and attenuated figure, the shoulders contracted and drawn in, the face dead and of the color of ashes. . . . He had little variety of gesture, and what he used seemed perfectly unstudied. He was evidently so thoroughly absorbed in his subject as to be quite unconscious that he had hands and arms to manage . . . he occasionally raised one hand, and then suddenly struck it down with extraordinary force." [79] His likeness to John Randolph of Roanoke was frequently commented on; and always, in spite of himself, the world remembered him by his personal peculiarities.

On March 4, 1857 James Buchanan was inaugurated. On the 6th, in the dingy basement chambers of the Supreme Court, the Dred Scott decision was read in an almost inaudible tone by Chief Justice Taney. No Court had ever been subjected to such vituperation as that which now burst out. Dred Scott, together with Bleeding Kansas and Brooks' assault on Sumner, became a drum on which the Republicans would pound interminably for the next four years. Gossip, speculation, and intrigue were rife all winter, while the case was being reheard; and Stephens mixed himself into it, urging "all the influence I could bring to bear" upon the Court to make it express an opinion upon the constitutionality of the Missouri Compromise. Of the judges he might have argued with, Robert Grier, of Pennsylvania, was a very distant relation; Taney and McLean he had messed with in 1845; and Wayne was a fellow Georgian. His contacts with all were sufficiently friendly to permit of some discussion, at home or in the street; yet what he accomplished, if anything, is now a matter of question.[79a]

[79] Mary J. Windle: *Life in Washington, and Life Here and There* (Philadelphia, 1859), 25–7. Of the speech she refers to, 40,000 copies were circulated; *MC*, January 15, 1857.

[79a] *MC*, December 15, 1856.

But in January of this year something happened which momentarily eclipsed even the Dred Scott case, and from which he did not fully recover for the rest of the year. Linton's marriage had been a brilliant success: for five years he and his wife had lived together and they were as passionately in love now as they had been at first. There were two daughters, Claude and Emma; a third had died in 1854, aged only nine months. Now in January 1857 another child was born; but Stephens soon heard that Emmeline had been taken seriously ill following the delivery. "Let me hear daily," he requested on the 15th; but there were not many days left. On the 27th Emmeline died, and for some months Linton was nearly insane with grief. His father-in-law took him in for a while, and wrote to Alexander: "He bears it very badly indeed there has been a portion of the time I have greatly feared his reason would be dethroned. . . ." Linton's nature, like his brother's, was intensely affectionate; his love for Emmeline had been one of complete dependence; and it was no wonder that when this support was so abruptly kicked out from under him, he reacted with blind, abandoned grief. Alexander, himself in great distress, wrote letter after letter from Washington, lavishing sympathy and advice. "Do not despair," was the burden of his letters, and "What would I not give to be with you"—for he feared his brother might do something irrevocable, perhaps even commit suicide. Judging by Linton's incoherent letters, it was a distinct possibility. Linton's nature was not only affectionate but extremely sensual; and in this first wild rush of sorrow he blamed himself for being the cause of his wife's death, saying that they had sinned in loving each other too intensely, and that she had been "taken away first because she was the greatest sinner"—an abyss of morbidity from which Alexander sharply tried to drag him away, saying: *"She is happy."* He would have left at once for Georgia, but heavy snow, and thick ice in the Potomac, prevented him from starting until February 4. All spring and summer he stayed at Crawfordville, watching, advising, suffering. When Linton, who was in his personal affairs something of a moral weakling, let completely go and tried to drink himself into forgetfulness, the elder brother again curtly interposed: "Rise early, take bodily exercise, devote your mind to some engaging object, and don't be much alone," adding sternly: "The great end of life is to do our duty towards man and our creator." At the same time he steadily—and quite unconsciously—began insinuating himself into the place in Linton's heart that Emmeline had occupied, impressing Linton with the fact of his utter dependence on him—"I have no mortal on earth," he insisted, "I can unbosom myself to but you. . . ." [80] It was for both of them a frightful year, made even more frightful by their incorrigibly romantic way of acting and feeling. Neither of them ever experienced an emotion that he could subdue. What was felt was expressed, and as vehemently as possible. Like grass in the wind they bent now this way and now that, as emotion drove them, helpless in passion.

During the summer, however, there was a diversion: the gubernatorial election. For Stephens there was yet another, since he was standing again for Congress. On June 24 the Democratic convention met at Milledgeville, embarrassed by a plethora of prospective candidates, each determined to get the nomination, since, with no party but the shattered Know-Nothings to oppose, nomination was virtual election. Nineteen ballots were taken without a choice, and a committee was appointed to take the nomination out of the convention's hands. Linton was a member of the committee; being told that Joseph E. Brown, an

[80] *LC*, J. Thomas to A.H.S., February 7, 1857; *MC*, January 29, 30, March 2, 14, July 31, 1857; Linton to A.H.S., February 27, 1857.

obscure northwestern politician, was a good man, he proposed Brown's name and succeeded in getting him nominated by a voice vote. The convention quickly ratified the
nomination. "Brown," Linton assured his brother, "is a
man that I know to have decided ability. . . . He was a
firm Southern-rights man, and one of the most prudent.
. . ." [81] It was indicative of how far Stephens had swung
toward the radicals that he had to be persuaded of Brown's
Southern-rightism.

The campaign was brisk, for Hill opposed Brown, and
the upcountry man was no match for him. But under
Toombs' and Stephens' guidance he did well enough, beating Hill by 10,000 votes, a margin whose slimness could
be ascribed largely to Hill's personal popularity. In Stephens' own district things did not turn out so well. The
Know-Nothings, determined to "get" him once and for all,
were still powerful enough to cut Brown's majority in the
8th district to a mere 810, and, more important, to lop
Stephens' percentage of the total vote cast to a sorrowful
54.6 per cent.

And so Joseph E. Brown, humorless, fanatical, impec-
cably moral, a native of South Carolina who had settled in
northwest Georgia as a boy, eleven years younger than
Stephens, tall, slender, square-faced, a violent teetotaler
and a timesaver, became Governor of Georgia—an event
that was to have great consequences for himself, for Stephens, who had helped to put him in the Governor's chair,
and for the South.

During the summer of 1857 an election was held in
Kansas for delegates to a constitutional convention. The
Free-Soil men, still active and unreconciled, refused to
participate in this election, with the result that the con-

---

[81] *Avery*, 33–8; Louise B. Hill: *Joseph E. Brown and the Confederacy*
(Chapel Hill, 1939) (cited hereafter as *Brown*), 6–8; James D. Waddell:
A Biographical Sketch of Linton Stephens (Atlanta, 1877), 127.

vention exclusively represented the proslavery element, which was by this time identified with the national Democratic organization, and drafted a constitution guaranteeing the right to hold slaves. The constitution was not to be submitted to popular ratification as a whole, but merely in its slavery clause. It was the constitution with or without slavery, but the constitution in any case. The Democratic leadership was convinced that Kansas could not become a slave state, and all they wanted to do was to make it a Democratic one. With this end in view Buchanan had sent out to Kansas in the spring a new Governor, Robert J. Walker, whose job was to persuade the proslavery machine, determined not to submit any part of its proposed constitution to the people, to submit at least one part if not the whole, so that what Northern Democratic support the Administration had would not be wholly alienated. Walker therefore told the people of Kansas that the Administration would support no constitution that had not been submitted to popular ratification; and Cobb, now Secretary of the Treasury, applied pressure to the convention delegates to do as they were told. The outcome was a compromise—submission of merely the slave clause of the Lecompton constitution to the people.

Walker's pledge raised a howl of rage from Southern radicals, who would not admit that Kansas had been lost as a slave state; and it considerably embarrassed men like Stephens, who had no idea of what was really going on. Speaking in the dark, Stephens told his constituents on August 14 that Walker was a traitor, and he asserted the power of the minority of voters which had nominated the convention delegates to draft a constitution. "If anyone refused to vote," he said, "it was their own choice not to do it." And he added that Congress would have no power to investigate the election of delegates. Buchanan he strongly defended, believing it impossible that the Presi-

dent could have upheld Walker; and he flayed the radicals
who were now cursing Buchanan because of his insistence
on the doctrine of popular sovereignty—the theory that
the people of a territory had the right to determine all
questions of internal policy for themselves.[81a] The radicals
held and had always held that not only not the people
of a territory, but no power on earth, could exclude slavery
from a territory—until the territory was ready to become
a state. Douglas' doctrine, on the other hand, insisted that
the people of a territory could legislate as they pleased
the day after the territory had begun to be peopled. And
Buchanan stood somewhere in between.

Douglas and Buchanan were somewhat cool toward each
other as a result of the Presidential elections; and when
Douglas returned to Washington in December 1857, with
the proslavery Lecompton constitution being backed by
the Administration, coolness gave way to heat. Douglas
thought the restriction of popular suffrage on the constitution to the slavery clause was an out-and-out fraud, and
told Buchanan so. It was not true "popular sovereignty."
Stephens, who had always admired Douglas, could not at
first believe him to be opposed to the Lecompton constitution, but on December 4 he heard Douglas' opinion from
his own mouth. The prospect of an open split in the party
greatly disturbed him, and he did not at first quite know
where to stand. His loyalty to Lecompton at last triumphed, and he went over bag and baggage to Buchanan.[82]

Open warfare between the Douglas and Buchanan factions began at once, with the President defending Lecompton in his annual message, and Douglas delivering a fierce
attack next day, saying he did not care whether slavery
were voted up or down in Kansas, but he did want every
clause of the constitution to be submitted to the people.

[81a] *TSC*, 409–20.
[82] *MC*, December 1, 4, 1857.

On the 21st of December the Lecompton constitution was ratified by proslavery votes, the free-state men staying away and having their own balloting on January 4, 1858, when the constitution with slavery was overwhelmingly defeated. The Administration took no notice of this second vote; and on February 2 Buchanan sent in to Congress the Lecompton constitution, pleading its legality and justice, and arguing that by admitting Kansas under its terms, Congress would put an end to sectional agitation forever. Stephens, who had this session been appointed chairman of the House Territorial Committee, and was therefore Administration floor leader on territorial matters, had called on Buchanan and gone over the text of the President's message before it was sent in: its point of view, therefore, closely coincided with his own.[83]

As soon as the message was read he moved that the Lecompton constitution be referred to his committee. Douglas men objected; and after several days of angry debate the motion was defeated, 114–113, and on February 8 the House decided it wanted a special committee to look into the Kansas situation. This was bad. Stephens was personally persuaded that Lecompton was done for; and Linton wrote back that if Kansas were not admitted under it, he for one would favor disunion. On February 11, Stephens' forty-sixth birthday, the special committee was appointed by Speaker Orr—very likely in consultation with Stephens, for though Harris of Illinois, a Douglasite, was made chairman, the committee was packed with a majority of pro-Lecompton men, Stephens at their head, comprising eight of the fifteen members. A report, favorable to the Lecompton constitution, and written by Stephens, was adopted on March 3 by 8 to 7. When Stephens announced a week later that the report was ready, there was instant opposition to its being read in the House; and Stephens,

83 *MC,* February 3, 1858.

who had concluded: "patriotism is defunct in this country —statesmanship is defunct," said curtly: "I will take the responsibility myself of having it printed and sent before the House," which he did, publishing it in the *Union*. Next day he and Harris became involved in an acrimonious debate, Harris charging that the committee, in failing to inquire fully into all facts relevant to the drafting of the constitution, had not done its duty, and Stephens countercharging that Harris wanted to keep the committee's report from ever being seen. The affair profoundly disturbed him; on the night of the 11th he exclaimed to Linton: "My country my country what is to become of it"—meaning, not America, but Georgia.[84]

On March 23, after much axe-wielding by the Administration, the Senate passed a bill admitting Kansas to the Union under the Lecompton constitution. Stephens tried to have this bill taken up for debate in the House on April 1; but an attempt was instead made to reject it. The attempt failed; whereupon Montgomery, a Pennsylvania anti-Lecompton Democrat, moved an amendment in the shape of another bill, providing for a popular referendum on the Lecompton constitution. If it were approved, the state would be immediately admitted; if not, a new convention would be called. Stephens, who had an idea—to let the Senate bill be amended and sent back, so that the Senate, refusing to accept the amendment, would ask for a conference committee, which would thereupon draft some kind of compromise—moved the previous question and let Montgomery's bill be carried, to the chagrin of Southerners and the open delight of the Republicans. Buchanan had tried to prevent the passage of Montgomery's amendment, being perhaps afraid the Senate might

[84] 35 *CG*, I, 679, 1037, 1075-7, 1103-10; *MC*, February 28, March 7, 11, 1858.

accept it; but he was overborne, only 29 Northern Democrats voting with the Administration.[85]

Senate and House locked on the measure: so far so good. On April 13 the Senate asked for a conference: better still. Patronage had to be vigorously used to whip the House into agreeing to confer; but the trick was turned, and on the 16th Speaker Orr appointed the House members, W. H. English, a young Indiana Democrat, Stephens, and W. A. Howard of Michigan. Between them, Stephens and English concocted a compromise, based upon the rather outrageous demand of Walker and a Kansas clique that when admitted as a state Kansas be given a land grant about three times larger than the usual one. If, the compromise said, the people of Kansas agreed to take merely the normal land grant, the state would be admitted under the Lecompton constitution; if they refused, they would have to wait until their territory had accumulated the population required to elect one Congressman. Stephens, though unwell, had the plan approved by the committee, and spent several days persuading as many Southerners as he could reach to lend it their support as the best compromise they could hope to get. The bill was reported on the 23rd, and Stephens, directing its passage, sought earnestly to bring it to a quick vote; but the House took its own time, and debate did not begin until the 28th. Douglas and his followers attacked it as a "fraud," which it was not—it might better have been called a blackjack—but Administration pressure was too much for him, and by the end of April both Houses had passed the bill. The long Kansas fight was done; and Ste-

---

85 *MC*, April 2, 1858. For much of the material on this and the next page I am indebted to Roy F. Nichols, who generously permitted me to pillage portions of his forthcoming book: *The Disruption of the American Democracy.*

phens had done much to end it. But what was his personal triumph was a disaster for the South.[86]

At this session of the Thirty-fifth Congress he stood at the top of his power in Washington. He held the whip, he represented the Administration, and he rammed its measures through the legislature against an opposition that resisted with the vehemence of desperation. From his eminence as chairman of the Territorial Committee he looked down, pale, brusque, impatient, dyspeptic, and terribly serious. "Members," one of them testified, "are afraid of him. They submit to him their measures and if he does not approve them, it is no use to argue, he will oppose. If he approves and consents to take charge of a Bill you have to let him take his own course—he will not take any suggestions." [87]

The majority report of the committee of fifteen had contended that Congress had no power to go behind the acts of the Lecompton convention. "No new state," it said (and remember that Stephens wrote it), "has ever presented herself for admission with a constitution formed and adopted with greater regularity and more strictly in conformity to law." And yet, ruthlessly gagged by Stephens himself, the committee had decided that the popular vote of January 4, by which Lecompton had been voted down, was none of its concern. And a little later, when it no longer mattered, Stephens admitted to Richard M. Johnston that the Lecompton constitution had been "procured by fraud." "I wished it might be covered up from the world," he then said, explaining that he had supported it "because it gave us only what we were entitled to under the Kansas Act." [88] But under the Kansas Act the South

[86] 35 *CG*, I, 1765ff., 1779ff., 1856ff., 1900–6.

[87] L. F. Grover to Asahel Bush, March 5, 1859, in Bush transcripts, University of Oregon. This enlightening fragment I also owe to Professor Nichols' kindness.

[88] H. Rep. 377, 35th Cong., 1st sess., 15; R. M. Johnston: *Autobiography*, 151.

was entitled to exactly nothing. Was he going over to the radical position that slavery could not be excluded from a territory? Was he one of those who would not admit that Kansas was certain to be a free state? It sounded suspiciously like it.

From this time on, the break between Douglas and Buchanan was final and catastrophic. When Douglas ran against Lincoln for the Senate, the Administration almost leagued with Republicans to smash the Douglas machine in Illinois; and Southerners could not understand it; for after all was said and done, "Douglas is *sound on niggers,*" even though he did say at Freeport that the people of a territory could lawfully exclude slavery.[89] Stephens took a trip in August through the Northwest with Linton, and on the way made a point of visiting leading Democrats in an effort to arrange some sort of deal between Douglas and the Administration. But Buchanan's hatred of Douglas was by now an obsession, and he was abetted by Cobb, who was angling for the Presidential nomination in 1860. Cobb's insistence on ruining Douglas led to a cooling between him and Stephens, who, for all that he had opposed Douglas, could not let him go so easily.[90]

When he returned to Washington in December 1858 he saw Buchanan and told him that if the war on Douglas persisted there would be a "burst-up" in the Democratic convention in 1860, and with that a disruption of the Union. Buchanan, though surprised at such a line of thought, could no longer abandon his position; and Stephens left the White House, satisfied that he could do nothing to stave off the disaster he felt was coming—and indeed had done something to hasten.[91]

Save for a mild battle over the admission of Oregon as

[89] *LC,* J. H. Smith to A.H.S., August 3, 1858; S. Anderson to A.H.S., August 26, 1858; J. W. Stevenson to A.H.S., October 9, 1858.
[90] *J&B,* 337–8; *TSC,* 442–4, 448–9.
[91] *J&B,* 347–8; *Recollections,* 28–9.

a state, it was an uneventful session. Republicans and anti-Lecompton Democrats tried to defeat the Oregon bill because they felt themselves cheated by the English measure; for Kansas had rejected the proffered land grant and therefore could not yet become a state. Stephens, still chairman of the Territorial Committee, had to work hard to get the bill considered by the House, and on February 12, 1859 delivered his last major speech in its support.[92] He castigated the spiteful Republicans for their childishness, and then addressed himself to some of his Southern colleagues who objected to the admission of Oregon because it would increase the number of free states and tilt the balance of sectional power too far northward. "That balance," he told them, "is already gone—lost by causes beyond your or my control. . . . This immense territory to the west has to be peopled. It is now peopling. . . . Progress and development mark every thing in nature—human societies, as well as every thing else"; and he reminded them that since he had entered Congress, sixteen years before, the United States had added to itself a land surface greater than its whole area in 1783. Population was growing with frightening rapidity, would soon reach a hundred million and then not cease. What if all this growth took place mainly in regions where slavery was impracticable? What if it strengthened the North? "Principles," he said, "not numbers, are our protection"; and refused to speculate upon the future, hoping only it would be a prosperous one if the principles of the sovereignty of the states and that of the people of the states were maintained.

It was a surprisingly philosophic speech for one who had just aided in the commission of what he admitted was a fraud in order to try to reverse this irresistible process of which he now so eloquently spoke. It was almost concilia-

<hr/>

[92] 35 *CG*, II, 266, 335, 408, 544, 700, 865–6, 943ff. Speech in *Cleveland*, 621–37.

tory, almost a confession of error. Perhaps he could afford to relax and say what he wanted because he had decided not to run for Congress again. Soon after his birthday the news of his retirement became public; and there were many who wrote expressing disappointment and their wish that he might yet change his mind. Some frankly refused to believe it. The finest touch came on March 1, when he received a letter saying: "The undersigned, your personal friends, desire to express their admiration of your character and public services; and upon the occasion of your retirement from Congress, urgently request that you will accept, at their hands, the compliment of a dinner, in this city, on Friday, the 4th instant." Sixty-six men signed the letter, among whom were Vice-President Breckinridge, Speaker Orr, Andrew Johnson, Douglas, Douglas' enemies, Senators Bigler, Bright, and Fitch, William H. Seward, Simon Cameron, Judah P. Benjamin, Lucius Q. C. Lamar, Erastus Corning, and Clement L. Vallandigham.[93] The compliment must have touched him deeply; but he declined the dinner, because, he said, of business engagements; and on March 5, a clear, cold day, stood at the stern of the coastal steamer as it moved downstream. To one who wished to know why he was retiring now, he explained himself: "When I am on one of two trains coming in opposite directions on a single track, both engines at high speed, and both engineers drunk, I get off at the first station." And there is a story that as he watched the white shape of the Capitol blur and recede into the past, someone inquired if he did not expect to return as a senator. "No," he replied. "I never expect to see Washington again, unless I am brought here as a prisoner of war." [94]

93 The MS. of the invitation is in the Illinois Historical Society. It shows what must be borne in mind all through this period, that these gentlemen were not incapable of cursing in the Capitol and kissing in the kitchen.

94 *J&B*, 348, 353.

INTERLUDE

(*1859–61*)

"SOME of the papers say that no man ever retired from public life with more general good will and favour than I have—So be it—I am content—and whether it be so or not I am content—" [1] In this spirit, or apparently so, he turned from a public wilderness to cultivate his gardens. He never gave a reason for his retirement, except the parable about the two trains. And that does not suffice. The real reason—or reasons—are almost impossible to find. No man whose public career has arrived at such a point as his—a point from which it can go on in a steady ascent—voluntarily chooses to cast over the work of a lifetime. If he has gone so far he will go farther unless something bars the way. Stephens in 1859 was only at the beginning of a career in national affairs. His power was only then beginning to manifest itself. And he must have sensed that as well as any latter-day observer. Yet he retired. One possible explanation may lie in the curve of the election returns in his district, according to which the peak of his local popularity had been touched in 1851–3 and was on a dangerous toboggan, having at the 1857 election reached its lowest point since 1843. He had held a tight hand over his domain, had maintained constant communication with county leaders; and all candidacies for state legislature and county offices had been subject to his approval: yet it might be that he felt his grasp being loosened by the

[1] *MC*, March 18, 1859.

Know-Nothing machine in Augusta, which went on opposing him no matter by what name it was called.

Then too, he may have sensed, with that peculiar kind of sagacity exhibited by intelligent politicians, that in the general debacle which he was sure was coming, his name might retain its prestige more readily if he were out of politics, aloof and ready to join in at some strategic moment.

Whatever it was, it was not a matter of money. During the decade his estate had grown considerably. In 1850 he had reported his total wealth to be $8,000. He then had 13 slaves, 5,000 acres of land, scattered about the state, 2 horses, 3 cows, 2 oxen, and 2 swine. In 1860 he reported himself to be worth $53,000 (both these total valuations were distinct underestimates), and he had 32 slaves, 2 horses, 4 mules, 6 milch cows, 14 cattle, 38 sheep, and 64 hogs; and his plantation produced 20 bales of cotton, 60 bushels of peas, 100 of sweet and 50 of Irish potatoes, 150 of wheat and 1,250 of corn. He was by this time one of the larger slaveholders in his county. And during the next two years, which he devoted heavily to the practice of law, he made another $22,000. Liberty Hall admirably mirrored this state of well-being, for he had spent much time and money on house and grounds since 1845. From across the little valley, from the courthouse corner, a stranger in 1859 or 1860 would have seen a long gray board fence, broken by high gates; behind the fence, a shade-streaked mass of foliage, oak, locust, hickory, and cedar; and peering out here and there through the leaves, hints of white clapboard and shuttered windows. If he walked up the slope and through the gates, he would see, at the end of a long straight drive cutting through cropped turf, a house, not large, with a piazza, a large doorway, and eight windows in its façade. The plan of the building was typical and simple: each of the two floors had four rooms opening off a central hall that ran directly through the house and was wide enough to be considered another room. At the back was a covered piazza and an annex of two small rooms, the library and the master's bedchamber, which Stephens had himself added. Behind the house were an orchard of peach and apple trees, and a sizable vegetable garden, from which the dining-table was kept supplied with tomatoes, peas, beans, potatoes, and corn. The whole estate at this time comprised about thirty acres of rolling land. Neither it nor the house was in any respect magnificent or vast—very few Southern estates were. But it was beautiful and quiet, secluded, yet only a moment's walk from the town and railroad station: the red brick of the courthouse could be glimpsed from the front piazza. The house was appointed in characteristic mid-nineteenth-century taste, with green predominating in the color pattern. There were the inevitable Brussels carpets, the elaborately papered walls, the lamps with their grotesque bulging milk-glass bowls, the portraits scattered here and there, the old grandfather clock, the typical drawing-room furniture of the day, uncomfortable and overstuffed, and in the library the rows and rows of books, with a bronze bust of Webster, crowned with dust, brooding over them and over the trunks filled with correspondence in fading ink; from many persons, living and dead. Wherever the visitor went in this house, he was certain to stumble over a dog, the poodle Rio, or a terrier, or a yellow houn' dawg, or a mastiff. These dogs were the most constant and, one suspects, most coddled guests at Liberty Hall, though the entire upper floor of the house consisted of bedrooms kept always ready for overnight human company. And so, what with dogs and servants and passing travelers and friends and members of the family, the master of the Hall was scarcely ever left to himself when he was at home. A day

without visitors was a rarity. He had done well by himself
since those frightening days in 1832.[2]

Perhaps this substantial vested interest, these acres and
these thirty-two slaves, had some slight effect all through
the decade upon his public utterances and behavior. On
July 2 of this year 1859 he attended a public dinner held
in his honor at Augusta—a testimonial from those he had
served for nearly sixteen years. It took him four days to
prepare the speech he delivered that evening. As a swan
song it was temperate and calm, some thought too calm,
and a little peculiar. It was optimistic, perhaps a bit too
optimistic. "I leave the country," he said, "not only in as
good, but in a better condition than I found it . . . the
republic has sustained no serious detriment, either in her
material resources, intellectual advancement, social condition, or political status"; and he added: "I see no cause
of danger, either to the Union, or southern security in it."
And he reviewed the past to prove it. As for slavery, it
"rests upon principles that can never be successfully as-
sailed . . ." and to attempt to overthrow it is "the ab-
surdest of all crusades. It has grown stronger by discussion;
and will grow still stronger as discussion proceeds, and as
time rolls on. . . . The world is growing wiser, and upon
no subject more rapidly than that of the proper status of the
negro." And what was that status? It was one of natural
subordination: and here Stephens' basic concept of human
society as a hierarchy is given expression. "Order is nature's
first law," he quoted, and went on: "with it, come gradation and subordination. . . . We see it in the heavens
above—in the greater and lesser lights—in the stars that
differ from each other in magnitude and lustre; we see it in

2 These statistics are from the MS. census returns for 1850 and 1860 in
the Ordinary's Office, Crawfordville, Ga. Liberty Hall is preserved as
nearly as possible as it was in the 1870's, and is open to visitors. A description of it in 1860 is in *Cleveland,* 20–9.

the earth below—in the vegetable and animal kingdoms—
ranging from the stateliest trees of the forest to the rudest
mosses and ferns. . . . We see similar distinctions and
gradations in the races of men . . ." and he concluded that
such gradations were "mysteries in creation which are not
for us to explain." The Negro was inferior, as inevitably so
as the amœba; and his logical place in the social organism
was that of a slave; and in the Southern social organism his place was clearly fixed, on the whole to his comfort
and satisfaction. The system was strong and excellent
—at most points. Then came the peculiar sentence:
"Without an increase of African slaves from abroad," he
wished to point out, "you may not expect or look for many
more slave states," because the South could no longer
compete with the North in the race to settle the West.
Therefore, if the *status quo* remained the *status quo*, politically speaking, the South had nothing to fear. Why?
Because slavery was guaranteed by the North—in principle
—and it was on principle that the South should stand. If
the North acted according to its principles, all would be
well. All this was especially interesting in view of the fact
that Stephens was in correspondence with William Walker,
the notorious Nicaraguan filibuster, about this time. At
any rate, he went on, in this calm and quiet speech, "The
world, by wise men, is to be taken as they find it"; qualify-
ing himself, "If our system is not the best . . . it is wrong.
I utterly repudiate the doctrine of the greatest good for
the greatest number." And he concluded: "My race is run
—my career is ended. . . . I see no cause to regret any of
my acts"; and he begged pardon of any to whom in the
course of his political life he had given offense by word or
deed.[3]

There is no denying the fact that his words and deeds
over the past decade had been more and more closely ap-

3 *Cleveland,* 637–51; *LC,* W. Walker to A.H.S., March 13, 1858.

proaching those of the Rhetts and Yanceys, at the same
time that his stake in Southern society had grown. The
connection may be purely accidental. It may also mean
something. For the attack upon his society from the outside had been growing stronger, too. The Republicans
were a powerful party, and in Southern eyes were dominated by "abolitionists" like Seward and Lincoln. Even as
he spoke, his soothing words were being belied by events
—and he must have been aware of their speciousness.
Buchanan and Cobb were waiting to avenge themselves on
Douglas at the Charleston convention next year. The
Southern hotheads were equally bent on wrecking Douglas, and if they could not succeed in that, they would let
the Democratic party go and secede from the Union. And
at the end of 1859 John Brown stormed Harpers Ferry in
what most Southerners felt was a North-inspired raid, applauded by most Northerners—though most Northerners
did not applaud. With such madmen on the loose, what
safety was there in the Union? There were wild visions of
mass uprisings fostered by Northern agents. More and
more swiftly, more and more inevitably, the masses of people everywhere in the nation were being caught up in a
whirlpool of hysteria from which there was no escape but
war.

And yet, however close he had come to the hotheads,
Stephens was not one of them, as his behavior at the critical moment was to show. Something held him back.

Meanwhile he spent two relatively quiet years attending
to business, to the plantation and to his little "family,"
which included a young lawyer named George Bristow,
for whose education he had provided, and Quinea O'Neal,
the old Ordinary of Taliaferro County. Besides these two
there were always guests passing in and out; and Linton,
who in May 1859 was appointed to the state Supreme
Court by Governor Brown, was not far away and would

often come to Crawfordville. The brothers, at such times, would watch the clock like lovers, and when they had to part, the elder would write: "I had no idea that I should miss you so much. . . . All the evening and night long I shall think of you"; while the younger would reply as he drove away: "I felt as if I were going into exile." Or the two would vie with each other in stating the magnitudes of the debts they owed: "You have formed my character," Linton would insist, "so far as it contains elements of good"; and Alexander would try to top him with: "For thirty odd years you have been the polar star of my existence." [4] And it was always like this. In the correspondence of twenty years there is scarcely the hint of a disagreement, much less an outright quarrel. Once, in an unthinking moment, Alexander did or said something curt and brusque; Linton's reply was that of a wounded child; and the brother had no sooner received it than he all but got on his knees and begged forgiveness. In this affection there was no pride and no restraint; and both men practiced daily Antony's reply to Cleopatra, when she asks how much he loves her: "There's beggary in the love that can be reckon'd." No beggary existed here, not the slightest hesitation, only an astonishing and beautiful unanimity of thought and feeling. Each was the other's echo, and proud to be.

Such unity was utterly lacking in the country at large. The session of Congress that opened in December was vicious and snarling. Most members went armed. Martin J. Crawford of Georgia, a close friend of Stephens, said bluntly: "We will not submit to the inauguration of a Black Republican President." And everybody was waiting for the Charleston convention—Douglas, who wanted the

[4] *MC,* October 1, 1859; January 29, 1860; Linton to A.H.S., October 4, 19, 1859.

nomination, the Southern fire-eaters, who wanted the party to guarantee unconditionally their so-called Southern rights, Buchanan and Cobb, who were out for Douglas' hide. The Cobb movement, indeed, had been assuming some proportions in Georgia; a caucus of his supporters met on December 8, 1859 and appointed delegates to Charleston, endorsing his candidacy. The state executive committee countered by calling a convention to meet on March 14, 1860. This split might become serious, and Governor Brown asked Stephens what to do. Stephens wisely recommended that the March convention merely ratify the December nominations, but said nothing about the endorsement of Cobb.[5]

As early as 1858 there had been talk of Stephens and the Presidency; and in December of that year he had been sufficiently irritated to write to Linton: "I do wish an end put to all such use of my name." [6] But there were those who would not take Douglas or a Buchanan nominee who might take Stephens as an alternative. Douglas, too, was looking for a Southern vice-president, and in the summer of 1859 told one of Stephens' friends that if he, Douglas, could not be nominated at Charleston, he would throw his influence in Stephens' favor—a polite way of feeling Stephens out. But Stephens for the moment held his peace upon the possibilities of a reunion with Douglas. The only thing he said publicly before the convention was: "The Presidency is an office I do not want"; and this he repeated several times to whoever would listen. He did not want it, but he did not say he would not take it if it were offered him. He did, however, tell a Douglas party worker who came down to Liberty Hall in March that he thought Douglas would be the only man who could be

5 *Avery*, 107–8; *TSC*, 453, 454.
6 *MC*, December 8, 1858.

elected, and that he would be willing to run as Douglas' vice-president.[7] Barely two years ago he and Douglas had been at loggerheads over Lecompton: why this sudden amiability? Did Stephens seriously imagine that Douglas could be nominated? Perhaps; perhaps not; but Toombs had told him that Douglas could throw the nomination to whomever he pleased. . . .

The Charleston convention opened on April 23 in an atmosphere of distrust, anger, suspicion, hatred, and utter confusion of purpose. The Georgia delegation came pledged to no one, and, as it happened, no one was ever to know for whom it or any other delegation might have voted. For the Yancey-Rhett clique of extremists had come determined to cram their newest brain child—an affirmation of the Federal government's positive duty to enact a slave code for the territories—down the Democratic party's throat. And when they tried to put a plank to that effect into the platform, Northern Democrats revolted and defiantly substituted a plank that merely restated the Cincinnati platform, whose principle was "non-intervention," not "intervention," in the internal affairs of territories. And when the thing was done, while some frightened Southerners pleaded with the North to reconsider, and Yancey himself, smiling, comfortably studied the agony around him, then, one by one, the Southern delegations began withdrawing from the convention, first Alabama, then Mississippi, pale, determined men leaving a suddenly silent hall. The Georgia delegation divided, its Cobb wing leaving, the rest staying on. The rump of the convention balloted fifty-seven times for a candidate with no result, and then adjourned to meet in Baltimore on June 18; the seceders promptly agreed to meet in Richmond at about the same time.

7 *LC*, C. P. Culver to A.H.S., August 29, 1859; J. H. Smith to A.H.S., February 29, 1860; *Avery*, 109–10; Milton: *Eve of Conflict*, 413.

Stephens heard the news while on his way home from a court session. "I was not much surprised, but for it I was truly sorry," he said, "Sorry as I should be to see the paroxysms of a dear friend in a fit of delirium tremens." He was deeply disturbed despite the half-cynicism of this remark. "Since 1850 I have stood upon non-intervention by Congress on the subject of slavery in the territories" — and in the main this was true, and it was the thing that most clearly kept him from joining the radicals. Now he could only conclude: "Bad men have got control of the country." [8] To Richard M. Johnston, visiting him soon after the convention, he said more. Johnston inquired what he thought of the state of the nation, and the black eyes flared, the shrill voice said: "Think of them? Why, that men will be cutting one another's throats in a little while. In less than twelve months we shall be in a war, and that the bloodiest in history." Walking nervously up and down, he said that the Democrats were split "for ever." He did not think Douglas would give up seeking the nomination, but he supposed someone else would get it. Why, Johnston wanted to know, if a Republican President were elected, must there be war? With an impatient gesture, Stephens turned on him: "Because there are not virtue and patriotism and sense enough left in the country to avoid it." South Carolina would surely secede if a Republican were elected; and the Gulf states would follow her, though as far as he was concerned, she could go to the devil for all for him. Then he became thoughtful for an instant: If a strong government could be established it might not be so bad . . . but . . . what chance of a strong government was there? He had said long ago of the radicals that they might create a revolution, but they could not build up a good government. And in a public letter of May 5 he set himself squarely against the seceders, urging

8 *TSC,* 470–1; *J&B,* 355.

Georgia to send delegates to Baltimore. "If . . . there be a failure, let the responsibility not rest upon us," was his tone.[9] In this he differed from Toombs, who, disgusted and rebellious, irresponsibly decided to go with the seceders and "let things rock on." But Toombs took adolescent delight in a rocking world.

When a state convention met to consider the problem of where to send delegates, it was packed with Cobb disciples, and quickly broke up into two factions, the majority sending delegates first to Baltimore to insist on slave protection in the territories, failing to obtain which they were to go to Richmond; the minority, led by Herschel V. Johnson, sending delegates to Baltimore only.[10] But the Baltimore convention proved little wiser than that of Charleston. From Alabama, Louisiana, and Georgia there were two delegations contesting for each state's vote—seceders and new appointees—and over the question of which groups to admit a struggle arose. When it was finally determined to admit the Alabama and Louisiana conservatives and split the Georgia representation between the contending groups, the radicals prepared to make another withdrawal. Douglas immediately sent a letter to Richardson, who represented him at the convention, giving him the power to withdraw his name if he thought it expedient, and substitute that of a "non-intervention and Union-loving Democrat." But the radicals, whether they knew of the letter or not, carried out their threat and seceded on the 22nd. The convention that remained nominated Douglas. The Vice-Presidency was left to the few lingering Southerners, who, influenced by Cobb's and Toombs' rumoring that Stephens was too ill to serve, passed him by, and after Benjamin Fitzpatrick of Alabama had declined, chose

9 *J&B*, 355–64.
10 *LC*, J. P. Hambleton to A.H.S., May 23, 1860; Flippin: *Johnson*, 104–11; *Phillips*, 190.

Herschel V. Johnson. The seceders at Richmond nominated John C. Breckinridge and Joseph Lane as their candidates. Lincoln was already in the field. And that was that. Douglas' letter of withdrawal was never used. Apparently his personal preference for a substitute to himself was Stephens; but he seems not to have expended any energy in urging Stephens as his running-mate. Perhaps it was because in his own state Stephens was under heavy fire, Toombs and Cobb, furious at his sudden moderation, spitefully saying that he would never be sustained in the South on account of his Mexican War record, and that a Presidential nomination would probably kill him. In Cobb this was not surprising, for Cobb's friendship had never been more than skin-deep; but in Toombs it was a little unexpected, and explicable only in terms of Toombs' abnormal impetuosity.[11]

Unable to endure the direct heat of the sun, Stephens stayed at home all summer, sick and moody, wondering how much longer he had to live, watching history with a jaundiced eye. "I shall take no active part—can do no good," he said. He would stick by Douglas and by "the national flag of Non Intervention so long as it floats." [12] He had no other choice. So far as strength permitted, he went about his affairs, visiting Linton, who had just resigned his Supreme Court seat, in the middle of August for a few weeks, to rest and think. While he was there the Cobb men named a Breckinridge and Lane electoral ticket, and a little later the Douglas minority did likewise, naming Stephens as one of its electors at large. Though he still did not feel able to go stumping for Douglas, he began

---

[11] *LC*, J. P. Hambleton to A.H.S., July 2, 1860. Hambleton was at the convention himself, and gave the impression that Douglas had rather wished Stephens might get the nomination. But wishes are not horses, especially not the wishes of politicians.

[12] *TSC*, 486; A.H.S. to J. P. Hambleton, July 7, 1860, Hambleton MSS., Emory University.

to study events with more excitement. He was sure Douglas could not win in Georgia, and this certainty may have accentuated his disposition to remain inactive and uninvolved. But on September 1 he went to Augusta and began a speech in support of Douglas. After an hour or so he had to sit down and rest before going on; and when this speech was done he said no more in public for some time,[13] until, in October, with the Pennsylvania and Indiana state elections indicating an almost certain Lincoln victory, he went on a belated speaking tour of the state. But it was a hopeless job. The radicals had done too well. When Douglas arrived in Georgia in the course of his Southern tour—an intense effort to persuade people everywhere that Lincoln's election would be no cause for disunion—Stephens met him at Atlanta and introduced him to the crowd. The demonstration was loud and enthusiastic, but hollow. How hollow, election day showed, when Breckinridge received 51,893 votes, Bell 42,855, and Douglas 11,580.[14] So far as Georgia went, the Little Giant might more accurately have been called the Big Dwarf. Stephens' own district in a sense repudiated him, for Douglas won in only four of eleven counties. Bell carried four others, and Breckinridge the remaining three. And in the light of subsequent events, a vote for Bell was more often than not considered by the voter as much a vote for secession as was a vote for Breckinridge.

Expecting Lincoln's victory, Stephens wrote: "We shall I apprehend have trouble." [15] And quickly. On election day, not deigning to wait for the official count of the vote, Governor Brown recommended to the state legislature the summoning of a convention to consider Georgia's future,

---

13 *Avery*, 126; *TSC*, 494; A.H.S. to Willian H. Hidell, September 14, 1860, Alexander H. Stephens MSS., Pennsylvania Historical Society (cited hereafter as *PHS*).
14 Milton: *Eve of Conflict*, 499; statistics from *Phillips*, 191.
15 *TSC*, 502.

and he asked for a million dollars to defend the state. All over Georgia mass meetings were being held and resolutions bombastically favoring secession passed and sent in to Milledgeville. And the legislature, considering Brown's requests, summoned its political leaders for advice. On November 12 T. R. R. Cobb, Howell's brother, argued for secession on the ground that Lincoln's election justified it; next night Toombs warned that after the 4th of March next all the power of the Federal government would be in the hands of "the enemy," and cried: "Will you let him have it?" On the 14th Stephens delivered his appeal to reason.

His speech was widely noticed and commented on, reprinted in many Northern papers, and brought letters from all parts of the country, including a note from George Ticknor Curtis and a printed testimonial of thanks from a group of Philadelphians.[16] Most important of all, it provoked Lincoln to write, requesting a copy of the speech, after studying which he asked Stephens the simple question: "Do the people of the South really entertain fears that a Republican Administration would, directly or indirectly, interfere with the slaves . . . ?" promising him: "there is no cause for such fears." But, Lincoln concluded, that was not all. "You think slavery is *right,* and ought to be extended; while we think it is *wrong,* and ought to be restricted. That, I suppose, is the rub. It certainly is the only substantial difference between us." Stephens replied by attacking the principles of the Republican party, and begged Lincoln not to hold the Union together by force. There the correspondence ceased.

While, all through December, Cobb, Brown, and a hundred others waved their arms and shouted for immediate

16 *MC*, November 24, 1860; *LC*, W. W. Corcoran to A.H.S., November 22, 1860; G. T. Curtis to A.H.S., November 23, 1860; Horace B. Sargent to A.H.S., November 24, 1860; citizens of Philadelphia to A.H.S., December 1, 1860.

secession, the conservatives were curiously inactive. In November, while he was at Milledgeville, Stephens had got fifty-two members of the legislature to adopt resolutions asking the voters to secure pledges from all candidates for the convention which had been called to meet in January, that they would resort to every other remedy before seceding; [17] but after this he retired to Liberty Hall, and spent his time slaughtering hogs and writing Linton long snatches of breakfast or evening dialogue between himself, his nephew John A. Stephens (son of his brother John), and old Quinea O'Neal, who never smiled except when he heard Stephens in the morning trying to sing as he was being rubbed down by Harry, his body servant. On December 20 South Carolina seceded, and Stephens did not think she was "entitled to . . . great sympathy on the part of her Southern Confederates," and went on, surprisingly enough, to say that "The South, so far from having become an abject minority . . . has controlled the Government, united our Presidents and sustained their Administration for 60 out of the 72 of our national existence. . . ." [18]

Perhaps it was not so surprising that he took up such a position. His adoration of the twin concepts of justice and law amounted to a religion. Lincoln had been legally elected; there could therefore be no possible ground for secession. In his very first term in Congress he had questioned his own right to hold a seat. His opposition to Polk's conduct of the Mexican War, whatever its root causes, had always been expressed in terms of justice and constitutional powers. His support of the repeal of the Missouri Compromise had been based, as had his point of view in relation to Texas, upon the strict notion of an equal and equitable division of public territory between the two

17 Pearce: *Hill,* 47.
18 *MC,* January 2, 1861.

great sections. Law was for him the written and procedural expression of a concept of justice, according to the terms of which human society, to be civilized, must operate. And justice, for him, was a simple Platonic justice: justice is every man's having and doing what is his own. The political rights he insisted on were rights determined by the simple logic of the situation: since North and South were united in one government, the property of that government was the property of both sections, each of which, in equity, was entitled to share in the benefits of such property. The nature of their respective societies had nothing whatever to do with it. Therefore his willingness to divide the territories on the 36° 30′ line: it would be the most practical solution of the problem, and it would not sacrifice any principles. Now the radicals were insisting that a legal election in which the South happened to have lost was sufficient cause for secession. This was irresponsibility; it was lawlessness; it was rash. Therefore he opposed it. He would fight for the South if the overt attack came; he made that clear: but Lincoln's election was not that attack. It was not yet right to revolt. Oppression had not yet come. If the majority of conservatives were convinced that their lives and positions were at last in deadly danger, he was not.

But as conciliation failed and failed, in Congress and at the White House, as Governor Brown ordered the occupation by state militia of Fort Pulaski on the Savannah River, as the situation in Charleston harbor grew daily tenser, he could not but conclude that whether he liked it or not he would have to follow Georgia. On January 2, 1861, the day when delegates to the state convention were to be elected, he went down the hill and under the railroad bridge and up the other slope and into the courthouse, through rain and wind, to cast his ballot and make a little speech. There were about a hundred people inside, dripping wet, standing by stoves, bewildered and subdued. He had a headache, did not much relish talking, but spoke a little to them, quietly, telling them not to be afraid, and pledging himself to do all he could to maintain the Union and Georgia's rights. When he was done, somebody tried to whoop up three cheers for South Carolina—but no one responded.[19]

And after that it went faster and faster, the whole machine wild and beyond control, racing to destruction. On January 9 Mississippi seceded; on the 10th the arsenal at Baton Rouge was occupied by Louisiana militia; on the 11th Florida and Alabama seceded; on the 13th the navy yard at Pensacola was surrendered; on the 16th the Georgia convention met; and on the 21st its ordinance of secession was signed by all but six delegates. On the 24th ten delegates were chosen to represent the state in a congress that was to meet at Montgomery, Alabama, on February 4. Toombs and Cobb were made delegates at large; Hill and Stephens represented their respective districts. Stephens did not want to go. It would be disagreeable. Toombs and Cobb were unpleasant and overbearing; Hill was unfriendly; Stephens was in a position, it seemed to him, of extreme impotence. At length he allowed himself to be persuaded, but only after the convention had pledged the delegates to organize a permanent government for the seceded states on the basis of the old Constitution. If he had to leave what he considered the best government in the world, he would do so only if he were assured of exchanging it for a reasonable facsimile.[20]

Leaving Liberty Hall on the evening of February 3, he drove down the hill past the white Baptist church to the station, where in the darkness a crowd of neighbors waited,

19 Ibid., January 3, 1861.
20 *The Confederate Records of the State of Georgia*, ed. A. D. Candler (Atlanta, 1909–11) (cited hereafter as *CR*), I, 331; *J&B*, 383.

silent and chilled, to see him off. There was no exhilaration here. The train came in, shuddered to a stop, sparks flying from the wheels, smoke blowing down. He spoke his brief farewells, shook as many hands as he could take, climbed aboard, turned on the open platform, tall and emaciated in the gloom, waved once more, and went into the car. In a moment more the train moved slowly off, round the curve, past Liberty Hall, into the west. In the hot, smoky, drafty, dim-lit coach he found Toombs and several other friends, including Colonel James Chesnut of South Carolina and his wife. She was a clever, interesting woman, and he admired clever, interesting women; they in their turn seemed somehow drawn to him. He sat beside her and they talked while the train swayed and rattled on, the sick yellow light flickering upon their faces. At Union Point T. R. R. Cobb and Francis Bartow came aboard. It was a dull, uneventful trip, except that in the early morning, three miles out of Montgomery, the train was delayed three hours when several cars went off the track. "This," said Chesnut, "is what comes of traveling on Sunday." [21] Stephens, pallid as always, fragile as always, sat in his seat as always like a collection of old bones that someone had absently tossed there, brushing the chestnut hair out of his eyes. Once an old man standing by the station at Madison had been shown this being sitting calmly in a coach, smoking; and when he was told who it was, stared and could think of nothing to say but "Good Lord!" That was ten years ago. . . . And now this same being was

[21] *J&B*, 383–4; T. R. R. Cobb to his wife in *Southern Historical Society Papers*, XXVIII, 281. The force of Chesnut's remark must not be underestimated. This was Victorian America, and these gentlemen were for the most part circumscribed and permeated by a religious piety and austerity quite incomprehensible to later, less whitened bosoms. God was the chairman of the Montgomery convention: which was why Toombs, who made no bones about his love of drunkenness, did not become President of the Confederacy, and why Davis, the apotheosis of starched morality, did.

passing through Madison once more, bound on the most important journey he had ever taken. . . . And now he was stepping carefully down from the platform in the clear Monday morning light. "Montgomery!"

CHAPTER FOUR

Power (*1861–5*)

THERE followed a strange four years, the most important of his life, beginning here in a small dusty country town in Alabama, in a circular room in a white building on a free eminence, where at noon on February 4, 1861 the Provisional Congress of the Confederate States—though it was not yet that—assembled. Of the thirty-seven men present, ten were Georgians, and they dominated. Save for Rhett and Porcher Miles of South Carolina, there were no names of great consequence on the roster except for those of Georgians. Yancey, Benjamin, Davis, were all absent. Yet it was an impressive convocation. These men were intensely self-conscious and in deadly earnest about what they were doing.

The prestige of Georgia was merely recognized when Rhett proposed Howell Cobb as the permanent chairman; and as he, in acceptance, spoke of the "perpetual" character of the act of secession, Stephens, for the moment perhaps resigned to the inevitable, agreed, speaking a little later in the very same vein.[1] But this did not imply conversion. He was reluctant and uneasy, and it was whispered about by some that he was "a Union man at heart";[2] nor did his rather aloof and supercilious behavior toward the

[1] *TSC*, 537.
[2] Or so Henry Cleveland, Stephens' quondam biographer, told Davis long after the war. *Jefferson Davis, Constitutionalist*, ed. Dunbar Rowland (Jackson, Miss., 1923), X, 6. But Cleveland by then detested Stephens for various reasons.

rest of the members tend to detract from this impression. Noting, what was true, that the "crowd generally seemed green and not to know how to proceed," he got himself appointed chairman of a Committee on Rules, wrote the rules himself, presented them to the committee when it met at his boardinghouse, had them approved and then printed the same night at his own expense.[3] So long as he was here, his actions seemed to say, he intended to see things done as he desired, especially in the matter of drawing up a constitution for the new Confederacy. He was appointed to the committee chosen for this purpose, which reported a provisional constitution to the convention on February 7. To judge by the membership of the committee, this document was mainly his work: for with the exception of Robert W. Barnwell of South Carolina, he was the only member with a national reputation and long legislative experience, and his word very probably carried the most weight.[4] Certainly the constitution conformed to the pledge he had exacted from the Georgia convention before his departure. It was a virtual copy of the Federal Constitution, with some differences, at least one of which, that restraining Congress from appropriating money except upon the specific request of the President or a Cabinet officer, he claimed as his own proposal. This draft constitution, slightly amended in two days of debate, was passed on the evening of the 8th.

The next order of business was the election of a provisional President and Vice-President. In the dinner being dished up at Montgomery for the Southern people, this was the *pièce de résistance,* and every member of the convention wanted to be a cook. For the office there were several

[3] *MC,* February 5, 1861.

[4] Of the twelve members, four had served in their state legislatures, and five had had brief terms in the national House of Representatives. Most were planters or lawyers, another sign of the propertied conservatism of the executors of secession. *Dictionary of American Biography,* passim.

logical candidates and some not so logical. Among the former were Rhett, Yancey, Toombs, and Cobb, the leaders of the secession movement, each considering himself entitled to the Presidency as a reward for services. Among the latter were Jefferson Davis and Stephens. Now both Rhett and Yancey were pretty well out of the running: their usefulness was past and they on the road to being forgotten. The seriocomic shadow play that followed, the game of preference and withdrawal, had Davis as its central character. His popular reputation was military, and the Mississippi delegation came to Montgomery prepared to keep his name from being considered, so that he could head the state militia.[5] Despite this a definite Davis sentiment did exist, even before the convention opened.[6] And here Georgia's power bluntly showed, for both Cobb and Toombs had come to Alabama with the fixed intention of getting the Presidency. The action of the Georgia delegation could determine that of the whole convention; and if either Toombs or Cobb persisted, a serious battle would develop. On the other hand, such a battle was the last thing most of the delegates wanted: to the watching world the convention must present a façade of unshatterable unity, lest its prestige be ruined from the beginning.

It would have been unnatural had Stephens not also angled for an office from the eminence of which, were he elected, he could guide the direction of a movement with which he was identified only under protest. On his way to Montgomery he had been approached by James Chesnut with the remark that South Carolina looked to Georgia for the Presidency, to which he had replied that Toombs or Cobb would be a good man. Chesnut countered that he and his friends had been thinking of Toombs or Stephens.

5 Elisabeth Cutting: *Jefferson Davis, Political Soldier* (New York, 1930), 130.

6 T. R. R. Cobb, in *Southern Historical Society Papers*, XXVIII, 281–3, speaks of it on the 3rd.

To this bait Stephens appeared not to rise: he merely remarked that he could not be considered, having been opposed to secession. At Montgomery, however, Laurence
Keitt came to see him and reiterated what Chesnut had
said. This time Stephens wavered, saying he would not
commit himself, but that even if unanimously elected, he
would not accept unless he could form a cabinet with views
similar to his own. The South Carolinians, dissatisfied
with such hedging, turned to Davis.[7]

If he seriously wanted the position, Stephens would have
had to fight for it. Cobb wanted it too, and both he and
his brother despised Stephens as a milksop. Hill and Stephens were still estranged. Toombs, who was spending
most of his time getting as drunk as he could [8] and earning the disrespect of the intensely churchgoing Montgomery public, still nourished hopes for himself. Bartow
and Nisbet would support Cobb. At most Stephens could
count on Martin J. Crawford and A. H. Kenan. It mattered little that Louis Wigfall was telegraphing from Texas
that Stephens should be elected.[9]

The election was set for February 9. On the night of the
8th the delegations of every state but Georgia caucused
and, Mississippi excepted, agreed on Davis for the first
place. The Georgians met the next morning. Stephens
moved Toombs as their choice for the Presidency. T. R. R.
Cobb objected, saying that every other delegation had endorsed Davis. Toombs, annoyed, asked Crawford to go
and find out whether Cobb's contention were true; and
before Crawford left, either Toombs or Kenan put Stephens' name forward as the Vice-Presidential choice in case
the report were so. There was a moment of uncomfortable
silence, and then the Cobb brothers and Bartow got up

[7] *J&B*, 389–90; William E. Dodd: *Jefferson Davis* (Philadelphia, 1907),
220.

[8] *MC*, February 23, 1861.

[9] Cutting, op. cit., 150.

and walked out without a word, leaving the others to their own devices. Crawford, instructed to see whether Stephens would be acceptable to the other delegations for the second office, soon returned to say that Davis was the general choice and Stephens would be supported. When the election was held a little later, both men were unanimously voted in. To the radicals Stephens was a "bitter pill," [10] but one that had to be taken. Georgia could not be neglected; and the appointment of an ardent critic of secession to the secession government was good psychology. Few considered the possibilities of a backfire.

On the evening of the 9th Stephens was serenaded by the citizens of Montgomery; and on the 11th, his forty-ninth birthday, he was inaugurated at one in the afternoon. It was a clear, bright day.[11] Davis did not arrive until the 17th, and the ceremonies of his inaugural were held next day, Stephens riding with him from his hotel to the Capitol. In his address Davis stressed the irrevocability of secession, and, warning of impending war, recommended immediate military preparations. The Confederate States of America was set in motion, headed by a man who was disappointed because he could not be a soldier, and a man who was dubious about the Confederacy itself. Irony could scarcely go further. And Linton was writing that while Davis was a "safe" man he was also a "mean" one: [12] a suggestion pregnant with future trouble.

The machinery of government was put together day by day: executive departments were created on February 21, and Davis at once filled them with conservative men of moderate reputation. Toombs, as Secretary of State, was his one firebrand. Then the President turned to the problem of persuading the Union administration to withdraw

10 T. R. R. Cobb in *Southern Historical Society Papers,* XXVIII, 283.
11 *MC,* February 11, 1861.
12 Ibid., Linton to A.H.S., February 12, 1861.

its troops from the forts in Confederate territory of which it still held possession. On the 23rd he asked Stephens to head a commission that he proposed to send to Washington to treat of these and other matters. Stephens declined, being convinced that Buchanan could not recognize the Confederacy or deal with any of its agents,[13] and urged Davis to appoint H. V. Johnson in his place. Though Davis refused to accommodate him, the personnel of the commission as finally chosen was not distasteful to Stephens. Martin J. Crawford, a close friend, and John Forsyth of Alabama, an acquaintance of sorts, were members.

Until March 11 the self-styled Provisional Congress turned itself into a constitutional convention for the purpose of debating the report of the committee on a permanent constitution. Stephens was not on that committee, but Toombs was; and one provision in the permanent constitution interested both men much. It was that giving Congress the authority to empower cabinet officers to sit upon the floors of both houses and participate in debate on matters pertaining to their departments. Stephens was sorry that this recommendation had not been made mandatory;[14] and as it happened, Congress never took advantage of it because Congress disliked most cabinet officers. The permanent Constitution, as altered from the provisional draft, omitted a phrase Stephens had inserted into the notorious "necessary and proper" clause. He had rewritten the old Constitution's clause to state that Congress had power to make all laws necessary and proper to carry into execution the specified powers, and all other powers "expressly delegated" by the Constitution. Now the words "expressly delegated" were dropped and the wording of 1787, "vested by," substituted.

---

[13] Ibid., February 23, 1861.
[14] *View*, II, 338–9. Stephens was all his life something of an Anglophile.

Besides establishing itself as a government, the Congress undertook, albeit circumspectly, to defend the Constitution, which it passed in an atmosphere of confusion and haste on March 11, and which Stephens accepted mainly because he had to, though considerably dissatisfied with it.[15] Acts were passed giving Davis power to accept levies of arms, munitions, and volunteers from the various states, and to call out 100,000 twelve-month volunteers. War was becoming less and less a matter of speculation, more and more a certainty. Lincoln had been inaugurated; the three Confederate commissioners were in Washington, received in polite society but not by the government, conducting backstairs conversations with Seward, and being misled into thinking that Fort Sumter would be evacuated. Lincoln, in agony lest the border states should secede, was not yet himself sure whether he would give up the fort or not, and did not finally decide until the beginning of April. But at Sumter and elsewhere soldiers faced soldiers, and a chance shot might make the nation run with blood.

Stephens was glad when the permanent Constitution was passed; Montgomery life bored him; and even though he was on excellent terms with the President and spent a good many hours closeted with him, he did not feel as though he had an influential, directing part in things. Leaving Montgomery on the 11th, he went home, delivering a half-hour speech at Atlanta on the way.[16] At Savannah, on the evening of the 21st, he spoke again to an enormous crowd, most of whom could not hear him because they were outside the hall. He expounded the new Constitution and painted a sanguine picture of the future, interrupted by frequent bursts of "rapturous" applause. "We have intelligence, and virtue, and patriotism . . ." he

15 *J&B*, 393.
16 *MC*, March 12, 1861.

boasted, and "If . . . we are true to ourselves, true to
our cause, true to our destiny, true to our high mission, in
presenting to the world the highest type of civilization
ever exhibited by man—there will be found in our lexicon
no such word as fail." [17] In this workmanlike job of rab-
ble-rousing was one passage that became the most notorious
he ever delivered: "Our new government," he said, "is
founded upon exactly the opposite idea [of the equality of
races]; its foundations are laid, its corner-stone rests upon
the great truth, that the negro is not equal to the white
man. . . ." After uttering this profundity, which he did
not himself completely believe, at least not so unequivocally, he went back to Crawfordville and busied himself
at his plantation, waiting to see what would happen.

It happened swiftly. The surrender of Sumter was demanded on April 11; the fort was fired on the following
morning; and on the 15th appeared Lincoln's first call for
troops. Two days later Virginia seceded; and Stephens,
who had received a telegram from Davis asking him to
come immediately to Montgomery for conference, was requested by the President to go to Richmond to negotiate
an alliance between Virginia and the Confederacy. He
again attempted to beg off, but, according to his own account, was so strenuously urged by Davis and the Cabinet
that he could not but accept.[18] Arriving in Richmond on
April 22, he took up residence at the Ballard House and
prepared to meet the secession convention, which, await-
ing him, was still in session. Next day, shortly before noon,
he went up to the Capitol, saw Lee greeted by the convention as the commander-in-chief of Virginia's armed
forces, and then spoke to the convention for some time,
expounding his race theory, explaining why he had gone

17 Speech in *Cleveland*, 717–29.
18 *Richardson*, 213; *J&B*, 396–7.

with Georgia in her secession, and stressing the value of unity in defensive warfare.[19]

That night Lee called on him at his invitation. Stephens had feared the Virginia convention might refuse to enter into any military agreements with the Confederacy, should Lee choose to protest his having to take orders from a titular subordinate in the event of the merging of Virginian with Confederate forces, Lee being a major-general and Montgomery having no rank higher than brigadier. Lee, when this was explained, assured Stephens he would make no protest; [20] and after discussions during the 24th, an agreement placing all military operations in Virginia under control of the Confederate government was ratified by the convention on the 25th. "The Virginians," Stephens, who wanted to get away, complained, "*will* debate and speak, though war be at the gates of their city" [21] —a sentiment he might well have recalled three years later.

Tired and not happy, he traveled back to Montgomery, where the young government was handling a tremendous volume of business, getting itself started. In the midst of this bedlam of opportunism and sunshine patriotism Stephens was depressed and sober, writing to Linton: "I am prepared for, and expect, a long and bloody conflict." [22] He walked the dusty tree-lined streets, passing through mobs of hustling contractors and would-be soldiers, loud politicians and their sycophants, listening to their "Why,

19 *J&B*, 398; speech in *Cleveland*, 729–45. He sounded here more than ever like a schoolteacher: he actually presumed to explain to the Virginians why they had seceded. But then he did not think much of Virginians, saying once: "they think him a great man indeed that can play whist well—smoke a cigar—ride in a close bodied carriage without getting sick—and go it upon punch—hot apple toddy—and mint julips" (*MC*, January 12, 1845.) His own digestion was, unfortunately, as easily upset as a wagon with three wheels.
20 *View*, II, 384–7.
21 *J&B*, 399.
22 *MC*, May 3, 1861.

sir, those Yankee pups would never dare to fight us," and their "If you get me the contract I'll let you have fifteen per cent"; and he went from office to office, the dingy dirty little rooms pre-empted by the government, with chalk scrawls or pasted paper saying WAR DEPARTMENT or COMPTROLLER-GENERAL, listening; and he went from party to party and listened to the women rattle in their empty frivolous way, the way they had been taught so well they could not now forget it; and he listened and was saddened. Mrs. Chesnut found him "not cheerful in his views," and accused him of being "half-hearted." But she nevertheless found what he had to say "deeply interesting." [23] If he was indulging in croaking, he was not far from speaking truth.

II

From this time forward Stephens' contributions to the prosecution of the war became negligible, sporadic, unimportant. The office itself was, as someone told him, "a sop," one way of getting rid of a troublemaker. But Stephens would not make a good Throttlebottom: he was too energetic for that; and therefore, if he could not help, he would hinder. If things would not be done his way, he would impede their getting done at all.

An act of Congress providing for a $50,000,000 loan in twenty-year eight per cent bonds, to be subscribed for in specie, military stores, or produce, enlisted Stephens' attention in the summer and fall of 1861. His views on financial policy, with whose determination he had nothing to do, but about which he was consistently concerned, may briefly be disposed of in this connection. He was no economist, but he saw danger clearly. As the currency grew more and more inflated he became alarmed, and agreed with Secretary of the Treasury Memminger's insistence upon heavy taxation for war purposes as the only cure

23 Mary B. Chesnut: *A Diary from Dixie* (New York, 1929), 47.

for inflation.[24] "Independence," he once said, "will cost money as well as blood," and on this note he often harped. But direct taxation was highly unpopular in Congress and with the people, and was therefore never resorted to.

The produce loan of May 1861, in Stephens' opinion, fell far short of what ought to have been done. Like so many other Southerners, he was a victim of the "King Cotton" delusion in that he had enormous faith in the power of cotton as a weapon with which to win recognition for the Confederacy from European nations. But whereas their policy—and it was largely followed by Congress and the states—was to try to coerce Europe by withholding cotton from her, his based itself upon an immediate transfer of as much cotton as possible to warehouses in Europe, where it could be used as a fund on which credit could be obtained. He wanted the government to buy all the cotton available, paying in eight per cent bonds, and then, using it as security, contract for fifty-odd ironclad steamers to be built in Europe, which steamers would break the Federal blockade and carry the cotton across the Atlantic.[25] This scheme he submitted to the government, but it was never seriously considered. In point of fact, it was impossible to carry into execution. There was not nearly so much cotton available in the Confederacy in the spring of 1861 as Stephens erroneously imagined; the European nations would never have built ironclads on such a scale for the South, as the events of 1862–4 demonstrated; and the planters did not want to sell their cotton for bonds, but for paper that could be used as currency. Toombs saw these objections, as anyone with a little economic sense could, and earnestly criticized Stephens' notion, imploring him to stump the state for the produce loan, for if it should

[24] A.H.S. to T. J. Semmes, January 4, 1862; Semmes MSS., Duke University.

[25] *Cleveland*, 756–7.

fail, "we shall see the worst times we have seen yet." [26]
This was precisely what Stephens was doing all through the
summer and fall.

At the same time he was helping his old friend Judge
Thomas W. Thomas organize a regiment composed of the
social flowering of the northern judicial circuit; and when
the regiment, the 15th Georgia Volunteers, left Georgia
for Virginia on July 16, Linton went with it as a lieutenant-
colonel.[27] Alexander, throughout Linton's term of service,
showed the greatest solicitude for him, saying often that
the thought of Linton sleeping in the rain with nothing
but a blanket for protection kept him lying awake at night,
thinking apprehensive thoughts. As it happened, Linton
was never exposed to enemy fire during his stay in the
army. Unprepared for the nastiness of military life, he
quickly came down with the measles. Stephens, who had
gone to Richmond to attend the third session of the provisional Congress, spent much of August and September
traveling to and fro between the capital and the camp
near Centreville, until, upon the adjourning of Congress,
he returned to Crawfordville. Linton's sickness left him
pretty well disgusted with the army; and after five months
of waiting, now in a tent with rain making the landscape
a misty, boggy, soggy quagmire, now on picket duty in the
wet and cold, with never a shot being fired, his disgust
and his physical weariness impelled him to resign and go
back home. The inefficiency of army administration grated
incessantly upon his nerves; and, in any event, his moody,
depressive nature would have kept him from being a good
soldier. It was probably as well that he was out.

Alexander, again in Richmond in December, was also
out of sorts. At the close of the year he was stricken with a
particularly severe attack of facial neuralgia, could not

26 *Recollections*, 67.
27 Waddell: *Linton Stephens*, 242.

sleep, ate little or nothing, and spent several weeks in bed while his correspondence accumulated. Unofficially he had a secretary, a young man named William Hidell, whom he had put through school and of whom he seemed quite fond; but Hidell received no salary until 1862. Stephens' illness continued into January of the new year, so agonizing that he had to take quinine at regular intervals to ease the pain. It was no wonder that men spoke of him in these years, with a kind of cruel cynicism, as a "refugee from the graveyard." [28] He looked it. Yet, curiously, inexplicably, though his suffering increased from this time on and was never to diminish again until he died, his abysmal pessimism disappeared. He became almost cheerful, and remained so for the rest of his days. Though he had gloomy things to say, though he was often sad, there was no more romantic brooding on the evanescence of life and the vileness of man. The cause may have been religious, for he became, about this time, much more devout than he had ever been since his childhood; but it may also have been far more profound, possibly even physiological, for he was now past fifty.

. . . Enter now Joseph E. Brown, Governor of the sovereign state of Georgia for four consecutive terms, representing, or so it would seem, the people of his state during the most savage civil war in history. There were others like him, but taking him for all in all he was unique, and might have said with Huey Long: "Just call me sui generis and let it go at that." From the Executive Mansion in Milledgeville, this tall, thin, awkward, sallow "barebones," writing in a style as nasal as his voice, this pious, irascible, alpaca-clad country-boy-made-good hampered and harassed, for four long years, the efforts of the Confederate government to wage a war and win it. Nothing the Ad-

<hr>

28 Jabez L. M. Curry: *Civil History of the Government of the Confederate States* (Richmond, 1901), 57.

ministration did seemed to please him; everything it did seemed to annoy him. To his microscopic eye the toes of the sovereign Georgia people were continually being trod. den on by the elephant at Richmond; and whenever he perceived or thought he felt the horny foot descending, he shrieked as loudly as he could. Nothing, at such moments, took precedence over his anguish. The Confederacy could collapse if it liked, but Joseph E. Brown would be solaced and would have justice done to Georgia.

His cantankerousness began at the beginning. In 1861 he tried to get the government to accept the officers and a handful of enlisted men of two regiments, leaving all officers not essential to the regiments to stay in Georgia and complete their recruitment; and the government, though it protested, had to take the regiments as he offered them because it needed men too badly.[29] When the President was authorized to accept volunteers for the army directly, without having to requisition them from the governors, Brown lunged at this infringement of his authority and forbade all direct volunteers from taking arms with them out of Georgia. The government had pitifully few guns as it was, and Brown knew this very well. He was finally persuaded to revoke his order, but at once began squabbling over the appointing of officers.[30] Under existing law, field officers of regiments were elected by the men; when companies were offered the government, the President organized them into regiments and appointed the regimental officers; at all times he appointed officers of units higher than regiments. When the Secretary of War in July asked Brown for a number of companies for a reserve corps, and later for two regiments, Brown offered him a brigade fully officered, which the Secretary under the law could not accept. Begging him to send two regi-

[29] *CR*, III, 21–32.
[30] Ibid., III, 81, 86; *Brown*, 57.

ments only, leaving the extra three battalions in Georgia, the Secretary warned: "The crisis of our fate may depend upon your action. . . . If you refuse you will regret it." This was just before Manassaš. Brown replied in his nastiest manner, assuring Walker he was unintimidated by his threats; and he did not yield until the beginning of August.[31] And while he kept troops from the fighting fronts he begged the government to send arms and men to Georgia, because he was afraid of an invasion from the sea. Of all these bickerings he kept Stephens well informed, and otherwise demonstrated his friendship by naming a training camp Camp Stephens.[32]

At the same time he was running for re-election, against stiff opposition from most of the newspapers in the state; and he assiduously curried favor with Stephens all during the campaign, assuring him that in the forthcoming elections for permanent Confederate officers Stephens and Davis should be returned "by acclamation." [33] Stephens, for his own part, looked upon Brown's tussles with the War Department with a sympathetic eye, and tacitly supported his candidacy, fearing for a time that Brown's reputation had been so badly tarnished that he could not win.[34] But the Governor bore down his opposition by a handsome margin in October, though he had, from then until the end of the war, to deal with a more or less hostile legislature.

In the winter of 1861–2 and the spring of 1862, while McClellan lay camped on the Peninsula with an army nobody knew how many times the size of the Confederate, and while the Federals in the west were taking Forts Henry and Donelson and Island No. 10, and in the south were

31 *CR*, III, 101–17 *passim.*
32 *TSC*, 565, 571–2, 574.
33 Ibid., 574.
34 *LC*, P. Thweatt to A.H.S., July 16, 1861; F. Bristow to A.H.S., September 26, 1861.

capturing New Orleans, Brown went on arguing. After December 1861 the twelve-month volunteers whose terms expired could re-enlist for three years and elect their own officers up to those of regimental rank. Brown wanted to know who would commission those officers, he or the Secretary of War. Judah Benjamin, now occupying that office, blandly replied that the President would do it; whereupon Brown, saying some of the twelve-month men would not re-enlist, asked that those returning home be allowed to bring their arms back with them. This request G. W. Randolph, the third Secretary of War, flatly rejected, for the government had too few arms to relinquish any in its possession.[35]

All day long on the 22nd of February 1862 it rained in Richmond. The news of the fall of Donelson, and with it most of Kentucky and Tennessee, had just come to the capital. The city swarmed with people on the make, speculators, contractors, soldiers, Congressmen, pimps, and whores. Hotels and boardinghouses were crowded and dirty. Butter was fifty cents a pound, wood eight dollars a cord. Expensive, smoky gambling hells and red-light districts were doing a roaring trade with Congressmen and soldiers, smugglers and loafers. Transportation in and out of the town was uncertain and always late. To the north and east were armies. The newspapers were screaming for martial law and conscription. And it rained all day long. In the chamber of the House of Representatives, a little before noon, a crowd of Congressmen, Senators, and officials saw two pale, thin gentlemen in black enter the hall and sit down on the Speaker's dais: Alexander Stephens, Jefferson Davis. A slight pause; then a procession filed out of the Capitol, across the square, to a shelter erected under the Washington monument. Despite the rain there was a large crowd waiting under umbrellas to see the permanent President and Vice-President of the Confederate States inaugurated. The ceremony was brief, impressive, austere. The two men were sworn in; Davis delivered a movingly exhortatory address; and then the crowd dispersed; Stephens squeezing his way among the people and walking back to his boardinghouse alone through the rain.[36] Between him and Davis a coolness had set in; and he was unhappy and discontented whenever he had to be in Richmond. He was distressed by the government's military policy, believing it to be mainly interested in holding on to territory instead of, as Linton said, letting the enemy get "into the midst of our territory and then meeting him with *concentrated* forces." [37] With his view both Linton and Brown agreed. He in his turn was coming to view with greater concern the Governor's battles with the War Department, even though friends warned him that Brown was a "dirty lowdown man," [38] who ought not to be trusted. To these cautions he turned a deaf ear, and his friendship with Brown, rather than diminishing, increased. Nor was Brown the only influence at work upon him to accentuate his natural tendency to distrust Davis. From Manassas his old friend Judge Thomas was saying that the President was "the prince of humbugs," who would make a good county clerk but unfortunately was a king. Toombs, whose wife hated Mrs. Davis with jealous fury, was coming to the same conclusion.[39] And Stephens stood hesitant, on the point of following his friends. He was, by the beginning of March, so out of sympathy with the Administration of which he was titular deputy leader that

36 Cutting: *Jefferson Davis*, 182; Dodd: *Jefferson Davis*, 264; *MC*, February 25, 1862.
37 *MC*, Linton to A.H.S., February 18, 1862.
38 *LC*, J. H. Smith to A.H.S., October 16, 1861.
39 *TSC*, 580–1; Chesnut, *Diary*, 112.

he wrote Linton unsigned, unheaded letters so that the government would not be able to trace the sentiments contained in them to their source.

Davis, the strict constructionist, meanwhile was learning that life did not admit of strict constructions. Problems threw themselves upon him regardless of logic or of courtesy. The enemy was preparing a grand assault; the West appeared to be lost; the diplomatic situation was hopeless; and almost every state in the Confederacy was higgling and haggling with the government over the furnishing and command of troops. Prices were leaping upward; gold was almost unobtainable. In a very real sense the Confederacy was fighting two wars, one with the Union, one with itself.

The danger of impending attack caused Davis in March 1862 to suspend martial law in various areas of Virginia, under the authority of an act of Congress of late February; and at the end of March he requested Congress to enact a conscription law to ensure the maintenance of an army large enough to meet any contingency. The war hysteria of 1861 had waned; conscription was indubitably necessary; and on April 16 an act was passed covering able-bodied whites between eighteen and thirty-five, and holding in service 148 regiments of twelve-month men which were on the point of disbanding. A substitution system was also provided, as was the exemption of civilians essential to the prosecution of the war.[40]

Opposition to conscription was bitter and widespread. Yancey, Rhett, Toombs, all condemned the act; so did Joseph E. Brown; so did Stephens. Brown, the defender of what Stephens liked to call "constitutional liberty," narrow, suspicious, a parody of Othello, jealous lover guarding his mistress without understanding her, a paranoiac,

---

[40] Albert B. Moore: *Conscription and Conflict in the Confederacy* (New York, 1924), 13–14, 52–3.

JEFFERSON DAVIS, "PRESIDENT OF THE SOUTH."
(*National Archives, Photographic Records Office*)

JOSEPH E. BROWN, GOVERNOR OF GEORGIA,
1857–65.

(*Courtesy Mrs. John S. Spalding, Atlanta*)

insanely bent on maintaining her inviolability, might
have been a great unconscious buffoon had he not done
so much damage. As soon as the Conscription Act was
passed he opened a correspondence with Davis; and his attitude is well figured in a sentence he· wrote Stephens at
this time: "If the worst comes to the worst find an honorable grave in the last battle on the soil of the state." [41]
And he was speaking of a battle, not with McClellan, but
with Davis. His correspondence with the President was long
and exhausting and diabolically ingenious. He invented
every argument imaginable in condemnation of conscription; and Davis fatally erred by descending to argue with
him. In some respects Davis and Stephens were much alike.
The President, like his colleague, was a neurasthenic, easily
fatigued, often ill, and when confronted with urgent problems, apt to let his nerves give way. Like Stephens he was
excessively sensitive and self-conscious, and took himself
with great seriousness, being unable to conciliate or compromise where he knew himself to be right. As in Stephens,
this tended to make him a martinet, to make him resent
opposition, to be irritable and pettish. His failure to be
the great soldier of the Confederacy, his relegation to the
civil service, may conceivably have given rise to a conflict
and repression which accentuated his natural rigidity. He
was where he did not wish to be, set to solve insoluble
problems; and he could not, like Lincoln, climb above the
situation. So now, instead of meeting Brown's whinings
with humor, he debated, thereby giving his opponent an
opportunity he did not miss. It was a pleasant summer for
Brown. The Georgian's contention, summarized, was that

41 *LC*, J. E. Brown to A.H.S., March 21, 1862. Brown is a made-to-
order example of how a man may possess a hundred minor virtues and yet
be a moral monster. And because his virtues were those held in the
highest awe by the middle class, he could always draw a pious tear of
sympathy and a round of applause from that quarter, no matter how
flagrant his hypocrisies.

the word "militia" signified the whole arms-bearing population of a state, considered not as an organization but as
an aggregation of individuals; and since the militia included everybody able to fight, Congress could not con-
script a man into the regular army, which was filled solely
by volunteering. To Davis, for whom the militia was simply a body of soldiers in a state enrolled for service, this
was nonsense. But he failed to convince Brown of its non-
sensicality; and Brown, from April 1862 to April 1865,
systematically wrecked conscription in Georgia. He refused to let militia officers be drafted; and when a second,
more stringent Conscription Act was passed in September
1862, just at the time of Lee's retreat from Sharps-
burg, with extended exemption provisions and a clause
authorizing the President to suspend the act wherever it
could not be executed, Brown immediately told Davis to
suspend it in Georgia, flatly warning that he would not allow it to be enforced until the legislature met in November. To this Davis reluctantly consented. Lee retreated;
Braxton Bragg was retreating from Kentucky after an unsuccessful battle at Perryville; Price and Van Dorn in
Tennessee had been whipped by Rosecrans; and in the
teeth of all this Brown suspended conscription for at least
two weeks while he prepared a bombastic message to the
legislature, posing the question: "shall we continue to
have states . . . or shall we . . . have a consolidated military despotism?" [42] The legislature split on this problem,
and a committee appointed to study it reported both for
and against conscription, the majority being opposed. Linton Stephens, who was again in the legislature, uncorked
himself one day and said that if the Confederate government could take Georgia's fighting men away without her
consent she would have no sovereignty left, adding that
he would order the Georgia militia to Savannah and leave

42 *Brown,* 87.

them there "as a monument to Georgia's sovereignty." [43]
The state Supreme Court, in a test case, had sustained the
constitutionality of conscription, but Linton in his wrath
said the court had no power to bind the legislature. At
this point Benjamin Hill, who was Davis' right arm in the
Confederate Senate, being in Georgia trying to neutralize
Brown's cantankerousness, spoke to the legislature on December 11, so eloquently defending conscription that it
adjourned without doing anything one way or another
about Brown's recommendations. [44]

The Governor was not easily outfoxed. He spent the
next two years exempting every able-bodied man he could
put into the state service—clerks, sheriffs, notaries, tax-
collectors, militia officers (of whom by 1864 he had somewhere between 8,000 and 15,000). [45] And while he conducted this personal vendetta, the Confederacy was slowly
being strangled.

III

Stephens, playing the role of figurehead, uninvited to the
Administration council table, listened to denunciations
from all sides. The air he breathed was thick with vituperation; and month by month its effect upon him grew.
Toombs, until March 1863 a brigadier in Longstreet's
corps, did nothing but complain in his letters to Stephens,
writing just after the Seven Days: "Davis and his Janis-
saries [the regular army] conspire for the destruction of all
who will not bend to them, and avail themselves of the
public danger to aid them in their selfish and infamous
schemes." [46] And a few months before, a friend had written: "I can but think that if you had been President . . .

43 Moore, op. cit., 257–8.
44 Pearce: *Hill*, 68–74.
45 Davis estimated 15,000; cf. Frank L. Owsley: *State Rights in the Confederacy* (Chicago, 1925), 207. Moore: *Conscription*, 95, gives the lower figure.
46 *TSC*, 601.

there would have been a . . . happier state of things in
this country at this time. . . ." [47] Stephens listened to this
talk, and was thoughtful. Brown's controversy with Davis
over conscription interested him deeply: and he was, he
confessed to Linton, shocked by some of the President's
arguments. His definition of "militia" was something like
Brown's: to him the word meant all the "involuntary"
fighting force of a state—all, that is, who were subject by
state law to military service. The government, he said,
could not call these men into active duty save by req-
uisitioning them from state authorities.[48] The government, in other words, had no power to force men into the
army. It could only request the states to furnish them. The
power to raise armies delegated in the Constitution to
Congress he contended to be identical with that given by
the Secretary of War to any person he might select to raise
a regiment. No such person could "impress freemen" into
his force; neither could Congress. Beyond the technical
argument, he discerned a moral one, saying the war ought
to be abandoned the moment conscription became necessary to fill up the army. Conscripts, who might be effective
machines for erecting dynasties, could never be the means
of "establishing free Institutions or maintaining them!" [49]

And so, despite another warning that Brown was
"cranky" and "unsafe," [50] he found himself on the Governor's side, and wrote him a letter telling him so. Brown was
highly gratified.

When Stephens returned to Richmond in August 1862,
he had discovered another "usurpation" of which to com-

----

[47] *LC,* P. Thweatt to A.H.S., March 10, 1862. Thweatt was Comptroller-General of the state at one time, a fat little man who confided
secrets in a stage whisper and was an unspeakably garrulous correspondent.

[48] *MC,* June 20, 1862.

[49] *View,* II, 570–4.

[50] *LC,* J. H. Smith to A.H.S., June 21, 1862.

plain, and which eventually turned out to be the bitterest bone of contention of all between the Georgia clique
and the Administration. On August 21 General Bragg, to
secure the safety of railroad facilities and hospitals, and to
maintain discipline among the soldiers, proclaimed martial
law for Atlanta and environs. Atlanta was an important rail
center, and martial law was clearly desirable. But the law,
which was about to expire, vested the power to declare
martial law exclusively in the President. Stephens, smelling
a rat, went to work on Congress, which was considering the
renewal of the act, and got Senator Semmes of Louisiana
to agree with him that under the Constitution no power
on earth could establish martial law in the Confederacy.
The most that could be done was to suspend the writ of
habeas corpus, but not so as to interfere with regular and
speedy trial.[51] Semmes introduced a resolution in the Senate
for a committee to investigate the question; and in the
House the judiciary committee was ordered to do likewise.
Its report in substance concurred with Stephens' views,
denying the President the power to declare martial law,
and granting him merely that to suspend the writ, guaranteeing, however, any person arrested under a suspension a
trial according to the laws of the land.[52]

Stephens, busily lobbying for restrictions upon martial
law, kept in touch with his friends at home, bewailing with
Brown the apparent willingness with which the people
seemed "to be yielding to usurpations." Linton, at home in
Sparta, providing a chorus, intoned the antiphonal: "The
cry of *necessity* is not only the plea of tyrants . . . but

[51] The reasons for martial law in Atlanta were clearly set forth by
J. A. Campbell, acting Secretary of War, in a letter of October 27, 1862,
in *The War of the Rebellion, a Compilation of the Official Records of the
Union and Confederate Armies* (Washington, 1880–1901) (cited hereafter
as *OR*), ser. I, xvi, pt. 2, pp. 979–80. Stephens' proselytizing is in *J&B*,
417–18.

[52] *Journals* of the Confederate Congress (Washington, 1904–5), II, 237; V,
318, 373–7.

. . . a *lie* in *every instance.*" [53] And when the Mayor of
Atlanta, whom Bragg had appointed its civil governor
under martial law, wrote Benjamin Hill inquiring as to
the nature of his duties, and Hill, perhaps to draw Stephens
out, passed the letter on to him for reply, Stephens, on
September 8, told the Mayor bluntly that "your office is
unknown to the law. Gen. Bragg had no more authority
for appointing you civil governor of Atlanta, than I had;
and I . . . have no more authority than any street-walker
in your city." [54] Repeating that the most that could be done
was the suspension of habeas corpus, he still further hedged
it about by declaring that even then no person could be
arrested except upon probable cause, supported by oath.
But if nothing could be done under suspension that could
not be done when the writ was in force, the whole reason
for suspending it would utterly collapse. This may, in fact,
have been what Stephens was hinting at.

He did not again go to Richmond until late April 1863;
and spent the winter and spring at home, reading Scott and
writing Linton letters about conscription. On November
1, 1862 he delivered a spread-eagle speech in Crawfordville,
full of exhortation, but rounded off with a warning that
independence and "constitutional liberty" must be kept
steadily in view. "Away with the idea of getting independence first, and looking after liberty afterward. Our liberties
once lost, may be lost forever." Far better, he declared, that
the Confederacy should be beaten than that liberty should
be destroyed.[55]

Brown's third term of office expired in 1863; and early
in the year he wrote to Stephens saying he had decided
not to stand again and had selected Linton for the succession. What did Stephens think of that? Stephens thought

53 *J&B*, 420; *MC*, Linton to A.H.S., September 1, 1862.
54 Letter in *Cleveland*, 747–9.
55 Ibid., 749–60; *J&B*, 419–20.

little of it, and urged Brown to change his mind. Brown then replied that if Linton would not serve he would gladly let the mantle fall on Toombs; and he persisted in this line of talk until March, though Toombs' popularity in the state had suffered a considerable diminution on account of his arrogantly egocentric attitude toward the government, and he would probably not be elected. Brown, on the other hand, despite his clashes with Davis, had, by checking profiteering in salt, and seeing to it that Georgia soldiers were well shod and clothed, and supplying cotton cards to the families of soldiers, and giving fodder to the poor from his own farm, endeared himself to many of the common citizenry of the state.[56] He probably really wanted to run again, and Stephens' insistence that he do so prompted him in May to consent "reluctantly" to the request of a group of stooges that he allow his name to be used. To ensure victory and stop the Administration from running a candidate against him, he wrote Davis a letter reeking with flattery, promising he would do anything rather than embarrass the government.

Toward the end of March Stephens' favorite dog, Rio, died; and he, who had been deeply attached to the animal, fell for a few days into a melancholy reminiscent of his former moods. But the mood this time quickly passed off. There were so many subjects beyond the range of personal grief to be concerned about. The machinations of the Administration were a natural organ of woe for him to grind; and he never ceased to grind it, opposing, in March and April, an attempt in the state legislature to have the state endorse an issue of Confederate bonds. "The responsibility of creating debt, and paying it . . . ought to rest on the same shoulders," he contended, neatly dissociating Georgia from the Confederacy.[57] He need not

[56] *TSC*, 610–11, 614; *Brown*, 107–22, 125n.
[57] *J&B*, 441.

have troubled himself; for the scheme came to nothing because of hostile criticism.

In late April he went to Richmond, called on Davis, conversed for a few hours, and came home again, having accomplished very little. Linton was stigmatizing the President about this time as a "sly, secretive, malignant hypocrite," an estimate of the man to which his brother made no reply.[58] As he rambled over his fields, or talked with R. M. Johnston, Stephens thought much in these months of his father, whom Brown so strikingly resembled in so many characteristics.

On June 20 he was summoned to Richmond; the request was a reply to a letter he had written on the 11th, on the subject of the exchange of prisoners. No cartel for exchange had existed prior to July 1862, mainly because the Federal government did not want to do anything that would involve the recognition of the Confederacy as a legal government; but after considerable clamor had arisen North and South, a cartel was finally negotiated. Under it, however, serious difficulties had arisen, over what classes of men would come under the cartel, and over various proclamations and orders, such as Davis' that captured Negro troops were to be delivered to the authorities of the state in which captured, and an act of the Confederate Congress ordering the execution of white officers of Negro troops, and the execution by the Federals of two Confederate officers caught recruiting in Kentucky. By the end of May 1863 the exchange of officers had almost completely ceased.[59]

---

[58] *MC*, Linton to A.H.S., April 6, 1863. Linton was quite certain that Davis was the kind of man who would "shoot his enemy from behind a tree." If this was intended as an imputation of treachery it was false; otherwise it was rather complimentary to Davis' native prudence. After all, Linton's own grandfather had shot Indians from behind trees at Braddock's defeat.

[59] William B. Hesseltine: *Civil War Prisons, a Study in War Psychology* (Columbus, O.), 7-33 *passim*.

Circumstances stood thus when Stephens addressed Davis, tendering his services as a negotiator. He tendered more, asking to be given power to discuss *"any point* in relation to the *conduct* of the war," hoping that indirectly he might be able to bring about a general settlement, based, he quickly added, on the "recognition of the sovereignty of the States, and the right of each . . . to determine its own destiny," whether in a restored Union or the Confederacy he did not say. Davis, who did not trust Stephens, refused to give consent to any such discussions,[60] but decided to send him to Washington to talk solely about prisoners.

Through the last week of June Stephens lingered in Richmond, while Lee marched into Pennsylvania. One who saw him remarked that he seemed "doomed to speedy dissolution," but noted that "his eyes are magnificent, and his mind is in the meridian of intellectual vigor." [61] He did not hear of Lee's invasion until June 23, and then protested that he did not want to go to Washington now, for the invasion would strengthen the "War Party" in the North, rather than weaken it. Davis and the Cabinet insisted that he go anyhow; and on the afternoon of July 1 he was urged to leave before Vicksburg, whose fall was imminent, did surrender.[62] He left on the 3rd, accompanied by Robert Ould, who had been the Confederate agent of exchange under the cartel, taking the C. S. steamer *Torpedo* for Hampton Roads, armed with a letter from Davis declaring his mission "simply one of humanity and . . . no political aspect," and empowering him to settle all disputes arising out of the cartel.[63]

60 *View*, II, 558–61.
61 John B. Jones: *A Rebel War Clerk's Diary* (New York, 1935), I, 306. In view of what was going on inside that mind, the irony of Jones' remark approaches the magnificent.
62 *MC*, July 1, 1863.
63 *OR*, ser. I, vi, 74–6.

The *Torpedo* reached the Roads on July 4, and Stephens announced in a message to Admiral S. P. Lee what his mission was, asking to be permitted to go on to Washington. Lee acknowledged the message, telegraphing it to Secretary of the Navy Gideon Welles. The Union agent of exchange was also informed, and he telegraphed Secretary of War Stanton, who immediately ordered him to hold no communication with Stephens. While the *Torpedo* was moved away from Hampton Roads, in Washington Lincoln and his Cabinet considered the request. Stephens had not precisely stated his object, and while Lincoln at first toyed with the idea of going to the Roads himself, he yielded to the opposition of Seward and Stanton, who considered Stephens a dangerous man, and orders were sent out to refuse the Southerner's request. When Stephens, on the 6th, having heard nothing, again asked Admiral Lee how long he would have to wait, he received a note stating that his request was "inadmissible," and that "the customary agents and channels are adequate for all needful military communications and conference." [64] That was all. The *Torpedo* turned about and steamed back up the James. Stephens did not understand why he had been refused; but he did not yet know that Vicksburg had fallen and Lee had been beaten at Gettysburg. Lincoln could afford to be rude.

IV

Between July 1863 and December 1864 Stephens was in Georgia, engaged in the most inexcusable adventure of his life. Once in May 1864 he made a half-hearted attempt to get to Richmond; but the railroad between Danville and the capital was broken when he arrived, and he turned about and went back home, saying he was too ill to continue.

[64] Ibid., ser. I, vi, 79–80, 83–4; Gideon Welles: *Diary* (Boston, 1911), I. 358–62.

The rest of 1863 was prelude. Brown, in late August, was confronted with two opponents for the governorship, one a Unionist, the other an ardent secessionist. Stephens did not give Brown any help, but Toombs did in a public speech that fulminated against everything the government had ever done; and once again the Governor managed to pull himself through by a good margin, receiving a majority of the votes cast by the civilians and by the soldiers.[65]

Such a result could not but inspire him to newer and higher efforts in his war with the Administration. With the Confederate army in Tennessee being pushed back toward Georgia, concern over the state's safety grew acute. There were laws providing for the organization of local defense forces in threatened areas; and Brown was requisitioned in June for 8,000 men. Had he complied, the troops would have been under Davis' authority; so he, who could not countenance such usurpation, tendered the 8,000 as state militia so that he could appoint the officers. The government had to agree; and Brown went to work, getting by September 15,000 instead of 8,000 volunteers.[66] Linton was one of those who volunteered, and was elected commander of a battalion of cavalry stationed at Atlanta.[67] While he was there the bloody battles of Chickamauga, Lookout Mountain, and Missionary Ridge were fought, and the Confederacy lost Tennessee. The army withdrew into Georgia, and Bragg was superseded by Joseph E. Johnston as its commander. In the midst of this incontestable emergency Brown tried to appoint the field officers of his local defense troops and even wanted them to be released from service before their six-month term was out, contending that no emergency existed.[68]

Stephens, surrounded by all this, withdrew into himself,

65 *Brown,* 137.
66 *CR,* III, 344–58.
67 Waddell: *Linton Stephens,* 259–65.
68 *Brown,* 172–4; *CR,* III, 431–3.

watched Brown, listened to his brother, whose hatred of Davis by this time bordered on the paranoiac, and brooded upon the possibilities of peace. The opposition to the government was by no means confined to Georgia; it existed everywhere in some degree; but in Georgia it took on exceptional proportions, and affected the outcome of the war in a degree scarcely to be underestimated. The behavior of Brown, Stephens, and Toombs caused a distinct falling off in the number of enlistments from Georgia, and an increase in desertions.[69] Strong anti-Confederate elements existed in the mountain countries to begin with; and it was here that underground peace societies flourished, and bands of deserters plundered and pillaged with comparative impunity. Conditions in these mountain regions tended more and more toward anarchy as the war drew to a close, and Brown's pronouncements about the government were surely critical factors in the existence of such situations. And Stephens not only supported Brown, but acted as a principal in the attack upon the government he had sworn to defend.

His private correspondence was assuming a steadily treasonable color; and he was repeatedly told that he was and had been always right and that "Our President is our greatest misfortune," and that some way must be found to get in touch with "the friends of peace in the North." [70] Two of his old colleagues, H. V. Johnson and Howell Cobb, endeavored to bring him to an understanding of what it was he was doing; but their words were wasted. Johnson, who was in the Confederate Senate, pleaded with him to come to Richmond, saying: "the attitude of non-action, which you have unalterably assumed, is wrong. It is un-

[69] *Brown*, 104–6. Cf. Georgia L. Tatum: *Disloyalty in the Confederacy* (Chapel Hill, 1934), 73–9.
[70] *LC*, J. Finley to A.H.S., July 11, 1863; M. C. Fulton to A.H.S., August 2, 1863; W. F. Sanford to A.H.S., January 9, 1864.

just to yourself, unjust to our bleeding cause, and unjust to the country . . ." and Cobb, emphasizing his support of the Administration, proposed that a dictator be appointed to carry the war to a successful end—an idea of which Stephens naturally had a low opinion.[71]

In December Linton, attending the legislature in Milledgeville, fell sick and spent some days at the Governor's house; and a little later Brown wrote to Alexander expressing infinite pleasure at having had the opportunity to do Linton service, and praising his "honesty and stern integrity." [72] Alexander, he added, had better mark all his letters to Brown "private" across the seal, so that they would not be opened by secretaries.

Probably because of his illness Linton was thrown into a depressive mood of extraordinary intensity, suffering all the "horrors of Hell fire," as he wrote to his brother. The brother himself was unwell, having contracted a persistent pain in his side, and in the middle of January being stricken with a terrible kidney attack that made him unable to urinate for several days—an attack so severe it brought a telegram from Davis inquiring after his welfare.[73] Linton's emotional agony profoundly disturbed Alexander, who could not sleep nights because of it; and Linton threw himself hysterically upon him, crying in his letters: "You dont know how my very heart strings are gathered around you, and how *dependent* I am on you— It does seem to me that I could not live without you." [74] Since the death of his wife he had never quite been normal; to read her letters and look at her portrait, even

71 Flippin: *H. V. Johnson*, 249–50; *LC*, Cobb to A.H.S., September 1, 1863.

72 *TSC*, 631.

73 *MC*, Linton to A.H.S., December 28, 1863; Davis to A.H.S., January 19, 1864, Jefferson Davis MSS., Duke University.

74 *MC*, Linton to A.H.S., January 23, 1864.

at the distance of seven years, was an indulgence that brought violent paroxysms of grief, for even now he half believed himself guilty of killing her—had she not died in childbirth?

"And now Alexander H. Stephens becomes, for a season, very nearly the central figure of the Confederacy." [75] Responding to an appeal by the President, Congress, on February 11, again suspended the writ of habeas corpus, this time throughout the Confederacy, in thirteen groups of cases. The necessity was incontestable, for disloyalty and spying were assuming critical proportions, and in mere self-defense the government had to be able to deal summarily with them. Davis feared the act would cause some trouble. He was not disappointed.

Already before the 11th of February Joseph E. Brown, Governor of Georgia, in a note to Stephens, delivers a cryptic and confidential aside. "No one," he whispers, "but you and Linton know my purpose." What purpose? He says nothing more. Stephens has been meditating with Linton the possibilities of peace and restoration to the Union: does Brown know this? But Brown seems not to be looking for peace. . . . Late in January he thanks Stephens for telling him that the Administration plans to wage war upon him, and hopes he will "be prepared to meet it." He is thinking of calling a special session of the legislature: is that his secret purpose? But why does he want the legislature to meet? What will he tell it when it does? Two days after the writ is suspended he dashes off a note to Stephens, asking that Linton and he set a date when the three men can meet in Sparta—not Milledgeville —"where we can compare notes, etc., on the subject of which we have lately corresponded." That little *etc.*: what

[75] Nathaniel W. Stephenson: *The Day of the Confederacy* (New Haven, 1919), 172ff.

does it mean? "I wish," the Governor adds, "to call the legislature together in the early part of March." For what? Is it in connection with the suspension of the writ? Then how can Brown and Stephens have learned in January that Davis would deliver a secret message on the subject in February? [76]

Linton stops at Liberty Hall on February 8; next day Cobb drops in for several hours, spent in free conversation. Upon what topic? Toombs, still publicly attacking the government, makes a call toward the middle of the month. What is said to him? Stephens and Linton arrange to be at Sparta on the 25th; Brown is appraised of the date, and replies, saying he will bring his wife with him, and expresses his "horror" at the suspension of the writ. It is a "wicked act. . . ."

At Linton's house in Sparta the three men meet on the 25th, transact the business they have assigned themselves, and part. Stephens goes home on the 28th, tired and unwell. The day before, Brown has issued a call for a special meeting of the legislature on March 10. He is to compose a message; Linton, as a member of the House, is charged with the duty of drawing up a set of resolutions indicative of the views of the friends of constitutional liberty. Alexander solicitously coaches him: ". . . fix up your Resolutions with great care & attention—you have a wide & a great field before you. . . . Be calm under the most intense excitement. . . . The main attack should be made on the Habeas corpus suspension. . . ." Somewhat earlier Linton, in his rage, has shrieked: "I would strike a thousand blows to pull down this *infamous* government rather than one to sustain it," and thinks Davis should be impeached. To which his brother replies: "I beg of you for your own

[76] *MC*, J. E. Brown to A.H.S., January 15, 1864; A.H.S. to Linton, January 22, 1864; *TSC* 621–2, 632–3.

peace of mind not to let such things fret or annoy you—
If the people are willing to bear them you cant relieve
them. . . ." [77]

Abstaining for this interval from all stimulants, Linton
draws up his resolutions; "His whole soul is swallowed up
in them," says a friend. When they are perfected to his
and Alexander's satisfaction, he sets out for Milledgeville.
It is March 9, 1864.[78] Meanwhile Brown, with Stephens'
aid, is drafting his message. Benjamin Hill, Cobb, and
L. Q. C. Lamar of Mississippi are all in Georgia, standing
by and lending what aid they can in support of the
Administration; while from Richmond Johnson continues
to beg Stephens to reconsider, replying to Stephens' contention that the government ought to be forced out of
office: "You are evidently in a towering passion." "I will
fight the war according to the President's plan," Johnson
declares, inquiring: "Is denunciation the way to enlighten
the people?" [79] Stephens does not reply to this.

Then it is March 10. The legislature assembles. Stephens
is there, staying at the Governor's, hovering about the
Capitol, an anxious man on moral tiptoe, plucking men by
the sleeve and drawing them aside, whispering, arguing,
convincing, his burning eyes and tragic lips attesting to his
agitation, an earnest silhouette, tall and meager, in the
dusk upon the streets. Brown's message is sent in and read.
"I advised it," Stephens later claims, "from stem to stern
and approve it." It is long, wordy, vehement, intemperate.
Conscription and habeas corpus are mercilessly beaten
about: a terrifying picture is painted of innocent citizens
being dragged from their beds to nameless prisons. Then
out pops the nigger in the woodpile: peace, the Governor

[77] *MC,* January 23, 27, 29; February 10, 18, 19, 23, 28, 1864; Linton
to A.H.S., February 9, 1864; *TSC,* 633; *Brown,* 201–21, reviews the events
of the spring of 1864 so far as they involved Brown.
[78] *LC,* C. Connell to A.H.S., March 12, 1864.
[79] Flippin: *H. V. Johnson,* 249–54.

says, will not come save by negotiation, and proposes that after each victory the government should offer peace on condition that the "great fundamental principles of the Declaration of Independence" be recognized by the enemy.[80]

The message, an Alabama paper comments, is "a majestic pyramid of impregnable facts"; but the Savannah *News* thinks it a dangerous firebrand. Some papers hint that it is not solely the Governor's work; Hill, writing to Stephens, congratulates him on having done an excellent job.[81]

The message read, Linton rises and offers his resolutions, of which there are two sets, one condemning the suspension of the writ, the other declaring the terms on which peace should be offered the North. The resolutions are mere summations of Alexander's dogmas upon both points. He, for his part, waits until the 16th, when, according to plan, being invited to address the legislature, he does so. The pallid, slight, intense figure enters the hall, which is jammed to capacity, and speaks. It is the crucial speech of his life, and he knows it. For three hours he castigates the Administration. Conscription is "radically wrong"; the local defense system is an attempt to centralize power; the suspension of habeas corpus is dangerous to public liberty; traitors ought to be arrested by judicial warrant upon oath. Liberty and independence together, he says; not independence first and liberty later.[82] For three hours the shrill voice fills the hall with pitiless rancor, the Confederacy's mortal disease discharging bitter bile, and then the speaker ceases and sits down.

[80] Moore: *Conscription,* 271n. The speech is in CR, II, 587–655; Stephens' avowal of his assistance in its preparation in *OR,* ser. IV, iii, 281.

[81] *Avery,* 271; *Brown,* 208; *TSC,* 634–7. Hill was probably being rather catty at this point.

[82] *Cleveland,* 761–86, contains a report of the speech. As a speech it is a hundred per cent froth, the rigor of its logic being merely the surface tension that binds the bubbles together. This should not be surprising, for Stephens' alarm, like Brown's, had long ago vaulted into the hysterical.

Following him, Lamar appeals to the legislature to cease factious opposition and stand by the government. For three days following, the legislature struggles with Linton's resolutions, both the Administration and the Governor exerting all the persuasive power at their command. When an amendment expressing confidence in the President is offered, Linton leaps up, crying: "I am for the cause and not for dynasties!" Those supporting his resolutions are accused of trying to slide Georgia into a separate peace; this is indignantly denied. On March 19, baffled and bitter, the legislature votes to adjourn; Brown promptly summons them in extra session unless they agree to act on the resolutions; and, too weary to resist such implacability, the legislature succumbs and the resolutions are passed. It is nearly midnight before the battle ends. What has it accomplished? [83] Brown immediately has Stephens' speech, his own message, and the resolutions printed and distributed among the Georgia soldiers in the army. At the same time he offers Linton a circuit judgeship, which the latter declines, and casts about to get control of the Augusta *Constitutionalist. Allons, enfants . . .*

Stephens and Linton went home together, and the elder settled down to study the reactions to his speech. Toombs was delighted; Linton was convinced it was a "great" speech; R. M. Johnston thought it the "most unimpassioned effort" of his life.[84] There were those, however, who expressed their indignation at the whole play that had been played in Milledgeville. Howell Cobb said he would be glad to see Brown hanged; Benjamin Hill publicly called Stephens and Brown traitors. Some regiments in the army thought likewise. Johnson, writing to Stephens, de-

[83] Linton's admirable sentiment is quoted by *Avery*, 272. Votes in Georgia, House of Representatives, *Journal*, extra session, 1864, pp. 51, 97–8, 105, 116–17.

[84] *MC*, Linton to A.H.S., April 5, 7, 1864; *LC*, R. M. Johnston to A.H.S., April 18, 1864.

plored his having arrayed himself against the government.
"I did not expect it of you," he said, adding: "You have
allowed your antipathy to Davis to mislead your judge-
ment." [85] Stephens, on April 8, replied at length to this
criticism, denying any antipathy to the President, denying
any intention of forming or aligning himself with a party
in opposition to the government, affirming that he did not
consider Davis a great man but rather one of good intentions, "weak and vacillating, timid, petulant, peevish,
obstinate, but not firm," arguing that Davis' behavior
showed he was aiming at absolute power, assuring Johnson
he felt no more resentment for Davis personally than he
had toward the infirmities of his old dog Rio, but was full
of wrath at the course events were taking. The appeal to
sustain the Administration he called a "stupid, senseless
cacchination." [86] Johnson in answer pointed out that if
Davis should die, Stephens would become President: "Is
it not desirable that you should be identified with no
party?" But his appeals were pointless. Stephens was past
listening.

V

All during 1864 an army of a hundred thousand men
moved southeastward through Georgia, opposed by an
army of sixty thousand. Implacably, glacial, the larger
advanced; and for the smaller there was nothing to do but
retreat. The Confederate Conscription Act, in the face of
this crisis, was extended to cover men from seventeen to
fifty, who would be used as reserves. Brown, who was still
withholding from service some ten or fifteen thousand
assorted civil servants, sent some of his state militia to
General J. E. Johnston, commanding the army contesting

[85] Flippin: *H. V. Johnson,* 253.
[86] *OR,* ser. IV, iii, 278–81. His criticism of Davis, it may be remarked,
was, with some exceptions, extremely acute. The main reason for this was
that he was really criticizing himself.

Sherman's advance, but made it very clear that he retained authority over them and would exercise it whenever he conceived he should. Meanwhile he was frantically begging Davis to send reinforcements to Georgia, warning him that posterity might mourn the President's error if he refused. Davis did refuse, for Grant was pounding all summer long at the gates of Richmond; and Davis ordered the commandant of conscription in Georgia to proceed in his duties regardless of the Governor's opposition.[87] Brown rebounded with his most criminal retaliation of all: as soon as Sherman had taken Atlanta on September 3, he proclaimed that the emergency for which the militia had been called out was over, and disbanded them to go home and reap the harvest. The War Department had asked him for ten thousand additional men: instead he withdrew those he had contributed, and continued to spit froth at the Richmond authorities until Sherman, still advancing, drove him and his government out of Milledgeville in panic-stricken flight. Ten thousand additional men, the Secretary of War argued, could have hurled Sherman back. Not quite, perhaps; but they could surely have delayed him. To Sherman, as he moved forward, listening to Stephens, Toombs, and Brown, Georgia must have resembled an overripe fruit ready to drop from the tree. A few gentle taps . . .

The summer of 1864 was a strange one. The peace movement that had flared up in Georgia was echoed by others in the North, for there were war-weary men in the North too, who studied the casualty lists coming from Grant's army and wondered whether the sacrifice was worth it. There was, too, a wing of the Democratic party, centered in the Northwest, known as the Copperheads, the leaders of which were peace-at-any-price men engaged in surrepti-

---

[87] The details of this sordid story are in *CR*, III, 582–3, 587–8, and in *OR*, ser. IV, iii, 530–1.

tious intrigue with Confederate agents to stir up trouble in the Midwest. These Democrats aimed at capturing the national party and electing a peace President in the fall; and when the party convention met at the end of August, they almost succeeded. McClellan, who was not a peace man, was nominated; but the platform he represented declared the party's intention, if elected, to undertake immediate efforts for a cessation of hostilities and the calling of a convention of all the states. But after the fall of Atlanta the chances that the Democrats would win the elections were seriously diminished. The Copperheads were losing out.

In the meanwhile there had been a brief flurry of negotiation in Canada, when Horace Greeley, at Lincoln's insistence, went across the border to confer with Confederate agents there. They could not treat for peace, and would not treat on Lincoln's terms, and Greeley came back empty-handed. At the same time two Northern peace men went to Richmond to sound out Davis, and were met with equal inflexibility. "We are fighting," Davis coldly said, "for independence, and that, or extermination, we will have." [88]

Stephens kept an expectant eye on the Northern Democrats through July and August. He was convinced that all these peace movements, of which there were countless rumors, had been started by Georgia; though in this he was quite mistaken. Most Northerners interested in peace had been in that frame of mind for at least a year. But Stephens held that "if our officials and military make no blunders and only hold our own for ten weeks . . . Lincoln may be beaten—a Peace man elected . . . and with that result sooner or later Peace will come." [89] This hope the nomination of McClellan shook but did not destroy;

[88] Edward C. Kirkland: *The Peacemakers of 1864* (New York, 1927), deals with the whole subject in great detail.
[89] *MC*, September 28, 1864.

and he attributed the failure of the convention to do what he had wished to the lack of support of the Confederate government. Endeavoring to squeeze the last drop of comfort from the situation, he imagined the Democrats to have as their intentions, if elected, to attempt a restoration of the Union by negotiation, and, should that fail, to accept peace on the basis of Confederate independence. In a public letter written on September 22 he called the convention "the first ray of real light I have seen from the North since the war began," and welcomed the idea of a general convention of all the states for the purpose of discussing the subjects of conflict. To this letter there was much caustic response, critical of his intentions and allegiances; and in a letter to Senator Semmes he had to protest that he had not invited such a convention, but thought merely that since the Democratic platform pledged itself to one, the South ought to have "responded favorably." [90] Brown heartily agreed, and tried to get the governors of the states east of the Mississippi to demand a convention of all the states, but without success; and from then on until the end of the war he cursed the Administration for not taking steps in that direction.

Both Brown and Stephens were coming to consider either ousting the Davis government or Georgia's secession from the Confederacy as the only possible remedy for the evils they saw themselves being contaminated by. "Should any State at any time become satisfied that the war is not waged for purposes securing her best interests . . . she has a perfect right to withdraw, and would commit no breach of faith . . . in doing so," he wrote to Linton in October. A month before, he had been almost on the point of carrying out his speculations. In his mail were a dangerous number of letters complaining that "The people

90 Letter in *Cleveland*, 191–6; A.H.S. to T. J. Semmes, November 4, 1864, Semmes MSS., Duke University.

of Georgia are tired of the war," and imploring him to find some way to stop it. An opportunity to take his state out of the Confederacy came in the middle of September, in the person of an envoy from Sherman, who, settled in captured Atlanta, had been visited by Joshua Hill, an old Unionist politician who was convinced that for the South to go on fighting was insanity. Sherman, interested, asked Hill, should he see Brown, to request the Governor to visit Atlanta; and, to make certain Brown received his message, he sent two prominent Georgians, Augustus R. Wright and William King, to Milledgeville. Lincoln, hearing of all this, watched closely to see what would come of it, especially after Davis, deeply concerned over Brown and Stephens, made a flying excursion to Georgia to deliver some sharply phrased addresses aimed at discrediting the "croakers." [91]

Sherman's messenger arrived at Liberty Hall while Stephens was away, and left an oral message. Stephens was piqued by this disregard of formality; he expected Sherman to send him a letter; which sounds as if, had he got one, he would have gone to Atlanta, though Toombs was cautioning him under no circumstances to do so. He had time to think it over, for Sherman did not send William King to Crawfordville until September 30, with another oral invitation to conference, which Stephens declined because he had no power, he said, to enter into negotiations.[92] This little adventure created so much unfavorable comment that, being unable to ignore it any longer, he was compelled to have reprinted the first political address he ever made, the Fourth of July speech of 1834, in order to demonstrate the consistency over thirty years of his

[91] *J&B*, 474; *LC*, I. Scott, J. B. Ross, and J. H. R. Washington to A.H.S., September 14, 1864; W. H. F. Hall to A.H.S., September 18, 1864; H. Cleveland to A.H.S., June 8, 1864. Sherman's story is in his *Memoirs* (New York, 1876), II, 137ff.

[92] *MC*, September 22, 1864; *TSC*, 652; *J&B*, 472.

views on the nature of state sovereignty. Against Sherman's and Grant's guns it was a brittle, negligible weapon to be consistent; but this he never knew. He was right; and so long as he was right and those in power wrong, the whole Confederacy could go down at once—he would not care.

At the end of November he left for Richmond. The Georgia legislature was in session; Brown had delivered another foaming attack upon the President; Linton had introduced resolutions calling for a state convention to consider negotiation for a separate peace—resolutions that the legislature, after a powerful letter from Davis demolishing the whole idea, rejected, giving the President instead its vote of confidence. But Linton's resolutions demonstrated, if the fact required further demonstration, the lengths to which the opposition in its blind and factional hatred would go.

After a miserable journey Stephens arrived in the capital and took up residence with Senator Semmes, at thirty dollars a day for room and meals. The atmosphere in the city was ugly. Congress was in a sullen and intractable mood toward the President; the government's power to wage war was daily weakening; the enemy was gaining wherever he attacked; disloyalty and bad temper abounded. The act suspending the writ of habeas corpus had expired on August 1; it was a matter of life and death that it be renewed. The opposition, however, was convinced of Davis' desire to establish a dictatorship, and could not see such power in his hands.

Leading the coterie of malcontents were Louis T. Wigfall of Texas and Henry S. Foote of Tennessee, who, during December, engineered a systematic campaign in Congress designed to embarrass and thwart the government. Proposals were made for conventions of Southern states to discuss peace prospects, and for direct offers of negotiation to the Union government. On the other hand, the House bowed to necessity on December 7 by passing a bill renewing the habeas corpus suspension.

Stephens was determined to prevent the passage of any such bill; he was also determined to find some way of securing peace. Shortly after his arrival he was approached by two Tennessee Representatives bearing a set of resolutions "looking to a peace conference," which, after discussion, they left with him for revision. The next thing was to get them introduced in Congress. Foote, who was on the Foreign Affairs Committee of the House, was about to resign; it was decided to have Atkins, one of the two Tennesseans, succeed him and bring in the resolutions. Very likely with the connivance of Speaker Bocock, Atkins was appointed to Foote's vacated place on the committee.[93] So far so good. Stephens, though, was gloomy, expecting little from Congress, thinking of resigning the Vice-Presidency, and saying that if the suspension of habeas corpus were regarded by the courts as constitutional, "I shall feel very little further interest in the result of the conflict." "I almost regret," he wrote to his secretary, "that I came here. . . . I may be wrong myself—but my convictions are strong . . . that the error is not with me." [94] His position was uncomfortable and unenviable. His relations with the President were badly strained, as a result of a correspondence carried on in November and December over his public statement that Davis seemed to favor the election of Lincoln instead of McClellan—an accusation to which Davis somberly and cuttingly replied, wishing that Stephens instead of inspiring "distrust in me among the people," would devote "your great and ad-

[93] The account given is told by Colyar, the other Tennessean, in 1877, in *Jefferson Davis, Constitutionalist*, VIII, 213ff. The resolutions are printed in the *Journals* of the Confederate Congress, VII, 451–2, and in different form in *J&B*, 480–2. MS. copies in *MC* and *LC* (the latter not in A.H.S.' hand) agree with *J&B*, and probably represent the resolutions before revision.

[94] *MC*, December 23, 24, 1864; *PHS*, A.H.S. to Hidell, December 28, 1864.

mitted ability exclusively to upholding the confidence and animating the spirit of the people to unconquerable resistance against their foes." [95] Now there was a brush with the Senate, over which he presided, as it considered the habeas corpus bill. When a tie vote was counted on an amendment, Stephens wanted to cast the deciding ballot and address the Senate on his reasons for his vote. Rather than listen to the tirade he felt was coming, one Senator changed his vote, so that the matter was taken out of Stephens' hands. The Vice-President, outraged, stalked from the chamber fully intending to resign; but on January 6, 1865, after adjournment, the Senate remained in chambers and requested him to speak. "The whole took me by surprise," he wrote Linton that night; [96] but in his own words of twenty years before, he "piled it down upon them" for two hours, telling them "that unless there was a thorough and radical change of policy . . . we were doomed. I reviewed the past policy—Habeas corpus suspension, impressment, military usurpations, &c., and . . . told them such measures would ruin us. . . . I urged the importance of offering to the North negotiations. . . . By friends at the North," he explained, "I did not mean men who were in favour of disunion, but men who really had the same interests at stake . . . that we have . . . state rights and constitutional liberty." Black-eyed raven upon

[95] This little tiff centered on Stephens' indignation at Davis' alleged refusal to investigate one David F. Cable, a Federal prisoner at Andersonville who approached Stephens by mail in the summer of 1864, saying he was an agent of the peace party in the North, sent down to establish contact with peace men in the South. Cable was most likely hoaxing, but Stephens, by now incapable of distinguishing black from white where peace was concerned, believed every syllable, and communicated Cable's tale to Davis, who reluctantly ordered the man investigated. Before the officer detailed for that purpose could reach Andersonville, Cable was dead, and Stephens was not informed of this until some time later. He did not know of the officer's attempt either; hence his anger.

[96] *MC*, January 6, 1865; *Journals* of the Confederate Congress, IV, 385–7.

the housetop of the Confederacy, cawing an interminable prophecy of death. . . .

The resolutions drawn up by Stephens and Atkins were reported in the House on January 12 by the Foreign Affairs Committee. They called upon the President to appoint three commissioners to confer with the Washington government for the establishment of peace and the maintenance of the Monroe Doctrine. Though they were not voted on, it seemed at times that they might pass. The temper of Congress was worsening daily; it refused to act upon Davis' military recommendations and tried to take command of the army away from him. The army itself was weary and desperate, everywhere confronted with overwhelming numbers; great areas of North and South Carolina, Georgia, and Alabama were full of bands of plunderers and deserters; the currency was past repairing; in Richmond fuel was scarce, clothing scarcer; spies, gamblers, timeservers, and peanut-cracking Congressmen infested the streets. There was much to be seen in Richmond that winter.

And there was someone to see it: about the middle of January there came down from Washington Francis P. Blair, Sr., one-time member of Jackson's kitchen cabinet, powerful figure behind the scenes. He had an idea; Lincoln knew of it. He was closeted with Davis on the 12th and explained it to him. Napoleon III was interfering with American affairs by seeking to establish a puppet monarchy in Mexico. This was dangerous. Why should not North and South unite to exterminate Maximilian, rather than each other? Slavery and independence were the only reasons for continuing the war; and Blair dismissed both, saying that slavery was certain to go and with it would go the South's only reason for independence.

Davis listened, did not commit himself, wrote a note

for Blair to take to Lincoln, expressing his willingness to
negotiate for peace "to the two countries." Blair went back
through the lines, reported to Lincoln, who was uninter-
ested in the Mexican angle but much heartened by the
signs of disintegration in the Confederacy; and Blair was
back in Richmond on January 21 with a note from Lincoln expressing *his* willingness to treat for peace to the
people of "our one common country." While there, it is
said, he attended a breakfast at Mrs. Stanard's house—the
nearest thing to a salon in Richmond—where Stephens also
happened to be, and heard the Vice-President bitterly as-
sail the government.[97]

As soon as Blair had gone back to Washington, on January 27, R. M. T. Hunter, President pro tem. of the Senate,
came to Stephens with a request from the President to
come and consult on special and important business. Stephens, who did not know Blair's errand, probably suspected something unusual, for no such request had been
received since July 1863.

Davis began by giving him an account of Blair's proposals. Stephens immediately wanted to know whether
they represented the views of the Lincoln Administration,
and was told that Blair had stressed his private and un-
official character. Davis, though, did believe he spoke for
Lincoln. Stephens thereupon said he thought Blair's proposal should be acceded to, at least as far as a conference;
and suggested that Davis himself go to meet Lincoln. To
this the President objected; and after some moments Stephens named John A. Campbell, Assistant Secretary of
War, Brigadier-General Henry L. Benning of Georgia, and
Thomas S. Flournoy of Virginia. Davis seemed receptive
to these names, and Stephens left him, in the belief that
his recommendations would be carried out.

Next day he was invited to attend a Cabinet meeting,

[97] Or so it is said. *Jefferson Davis, Constitutionalist*, VIII, 211ff.

where, to his chagrin, he learned that he had been appointed one of the commissioners, the others being Campbell and R. M. T. Hunter. He protested, but vainly, that the absence of both himself and Hunter from the Senate would be the cause of too much comment—a protest that limped on both legs. The city was so agog over Blair's visits that the appointment of a church mouse to meet Lincoln would not have gone unnoticed. The truth was that he did not want to go. Perhaps he suspected Davis of seizing an opportunity to shut him up diplomatically, as was in fact the case,[98] and resented the implication that he was a baby whose whims had to be indulged, not for their own sake, but to keep him from bawling.

It did not matter that he declined; the plan was not altered. Later the same day he and the other commissioners saw Davis once more; and in the evening Campbell was given their letters of appointment, which had caused Davis some anguish in the drafting. Having rejected a version by Secretary Benjamin that mentioned the object of their mission as simply the "subject" of Lincoln's letter, he rewrote the instructions so that they contained the phrase: "for informal conference . . . for the purpose of securing peace to the two countries." [99]

At ten in the morning of January 29, 1865, the three men, accompanied by the Mayor of Richmond, drove out toward Petersburg in a carriage. The day was clear and cold. Rumors of their mission had leaked out, and as they approached the front lines they were the objects of considerable staring and conversation. Reaching the lines about three o'clock, they sent an officer under flag of truce into the Federal camp to ask permission for them to go on to Washington. While they waited for a reply they

[98] Davis in ibid., VIII, 28.

[99] *MC*, January 28, 1865; *Jefferson Davis, Constitutionalist*, VIII, 540–1, 570–1, 585.

remained in the carriage, conversing with Mrs. Roger A.
Pryor; and as they talked, there came to their ears the
sound of cheering, coming from the troops within sight
of the carriage. It would be good if the war were over. The
landscape round them was muddy and torn up by shell-
fire; the soldiers they could see were bearded, dirty, ragged
creatures who walked with an unutterable weariness. . . .
They waited all afternoon long, conversing, speculating,
while the vast machine of army organization was set in
motion. A message inquiring if the commissioners might
be permitted to enter the Union lines was received by
Major-General Ord at Grant's headquarters at six thirty
in the evening. Grant was absent; and Ord, not knowing
how to reply, sent the message along to Secretary Stanton
in Washington, who in turn submitted it to Lincoln at
eight thirty. Lincoln, deciding not to go himself, sent
Major T. T. Eckert, head of the War Department telegraph office, with instructions to see the commissioners,
learn whether they would come through the lines to confer
on the basis of his letter to Davis, and report back with
their answer. If they accepted the offer, they were to be
admitted; otherwise not. Meanwhile the commissioners,
disturbed by the delay, had written to Grant directly, asking to be admitted within the lines, either to go
to Washington or to confer with Grant himself. The
general, receiving this note on the evening of January 30,
decided on his own responsibility to bring Stephens,
Campbell, and Hunter to his headquarters at City Point;
and he informed Lincoln accordingly. The President immediately upon receipt of Grant's dispatch, early in the
afternoon of the 31st, ordered him to "detain the gentlemen in comfortable quarters," and sent instructions to
Secretary of State Seward to go to Fortress Monroe and
confer with the commissioners on the basis of the letter to

Davis—though Seward was cautioned not to "assume to definitely consummate anything."

So, in the evening of the last day of January, the three Confederates were driven across the lines, amid cheers and cries of "Peace! Peace!" from soldiers of both sides, and taken by rail to City Point, where they were conducted by Lieutenant-Colonel Orville Babcock of Grant's staff through a maze of buildings and stores to a small hut. Babcock knocked at the door, was told: "Come in," and ushered the three into a little room where, by the light of a kerosene lamp, a small bearded man sat writing. It was Grant. After a brief conversation he personally conducted them to the steamer *Mary Martin,* lying at anchor in Hampton Roads, where they spent the night. On the way to the steamer a bystander audibly queried: "Which is Stephens?" and upon being told, said bluntly: "He's dead now but he don't know it." Grant later remembered that he was particularly impressed by Stephens, and somewhat amused by the shrinkage in his size caused by his removing the huge woolen overcoat he wore against the cold.

For two days, while they fenced with Lincoln, the commissioners stayed aboard the steamer, though they were permitted to come ashore and visit Grant, and several times did so. Stephens was deeply impressed by the quiet soldier, and came away with the impression that he was anxious to see a conference take place, as he indubitably was. The three had also occasion to talk with numerous Federal officers, sounding and being sounded on the prospects of an early peace.[100]

100 Mrs. Roger A. Pryor: *Reminiscences of Peace and War* (New York, 1905), 328. The official correspondence concerning Hampton Roads is in *View,* II, 793–803, and in *OR,* ser. I, xlvi, pt. 2, 290–2, 301–2, 311–14, 341–3, 352–3, and 505–13. Details of the trip to City Point are in *View,* II, 597–8. Grant's recollections are in his *Personal Memoirs* (New York, 1895), II, 287–9. An undated, unsigned account, apparently dictated by Stephens about 1870, giving more details than appear in the *View,* is in *LC.*

Major Eckert arrived on February 1, delivered the message Lincoln had given, and received an unsatisfactory reply at six in the evening. The difficulty of "two countries" versus "one common country" was getting embarrassing. The commissioners were constrained under their instructions to deal on the basis of Davis' note to Lincoln; and they gave Eckert a copy of those instructions, addressing also a note to Grant, asking his aid. Eckert was adamant; they could not go on unless they accepted Lincoln's terms; but he notified the President of the impasse that had been reached. At the same time Grant telegraphed Lincoln that he had conversed with Stephens and Hunter and was satisfied of their good intentions, adding that he regretted Lincoln could not have seen them. On the morning of February 2 Lincoln read both Eckert's and Grant's dispatches, the latter causing him instantly to make up his mind to go and see the commissioners at Fortress Monroe as quickly as he could get there. He wired Grant to this effect. Before he left he learned that the commissioners, yielding to circumstance and their desire to get something done, had agreed to confer on the terms conveyed by Eckert, though they wished to be understood as not committing themselves to anything. A bad situation was growing intolerable. The three were being maneuvered into a position where after a great fuss they would meet Lincoln and have nothing substantial to say.

Lincoln arrived at Fortress Monroe before the day was out; but it was not until the following morning, February 3, that a rowboat put off from the side of his steamer, returning soon after with Stephens, Campbell, and Hunter. They were shown into the saloon, which was momentarily empty; as they took off their coats Lincoln came in, with Seward behind him, stood watching Stephens unwinding his several shawls, and then, hand outstretched, smiling, greeted him: "Never have I seen so small a nubbin come

LINTON STEPHENS AT THE TIME OF HIS VISIT
TO BOSTON IN 1865.

(Liberty Hall collection, Crawfordville)

"THE HARM OF YEARS IS ON HIM": STEPHENS IN
OLD AGE, 1878.

(Courtesy Manhattanville College, New York City)

out of so much husk." The two had not seen each other since 1848; and they began to talk about the old days, asking each other about the subsequent careers of some of their colleagues of that year.

But reminiscence was not the object; and Stephens soon broke off, saying: "Well, Mr. President, is there no way of putting an end to the present trouble, and bringing about a restoration of the general good feeling . . . *then* existing?" Lincoln replied that he knew of but one way: for those resisting the national authority to cease resisting. Stephens side-stepped by bringing up the Mexican business and the maintenance of the Monroe Doctrine as something that might "divert the attention" of both sides from their own war for the time being. Lincoln quietly rejoined that Blair had had no authority from himself to broach the Mexican topic; the restoration of the Union was, with him, a *sine qua non*. Campbell was not surprised at this; Hunter was inwardly chafing at Stephens' insistence upon discussing Blair's quixotic notions. When he and Lincoln had fenced over the idea awhile, there was a pause. Campbell then asked: How was the Union to be restored? whereupon Seward requested Stephens to elaborate his political philosophy, which Stephens gladly did, launching into a constitutional disquisition, explaining how the war could be legally suspended. A military convention, which Lincoln, he was sure, could enter into, would easily do the trick. Inflexibly, quietly, Lincoln remarked that he would not suspend the war until the national authority were restored everywhere in the United States. How restored? Campbell once more queried. By the disbanding of the rebel army and permitting the national authority to resume its functions, Lincoln said.

Slavery was considered; the commissioners heard Lincoln say he would not have interfered with it save that it became necessary to preserve the Union. He explained the

Thirteenth Amendment to them, and then, pensively looking down, addressed himself to Stephens, saying: "Stephens, if I were in Georgia, and entertained the sentiments I do—though, I suppose, I should not be permitted
to stay there long with them; but if I resided in Georgia,
with my present sentiments, I'll tell you what I would do,
if I were in your place; I would go home and get the
Governor of the State to call the Legislature together, and
get them to recall all the State troops from the war; elect
Senators and Members to Congress, and ratify this Constitutional Amendment *prospectively*—so as to take effect—
say in five years." This was an interesting suggestion: was
Lincoln remembering what he had heard from Sherman
at Atlanta in September?

Hunter tried to object that to refuse to deal with the
South until she had laid down her arms was simply a
cloaked demand for unconditional surrender; and to Seward's remark that if the South surrendered, it would be
back under the Constitution and therefore protected by
it, Hunter rejoined that there would be no guarantee that
the Federal government would use the Constitution to
protect the South; and he tried to be historical by pointing
out that Charles I had treated with those in arms against
his government. Lincoln, looking quizzical, answered
slowly: "I do not profess to be posted in history. On all
such matters I will turn you over to Seward. All I distinctly recollect about the case of Charles I is that he lost
his head in the end."

For four hours five men talked, sometimes half-humorously, about the life and death of the Confederate States
of America. It was a restrained, dignified, pleasant conversation. Courtesy ruled. Lincoln and Stephens dominated,
as old friends and men of high official standing. But even
pleasant conversation, with a steward bringing in refresh-
ments, cannot go on forever when there is so little to say.

The blunt opposition between "two countries" and "one common country" was too irreconcilable. It became at length a gag to further speech. And there was silence.

Stephens rose, remarking that the mission seemed to have been useless, and made one last effort to get Lincoln to consider the Mexican venture. Lincoln, taking Stephens' hand, earnestly said: "Well, Stephens, I will reconsider it, but I do not think my mind will change." He then asked Stephens whether there was anything he could do for him.

"Nothing—" then, remembering his nephew John A., who was a Federal prisoner of war: "Unless you can send me my nephew who has been for twenty months a prisoner on Johnson's Island."

Lincoln wrote the name down in a notebook and promised Stephens his nephew would be released—as, a few weeks later, he was, being given the freedom of Washington for two weeks, and a portrait of Lincoln when he set out for Georgia, Lincoln saying: "You had better take that along. It is considered quite a curiosity down your way, I believe."

And that was all. The commissioners got into the rowboat and were taken back to City Point, and from thence to Petersburg and Richmond. Lincoln and Seward returned to Washington, more conscious than ever of the full extent of their power. They held all the cards now; they were the masters; the Southerners were mice; and the end of the war was not far off.[101]

VI

What Stephens' mood was as he crossed the lines and, together with Campbell and Hunter, reported to the Presi-

101 Stephens' account of the meeting is in *View*, II, 599–618. Hunter's is in *Jefferson Davis, Constitutionalist*, VIII, 131ff. Campbell wrote, soon after his return, a memorandum of the meeting, which he published, with other matter, as *Reminiscences and Documents Relating to the Civil War during the Year 1865* (Baltimore, 1887).

dent in Richmond is a debatable matter; but, judging
from his actions, he was furious at having been made the
goat by Davis. His instructions as written had kept him
from accomplishing anything—a result the President had
doubtless anticipated when he wrote them. He, for his
part, was therefore probably not so disappointed as the
commissioners when they delivered their account of the
conference; and when Stephens tried to get the whole
matter forgotten by opposing the commissioners' making
any formal report, on the ground that no such report
could be full and explicit and would hence merely mislead
the public, Davis sternly insisted upon the writing of a
report.

For Davis himself the conference altered nothing. He
would fight on. He could not surrender; he would be
guilty of betrayal if he did. He was not made for defeat.
And he planned and held a great mass demonstration,
sponsored by the government and designed to offset the
disappointment that the failure of the conference inevitably would cause, and to show that the only honorable
course for the people of the South was mass suicide
through continued, fanatical, bitter-end resistance. The
demonstration was held on February 9; there were church
meetings and street processions. Davis spoke in the African
church, referring to "His Majesty Abraham the First,"
predicting a Confederate triumph within twelve months.
Stephens, who sat by, listening, called the speech, "bold,
undaunted and confident," concluding: "However much
I admired the heroism of the sentiments expressed, yet in
his general views of policy . . . I could not concur." Davis
had invited him to join the demonstration, but he had
declined, "because I could not . . . impress upon the
minds of the people the idea that they could do what I
believed to be impossible. . . ." This was not his whole
reason, though; he privately wished the government would

try to reach the peace party in the North, of which he still had hope.[102] As he declined to take part, Davis asked what he intended to do. To go home, he replied, and stay home, and say nothing. There the two parted. He was tired and dissatisfied and angry; he looked like a walking dead man. It was good to get back to Liberty Hall and rest.

The end was swift in coming. Sherman, in February and March, cut his way up through the underside of the Confederacy into North Carolina; Grant kept forcing Lee to spread out farther and farther his thin defense line before Petersburg. A great vise was closing on both Lee and Johnston; and in April it screwed itself shut. On the 1st and 2nd Lee was attacked; on the 2nd, a Sunday, he informed the President that he could no longer defend Petersburg, and that Richmond must be evacuated. The city was abandoned by the government that night; Davis and his Cabinet fled south to Danville, while at Appomattox, on the 9th, Lee, hopelessly caught, surrendered his little army. Day by day the Confederacy died, losing with each moment something more of its identity: "Little—less —nothing, and that ended it." The government, with hostile cavalry hovering somewhere near—no one knew how near—in rain and mud, amid desperate confusion, moved from Danville south, living in an old boxcar, eating bread and bacon and whatever else was to be found. At Greensboro a last council of war was held, with Johnston and Beauregard present. Davis, beyond reason, insisted the war must go on, yielding only with great reluctance to authorize Johnston to negotiate with Sherman. Then the government moved south again, in wagons and ambulances, with a cavalry escort, the railroads being all wrecked, arriving at Charlotte on April 18, leaving on the 26th, Davis planning to retreat into Texas and continue the war from there. Across South Carolina, with Federals

102 *MC*, February 18, 1865; *View*, II 623–5.

closing in, the government moved south, through Abbe-
ville, into Georgia, reaching Washington on May 3, leaving on the 4th, riding through the countryside about fifteen miles east of Crawfordville, down through Warrenton, Sandersville, and Irwinville, near which, on the
morning of May 9, it was surprised and captured. The
Confederate government was gone, vanished, dissolved.
It could command men no longer. Nothing a man might
write on a slip of paper headed *Confederate States of
America* or signed "By order of the President" could move
any other man to perform an act. Titles dropped from
men like leaves: Chief of Ordnance, A.A.G., Major-
General, Chief Clerk, Provost-Marshal, Secretary of War,
Comptroller, Vice-President. . . .

And the Vice-President?

The Vice-President was at home, silent, reticent, withdrawn into the role of spectator. The government of
which he was second officer fell into ruins for thousands
of miles around him; he merely watched. Authority
melted; he tended his plantation. He had refused time
after time to speak for the cause; [103] now when it no longer
mattered he kept silent, listening to the rumors of flight
and surrender that came down out of the north. On April
20 he wrote to Linton: "I wish you would come over here
and let us stand or fall together. . . . Organized war is or
soon will be over with us. . . . Almost anything is better
than guerilla warfare." [104] As he wrote, Federal columns
were advancing on Macon. By the end of the month they
were securely encamped there.

About the 1st of May Linton and his children came over
from Sparta; and all the Stephens blood in Georgia was
together—John A., who had brought from Washington a
letter from Lincoln, over which Stephens wept as he read,

---

103 *MC,* February 23, 1865.
104 Ibid., April 20, 1865.

for he knew that Lincoln was dead; John's brothers, Linton and William; their mother, widow of Stephens' brother John; and their sister Mary. On May 2 Toombs and Brown stopped by for a while. Then all left; the Vice-President standing at his gate in the warm May weather, saying good-by and watching the buggy roll away down the hill. Except for his servants and an occasional visitor he was alone, waiting for what he knew would come.[105]

It came on the morning of May 11 as Davis was being taken under guard to Macon. After breakfast the Vice-President attended to his correspondence; his secretary, Hidell, went into town, leaving him with a young man who had stayed overnight. After a while the two sat down to cassino. As they played, a Negro boy ran in with news that there were Yankees in town, riding all around. "I expect they have come for me," the Vice-President said; he excused himself, crossed the hall to his bedroom, and began putting his papers in order. In a little while, glancing through the window, he saw soldiers approaching. He went down the hall, into the library at the back of the house, and waited there until the officer commanding the party had come in and approached him.

There was brief dialogue.

"Is your name Stephens?"

"It is."

"Alexander H. Stephens?"

"That is my name."

"I am ordered to put you under arrest."

The Vice-President asked to see and was shown the order of arrest—charges unspecified, destination Atlanta, issued by Major-General Emory Upton. Remarking that a simple request to report to Atlanta would have sufficed, the Vice-President asked: "How am I to travel?"

[105] *Recollections*, 141-2; *MC*, May 3, 1865.

"On the cars."

"Am I to be permitted to take any clothing with me?"

"Yes."

"How long may I have to pack?"

"A few minutes—as long as necessary." And the captain stood waiting while Stephens quickly packed. Hidell came back from town with a few friends. Stephens wrote Linton a hasty note, but tore it up when the captain objected to his sending it at once. Possibly fifteen minutes after the soldiers had come, Stephens, walking with them, returned to the depot, where a train was waiting. Many people were there, his friends, the men and women he knew and understood. No one knew what would become of him. No one knew how long, if ever, it would be before they would meet again. Little was said; little needed to be said. He was put aboard the train, and after a long, chilly night ride reached Atlanta early next morning. He was taken to General Upton's headquarters, given a room and breakfast, after which, under guard, he walked about the ruined city. Upton did not see him until the 13th and then informed him that he was on parole and that his probable destination was Washington. Davis, the general went on, was also arrested. Did this mean, Stephens wondered, that he and Davis would have to travel together? Unfortunately, yes.[106] Late that night a train carrying Stephens and a guard of one hundred men headed east from Atlanta. At eleven next morning it paused briefly at Crawfordville, so that Stephens could get more clothing and put his affairs in order. It was Sunday; church was just out; a great crowd was at the station. He could not stay long; after saying what he could, for he had a severe sore throat, farewells were spoken. Linton was not there; he was at home, sick. But there were so many whose hands had to be grasped, and all the faces were so disturbed and

[106] The story of the arrest is in *Recollections*, 99–102 et seq.

sad, that, fearing he would break down, he asked that the train get under way. This it soon did.

At seven in the evening they reached Augusta, the train bearing Davis, C. C. Clay, Postmaster-General Reagan, and General Joseph Wheeler, behind them, and were put into carriages and driven under heavy guard through the town to the river, where a steamer waited. Stephens brought up the rear of the procession, carrying with him his greatcoat, carpetbag, shawl, cane, and umbrella. In the streets were crowds of people; some said: "There goes Stephens"; and several bowed to him, he bowing in return. Dark came; the carriages reached the landing. Stephens, feeble, suffering from headache, was helped down and over the plank leading to the tug that was to take them to Savannah. The tug was small, badly crowded; they were tired and depressed. The night was cool. Next morning Davis came on deck and briefly greeted Stephens in a remote but courteous fashion. The strain of anticipation, at least, was over; the two had met.

At Savannah the party was transferred, first to a coastal steamer and then to the *William P. Clyde,* a narrow-beamed brig-rigged steamer, which, guarded by a sloop of war whose guns were steadily kept on her, steamed north along the coast for three days, from the 16th to the 19th of May. Here, where there was little alternative, Davis and Stephens met frequently and talked more freely. They were, after all, sharing a common fate of whose precise nature neither was yet aware.

On the 19th the *Clyde* reached Hampton Roads and anchored there. All day long nothing happened, or the next. The prisoners wasted time as well as they could. Finally Stephens and Reagan were told that they were to be put aboard the sloop *Tuscarora* and taken to Boston. Stephens thought at once: Fort Warren; and began to worry about the climate, fearing it too cold and damp for

him. But it did not matter; the arrangements had been
made.

Thinking much of home and of Linton, Stephens spends
a bad night. Next morning, May 22, Sunday, he takes
leave of his friends, Mrs. Davis, the Clays, General
Wheeler, and Davis himself, who seems moved at parting,
squeezes Stephens' hand, and says "Good-by" in a voice
full of emotion. The tug conveys him to the ship; and at
eleven o'clock the *Tuscarora* stands out to sea. For two
days he and Reagan share the captain's cabin with him,
while the steamer moves north through the Atlantic. Thick
fog slows them near Block Island; but they are at anchor
in Boston harbor, just below Fort Warren, by ten on the
evening of the 24th.

For four months and nineteen days, from May 25 to
October 13, 1865, Stephens lived in Fort Warren. Until
July 29 he was confined to his cell, allowed no communication except through General Dix at New York, taken
out at intervals during the day for walks about the para-
pets; but under these conditions his health grew steadily
worse, and from July 29 until August 19 he was, while not
moved from his somewhat underground cell, given the
freedom of the fort and allowed to receive any friends he
might wish to see. And on August 20 he was removed, by
special order from President Johnson, to a larger, higher
room, in which he stayed until his release.

Life quickly settled into a routine. The prisoner, as he
often half-humorously called himself, woke early, break-
fasted at seven, walked on the parapet with a companion,
usually Lieutenant Woodman of the 1st Massachusetts
Volunteer Artillery, had dinner at three, walked out again
toward evening, had supper, went to bed at half past nine.
The intervals of time which no minor occupations, such
as bathing, shaving, or talking to the lieutenant, could fill,
he whiled away in reading, mostly the Bible and what

newspapers he might get. And he kept a diary, a long book that he deliberately made long to occupy himself.

Until September 1, when Linton finally arrived at the fort, he suffered much from loneliness and homesickness. He heard nothing from his brother before July 8; and he was cut off in most respects from all associations and connections with his customary life, though Woodman and Dr. Seaverns, the fort surgeon, treated him kindly and spent much time with him. There were other acquaintances too, but none that could make up for what he did not have, none that could supplant the relations of a lifetime. He spent the time as best he could, learning the whole routine of the fort, thinking, walking. The weather was not uncomfortable after a while; and he stayed much of the day outside his cell, watching the ships in the harbor. His old troubles did not let him go: he suffered from acute attacks of pain in his bowels, possibly brought on by the rough diet to which he was first confined; his kidney disease threatened several times to strike; and toward September he became so weak that he had to remain in his room. After Linton came, things were more endurable; there were visitors almost every day who would even stay and take dinner in the fort with him; and Linton himself voluntarily lived in prison so that the two would not even be separated for the space of a night.

Time passed, that summer, marked by the rising and falling of the sun, by the rhythm of breakfasts and dinners and walks on the parapet, by the fluctuations of the thermometer he kept outside the window, by the comings and goings of people and things, the stray cat that came in, stayed awhile, and then disappeared, the little daughter of the fort's commandant, who would occasionally bring him flowers, the mouse he saw once and tried to catch so that he could tame it. . . . And though time seemed to move more slowly, more of it seemed to be going: one felt oneself aging more rapidly than ever; looked into the mirror and saw a face parchment-pale, and hair in which the chestnut was streaked with growing lines of white. And one found glasses to be becoming every week more indispensable. . . . And time grew confused; the past insistently rose up and one passed from dreaming to wakefulness with scarcely a sensation of transition and friends long dead appeared in sleep beside the living and one almost imagined upon waking that they had walked into the room and spoken, so vivid was the image. The past: the past was so full; and now there was leisure to study it and judge one's part in it; for the long nightmare was over.

For himself there was nothing to regret. Believing as he did, what other course could he have taken but the one he did? For if you held, with him, that slavery was not the basic cause of the war, but rather the "gur-reat pur-rinciple" of state sovereignty and constitutional liberty— the notion that the people of the states were, as a people, sovereign over both their state and national governments, and could alter or obliterate either or both whenever they chose—if you held that the recognition of that principle was the issue of the war, what then could you do when you saw the government you had helped set in motion for the purpose of asserting that principle wantonly perverting it, but attack its usurpations with all your strength? How could you bear with tyranny for the emergency, for the unavoidable duration, and expect it mildly to abjure itself as soon as the emergency was past? What guarantee was there? Was it not the invariable experience of history that tyranny once begun, under no matter what pretext, never voluntarily resigned, but rather endeavored always to fasten itself more firmly upon the people who had accepted it under the guise of necessity? Power must always be guarded, even if the price to be paid was high, involving awkwardness and inefficiency in government.

"Usurpation never did and never will yield to gentle suasion." [107]

In as persuasive form as its nature allows, this is the argument. On it Stephens' behavior toward the Richmond Administration must be judged. If it stands, that stands; if it falls, he is condemned. And, in the main, it falls. What Stephens never fully understood was that the Confederacy was fighting for the naked right to exist, against an enemy who, powerful at the beginning, grew more powerful as the war progressed, while the South grew weaker. Jefferson Davis was no tyrant; he was neither a Napoleon, a Cromwell, nor a Cæsar. He was a man unfitted by character and disposition to handle successfully the inhumanly arduous job the Montgomery convention thrust upon him. He had to see that all the force his country could bring to bear was concentrated on the proper objects and at the proper times. Decisions had often to be made with scant knowledge of the factors involved. Men had to be dealt with in an infinitely subtle manner, cajoled, coaxed, flattered, commanded, or cursed according to their natures, in order that the most might be got out of them. The job demanded the wisdom of a serpent and the patience of a cow and the strength of an elephant; and Davis lacked them all. He had courage and loyalty and some sense; but he, like Stephens, was a neurotic invalid, and hence irritable and stiff-necked, especially when criticized. But he wished nothing for himself beyond the praise that victory would rightfully have brought. He held vast powers, but wielded them for the most part with circumspection and self-command. Without holding them he could not have fought the war; and had he been permitted to wield them more effectively, he might have won it.

[107] This account of the prison months is taken mostly from *Recollections,* which was written close on the heels of the event, and is probably accurate. Stephens' misgivings about power are in a letter to H. V. Johnson, in *Cleveland,* 790–5.

Stephens loved liberty too well to understand that it must sometimes be curbed to be preserved. There can be no palliation of his role in the collapse of the Confederacy. He lent the power of his name to the snivelings and evasions of men like Holden and Vance, Brown, Wigfall, and Foote, who, out of blindness, spite, and envy did the best they could to ruin the government in whose councils they had thought to take a larger part than was assigned. He comforted deserters and disloyal men. His incessant criticism embarrassed the government; his personal quarrels with Davis weakened the unity of the Confederacy. He had gone into the affair reluctantly, and it had not proceeded according to his plan. Therefore it was doubly bad. And so, with steadily increasing passion, during the dark years of war, he came to think of himself as waging a great and hopeless fight against the powers of tyranny and evil, as a heroic knight, wielding the sword of justice, alone against a thousand. At such times, in the fragrance of this vision, he could forget himself and the miserable body with which he was cursed, and stand, not merely equal with, but almost superior to, the men who were running the machine so blindly and in so sinister a spirit.

If Davis, in 1864, had been impeached or forced to resign, he himself would have become President. Linton pressed this idea on him; and he must surely have given it considerable thought. But would he have wanted the Presidency? He said no; but he always consciously declined to accept political trusts. Subconsciously, however, it was impossible for him to keep out of politics; and had the opportunity presented itself, he would have taken it. The efforts of March 1864 to arouse the popular indignation against the Administration, so that it would be obliged to resign, failed because they were not intense and coordinated enough; and from then on, Stephens, rather than change the Confederate government, was interested in playing for some kind of restoration of the Union through the Chicago convention on the basis of state sovereignty—not realizing that state sovereignty after the bloody baptismal of the new America was deader than Methuselah's grandmother. He hated war and loved peace; but the peace he longed for was a delusion. He could not utterly desert and become a Unionist; he could not remain with Davis, whom he had never much liked; he was neither here nor there, a lonely and bewildered figure, wandering through the twilight of the Confederacy with a copy of its Constitution in his hands. Reality could not conform to plan; he would not modify the plan because he believed in it and it was right. . . .

So here he was in prison, and for what? After much internal debate he wrote President Johnson on June 9, asking for pardon or a parole, under the terms of the amnesty proclamation of May 29, and setting forth at length his political theories and his course in opposition to the war. Johnson was flooded with such applications, and Stephens did not at once hear from him. Growing impatient, he asked that his application be considered withdrawn; then, thinking twice, wanted Johnson to let him come to Washington for a conference. Soon after this letter was received by the President, Linton saw him, bringing recommendations for his brother's release from James Johnson, provisional Governor of Georgia, from General J. B. Steedman, commanding the department of Georgia, from General George Thomas, and others. Herschel V. Johnson went to Washington in the latter part of September to lend his influence; Stephens wrote to Seward and Grant, the latter of whom spoke to the President several times about the case. At length, under a general order of October 12, Stephens and Reagan were both released.[108]

[108] Letters to the President in *Recollections*, 187–204, 286–8, 466–7. *MC*, Linton to A.H.S., August 27, 1865.

They left Fort Warren in the afternoon of the 13th
and went to Boston, where they stayed several days, called
on by crowds of visitors. Then they journeyed south by
way of New York, where they stopped at the Astor House,
and Washington, where, on the 20th, Stephens conversed
with President Johnson about Negro suffrage. From Washington on, it was less festive, more somber. Here nothing
was yet normal; the air was full of distress and bitterness;
everywhere were problems to be solved, adjustments to be
made. The old South was gone, and there was nothing
definite to take its place. "Oh, how changed are all things
here," Stephens wrote when they reached Atlanta.[109] And
as they passed through desolate, dead country to Crawfordville, and were met at the depot by crowds of friends, and
drove up to the house, and stopped, and looked at it, he
felt as if he were in a dream, one of those he had had so
often at Fort Warren. Then they went inside.

[109] *Recollections,* 539.

CHAPTER FIVE

Decline (1865–72)

THE rest is easily told. Before Stephens had come home from Fort Warren the old America was dying; and by the time that he himself was dead, the new America had largely taken its place. And in the new America there was no room for him. In lucid moments he understood it to be so, yet for the most part during these last seventeen years he fought to keep the position he once had held in that long past, so distant and so rapidly receding; and in a sentimental sense succeeded. He kept the hearts of his people to the end and past it; but the political power he had known in antebellum days was gone. While he struggled instinctively to win it back, however, failure did not too much disappoint him; and despite great suffering this was the happiest period of his life.

Even before his return his friends were working to keep him actively in politics. Their opportunity lay in the gubernatorial election that was to come in November. Since the end of the war civil government in the Southern states had been vested in a series of provisional governors appointed by President Johnson and empowered to call conventions of delegates who had taken the oath of amnesty and did not belong to any one of various classes of politically disqualified Confederate officers. These conventions were to draft new state constitutions and provide for the election of permanent governors. In Georgia the convention met in the latter part of October, and the elections for governor and legislature were held on November 15.[1] There was at first some factionalism. Joseph E. Brown, who had been among the first to beg pardon of the United States for having revolted against it, was pressed to run by those who had not lost faith in his morality, and he was naturally not averse to the idea. And many of Stephens' friends urged him to let himself become a candidate, even though he, more than any other Georgian, fell under the disqualifications of the amnesty proclamation.[2] A third name was being talked of: Charles J. Jenkins, who had the advantages of being safe and conservative without being a toady to the North. Stephens, who saw that it would be impossible for him to accept a nomination, quickly issued an emphatic declination; whereupon Brown, privately assuring himself that Jenkins' election would not diminish his own influence, publicly asked him to run. Jenkins, being unopposed, was then elected.[3]

If, Stephens' friends concluded, he could not be governor, he could be senator. Before the new legislature met on December 4, he was pondering the problem and asking Linton's advice.[4] It was a delicate question: for in the North he was far better known as the author of the cornerstone speech than as Davis' opponent. His election to the Senate so soon after the close of hostilities might not be understood in the proper spirit. President Johnson himself, when asked by General Steedman, with whom Stephens seemed to be rather friendly, whether it would be considered a violation of parole for Stephens to accept a senatorship, replied that "it would be exceedingly impoli-

[1] Clara M. Thompson: Reconstruction in Georgia (New York, 1915), 147–9.

[2] TSC, 670–1; LC, S. J. Anderson to A.H.S., November 7, 1865; A. R. Watson to A.H.S., November 6, 1865.

[3] Avery, 351.

[4] MC, November 17, 1865.

tic for Mr. A. H. Stephens' name to be used in connection with the senatorial election. If elected, he would not be permitted to take his seat . . ." assuring Steedman, however, that his personal feelings in the matter were quite kindly. At the same time there were those in Washington who told Stephens' friends that his election would be graciously received.[5]

The legislature that met in December had been elected by all the people of the state, in contradistinction to the convention, which had been chosen by a restricted number; and it quickly displayed a temper somewhat different from the convention's conservatism. During the session Stephens visited Milledgeville, and upon being approached by members of the legislature asking him to run for the senatorship, told them categorically it was impossible. Notwithstanding this, the pressure upon him was not lessened until the election was held, on January 30. He was formally requested in writing to allow the use of his name; he responded with an "explicit and emphatic" refusal. Undeterred, a group of legislators, on the day before the election, reminded him that their right to bestow was as good as his to refuse; to which he replied, weakening slightly, that he could not imagine himself refusing to serve his people if they should "assign" him to office. The result was that on the following day Stephens, running against Joshua Hill, the wartime Unionist, for the long term, won on the first ballot by 152 to 38. Herschel V. Johnson won the short-term seat after a more difficult fight. Northern newspapers at once deprecated the choice as unwise; but for both Stephens and Johnson it was an empty victory. Neither was ever admitted to his Senate seat.[6]

[5] Flippin: *H. V. Johnson*, 272.
[6] *PHS*, A.H.S. to Hidell, December 13, 1865; *J&B*, 489–90; Thompson: *Reconstruction*, 154–5.

II

"It seems," wrote Stephens in November 1865, "to be a hard matter for our people to realize the fact that old things have passed away." [7] The dimensions of change were great enough to excuse a certain inability to comprehend. The civilization men in the South had known had, as they remembered it, disappeared. Much, to be sure, remained; but much more was altered. How, after such civil war, could it be otherwise?

The South was economically ruined. Most cities of any size were deserted or destroyed. Whole regions of Virginia, North and South Carolina, Georgia, Alabama, and Mississippi were wastelands. Debt was a general condition. And three billion dollars' worth of human property had ceased to be property. Men who had once been rich were level with their yeoman neighbors. The whole system of social and economic relations based on slavery was gone and waiting to be replaced with something else.

The solution of such a problem seemed at first remote. In Georgia the summer and fall of 1865 saw a general crop failure, and the gathering of crowds of freedmen in the larger towns, where they mostly refused to work, for they were too interested in the taste of liberty. The Freedmen's Bureau, originally set up during the war to take care of the Negro population in liberated areas, gradually began instituting a system of compulsions aimed at the freedmen, to direct them into useful labor; and the Bureau was valuable also as a liaison between planters and freedmen, arranging the terms of labor contracts.

Besides the difficulty of getting labor, the planter had to hold on to it when he got it, and he had to pay for it. The freedmen, thrown off balance by emancipation, were unaccustomed to working under new conditions, and they

[7] *MC*, November 19, 1865.

generally wanted to assert their freedom in the most obvious manner, by going off whenever and wherever they
chose: exercising that mobility which had so long been
denied them. The planter could never be certain that his
laborers would stay with him, even if he had a contract
written out; and planters from Louisiana and Mississippi,
where labor was more in demand and wages higher than
in Georgia, made a practice of seducing contracted freedmen away from their plantations simply by offering them
more money. The matter of money, too, was vexing the
planter in these years. Cash, in 1865 and 1866, was almost
nonexistent, and what there was went for tools and seed
and fertilizer. The freedmen were paid in cash if any
remained over; otherwise they were given a share of the
crop, though this system was not adopted without considerable grumbling. Until 1868, as if one set of problems
were not enough, cotton crops were failures, while steady
high prices impelled planters to involve themselves deeply
in debt to get as much cotton in the ground as they could
each year. After 1868, as crops grew richer, the price of
cotton sank, though the cost of growing it kept climbing.[8]

The disappearance of the old antebellum plantation and
the rise of share tenancy were the chief phenomena of the
economic revolution in Georgia—as indeed everywhere in
the South. The planters, rooted, conservative men, reacted to the shock of losing the war in the only way they
knew, and clung, amid the falling and the change, to the
old ways of doing things. Their desire after the war was
to perpetuate if they could the old plantation economy,
substituting contract for slave labor. All else they wished
to remain as it had been. But the freedmen had other
notions. They wanted to be independent, to have their
forty acres and a mule; and circumstances aided them, for

8 Cf. Robert P. Brooks: *The Agrarian Revolution in Georgia* (Madison,
Wis., 1914), 10–13.

the insolvency of many large planters obliged them to
break up their vast estates.

More farms, smaller farms, and more waste land, were
the characteristics of the Georgia agricultural landscape in
the decades following the war.[9] And at the same time the
planter's acreage shrank, his control over his workers disintegrated. For a time, under the stress of his impulse to
keep things as they had been in the old days, his contract
labor was closely supervised by foremen, and the freedmen
worked in gangs as formerly. But gradually the gangs grew
smaller, and supervision less thorough, until the freedmen
found themselves working their own farms as tenants of
the planter, who for his part had degenerated into a landlord. Of tenancy there soon came to exist two varieties,
rent and share, in the first of which the landlord bound
himself to furnish only the land and house and had nothing to say about what the tenant grew or how he grew it.
The freedmen liked this system, which attained some superiority over share tenancy, in which the landlord furnished, besides the land and house, the tools, seed, and
fertilizer, receiving in return a share of the crop and
being entitled to supervise the tenant at every step of his
work.

One change entailed innumerably more. Since the
planter no longer needed to purchase great quantities of
goods for his slaves, and since the number of customers
increased, the old credit structure was revised, and the
small country store, the itinerant peddler and his wagon,
began to grow more and more common. Life remained
rural, perhaps became more so, though the large towns
became larger and, because of the atomization of agriculture, an impetus was given to commerce and trade, and
the railroads of the state, badly damaged by the war, were
vigorously extended between 1867 and 1872.

9 Ibid., 41.

Change, though, was more than economic; it was political as well; and the political element at the moment probably hurt the most. The difficulty, so far as the Federal government was concerned, was clear: here were eleven states out of their normal political relations with the rest of the country. How get them back? President Johnson, in his appointments of provisional governors and in his amnesty proclamations, showed his intention to continue Lincoln's policy of restoration as nearly as he could. He, like Lincoln, was not a hater of the South. But there were those in Congress for whom the South was conquered land, to be dealt with in whatever spirit they, the conquerors, saw fit in their justice and magnanimity to invoke. These men, some sincere, some power-hungry, some frankly venal, led by old Thaddeus Stevens, undertook a systematic campaign to get control of the government, beginning in February 1866, when President Johnson challenged their pretensions by vetoing a bill designed to make the Freedmen's Bureau a permanent instrument to enable the Republican party to run the South. They passed a second bill over his veto in July: and the epilogue to the Civil War was on.

A Joint Congressional Committee on Reconstruction, dominated by the radicals, had been set up. This committee concocted an amendment to the Constitution, finally passed and submitted to the states for ratification as the Fourteenth Amendment, one clause of which debarred all former Confederate officials from holding Federal office except by enabling vote of two thirds of each House of Congress. It was understood that no Southern state would be readmitted to full participation in the government unless it ratified this amendment. There were many in the North who felt that this was carrying high-handedness somewhat too far: and on the issue of this amendment and the Freedmen's Bureau bill the Congressional campaign

of 1866 was fought, with a result so gratifying to the radicals that in the following spring they felt able, every Southern state but Tennessee having rejected the Fourteenth
Amendment,[10] to dissolve the state governments that had
been functioning and to remand the South to military rule.

The committee had been for some months gathering
testimony regarding the state of affairs in the South; and
among the witnesses called had been Stephens, who had
visited Washington in April 1866 for the purpose of giving
evidence. He had told the committee that the people of
Georgia were anxious for restoration to the Union; that
they had submitted the question of the right of secession
to the arbitrament of the sword, and that they were, by
and large, willing to abide the sword's decision. As to the
enfranchisement of the Negro, he thought himself that
such problems should be left to the individual states to
decide as they saw fit. His testimony was singularly unimpassioned, and in the South created a good impression: in
Georgia it was called a "calm, lucid, powerful and unan-
swerable argument." [11] Somewhat earlier, on February 22.
at the invitation of the Georgia legislature, he had addressed it, giving his view of the situation, counseling patience and forbearance, acceptance and open-mindedness,
urging the people to help the freedmen find themselves.
"The great body of the people here," wrote a Boston man
after reading the speech, "hail such sentiments . . . with
the highest satisfaction." [12]

But such a temper on the one side was not the rule; and
it was met, on the other, by a temper distinctly different.
On April 1, 1867, under the terms of the Reconstruction
Act of March, General John Pope became military com-

---

[10] Georgia rejected it on November 9, 1866.

[11] Macon *Telegraph*, April 26, 1866. Testimony in *Cleveland*, 819–33.
Stephens' wisdom in 1866 is as complimentary to him as his madness of
1864 is damaging. Perhaps imprisonment did him some good.

[12] *LC*, J. Kent to A.H.S., March 7, 1866. Speech in *Cleveland*, 804–18.

mander of Georgia. He remained in office until January 6, 1868, when General George Gordon Meade replaced him until civil rule was restored in July. Under these men the reconstruction struggle began.

There were those who favored co-operation with the military: among them was Brown, who, it was noticed, made it a business to cultivate Pope's friendship.[13] There were those who favored resistance: and their leader was Benjamin Hill, who, during this summer of 1867, published a flaming series of anti-reconstruction articles in the Augusta *Chronicle and Sentinel*. There were those who remained silent: and Stephens was among them. At the earnest request of Montgomery Blair and Clement L. Vallandigham, he had gone with Linton to Philadelphia in the summer of 1866, to attend the great Union convention called by the partisans of President Johnson.[14] But while there, he had been too ill to attend any of its meetings. That convention had failed; and he had gone home to mend his fences, convinced that the best way to serve his own political and personal interests was to be silent. "I do not see," he wrote, "the slightest prospect of my being able to tender the public the least possible good by anything . . . I can now either say or do. . . ."[15]

Pope's rule was irritating but not tyrannical: he tried to suppress newspaper criticism of his regime, and gave Negroes the right to serve on juries; but these were his most unpopular measures. Meade did more: he removed Governor Jenkins from office in January 1868 because he had refused to sign a requisition for $40,000 per diem demanded by the constitutional convention of 1867. It therefore became necessary to elect a new governor at the same time that a vote on the new Constitution was to be taken.

13 *LC*, P. Thweatt to A.H.S., serial 7127.
14 *MC*, July 21, 29, August 1, 1866.
15 A.H.S. to J. P. Hambleton, May 30, 1867, Hambleton MSS., Emory University.

This document had been written by scalawags and carpet-baggers and Negroes, the conservative Democratic whites mistakenly having abstained from the voting for delegates, and, while it was not too radical, it was not the kind of constitution they particularly desired. For the gubernatorial election the conservatives organized instead of passively sitting by; but two of their prospective candidates were disqualified by Meade as ineligible under the Fourteenth Amendment; and the one finally chosen, ex-General John B. Gordon, was defeated in April by Rufus B. Bullock, the Republican candidate, a Northerner who had come to Georgia before the war, and who remained Governor from July 22, 1868 to October 1871. The legislature that was elected with him ratified the Fourteenth Amendment the day before his inauguration; but it was nevertheless a conservatively dominated body, as was proved when, in September, the Negro members of both houses were ousted as being unqualified by the laws of the state to hold office, and when, in March of the following year, the legislature refused to ratify the Fifteenth Amendment. Military rule had ended with Bullock's inauguration; but these peevish and ill-considered actions, coupled with judiciously doctored accounts of Ku-Klux outrages in the state and with the lobbying of Bullock himself, whom the legislature had insulted by not electing his favorites Brown and Foster Blodgett to the United States Senate, led, in December 1869, to the restoration of military rule until July 1870.[16]

The Bullock regime, like most carpetbag governments, combined social progressivism—as in education—with political corruption. Its most flagrant irregular practice was that of issuing state-endorsed bonds to one railroad com-

---

[16] Thompson: *Reconstruction*, 175, 199ff.; *Avery*, 379, 389–90. The 1867 Constitution provided, among other things, for free, tax-supported, and *racially non-discriminative* education—a provision that was altered in 1877, when conservatives were back in power.

pany after another, on the flimsiest security, and very often before a foot of track was laid. There was evidence, later adduced, showing that members of the legislature were shadily involved in these transactions, being bribed to vote for certain bond issues. The state-owned railroad, the Western & Atlantic, was manipulated by the regime for all it was worth, and had always at least three times as many employees as it needed. Bullock himself had been connected with the Southern Express Company before the war, and his government, in contradistinction to prewar Georgia governments, was one in which economics ruled. Its point of view was that of making money and maintaining itself in power so that it could make more money. In order to remain in power it was eager to meet illegality with illegality. When Bullock called a meeting in January 1870 of the legislature elected in 1868, this fact was rendered peculiarly obvious by his "purging," with the aid of General Terry, the military commandant, a certain number of Democrats and replacing them with Republicans. He also saw to it that the Negroes who had been expelled in 1868 were reinstated, and so assured himself a solid Republican majority, which immediately ratified the Fifteenth Amendment.

The long holiday, however, was nearing sundown. Bullock worked desperately to keep Georgia under military rule, but, despite his propaganda and his lobbying, the feeling grew in Congress that all this was a little silly. And in July 1870 the radical Republicans were, for the first time in all their dealings with the South, defeated by the passage of a simple declaration that Georgia had complied with all conditions and was entitled to representation in Congress. The following December the Representatives elected in 1870 were admitted to the House; and in 1871 Joshua Hill and H. V. M. Miller took their seats in the Senate. Reconstruction had taken almost six years.

The Bullock government lingered on for a time. Half
the state legislature was due to be elected in December
1870; and with the collapse of the effort to maintain radical domination the outcome was predictable. The legislature became Democratic by a good majority. Bullock,
who knew very well that when this new legislature would
meet in November 1871, its main business would be his
own impeachment, could choose between waiting or running. He ran, resigning in October 1871 and appointing
the President of the Senate, a radical, Acting Governor.
This gentleman did his best to hold on to the office, but
was put out in December. A Democrat, James M. Smith,
Speaker of the House, became Governor on January 12,
1872. The house was at last swept clean and the time for
Democrats to squabble among themselves had begun.

III

Stephens, during these years of economic revolution and
political disturbance, remained for the most part isolated
and aloof. He thought he was through with politics and
went back to the practice of law. "A man must take things
as he finds them and do the best he can with them as they
are," [17] was his tone, and he held to it pretty well. He was
old, and he was sick; but he was no longer morbidly melancholy. Nor did he need to be. Liberty Hall was his, and
the plantation was still his, and most of his former slaves
stayed with him when they were free, those who had been
field hands renting little tracts from him, because he had
been kind to them and earned their love. Around him
gathered a collection of friends and relatives: his nephew
John A. Stephens, who practiced law in Crawfordville and
acted as his uncle's secretary; his other nephew Linton
Andrew Stephens, also living in Crawfordville; the old
Ordinary, Quinea O'Neal, who had left Liberty Hall dur-

17 *MC,* January 3, 1866.

ing the war but now returned to stay; and of course Linton, always Linton, the one most constant factor in his life, to whom he was writing: "When you are happy I am happy—when you suffer I suffer when you are miserable I am miserable!" And after June 1867 there was someone else. While in Boston in the summer of 1865, Linton had met again a certain Mrs. Salter, a woman he had first known in Washington in 1860. Mrs. Salter had a daughter named Mary, in whom Linton gradually became more and more interested. During 1866 and the spring of 1867 the friendship advanced to an engagement, under the solicitous eyes of Alexander and Mrs. Salter, who together did their best to match the pair; and on June 28 the two were married. Linton was not quite forty-four; Mary was about twenty. She had taken to her brother-in-law-to-be at once, and had made it clear to Linton before she married him—as if he did not feel the same—that the two should do all they could to make Alexander's last years the most peaceful of his life. Stephens, for whom the necessity of having to share Linton with another had never been acceptable or really enjoyable, betrayed this time no hint of sadness. "Oh you will be very dear & close friends to each other," Mrs. Salter told him, and it was so.[18]

July 1868 again brought his name into brief political prominence. When the legislature elected with Bullock proceeded to the choice of United States senators, the Democrats put him forward as their candidate for the long term. Bullock and his radicals wanted Brown; and on the first ballot he led Stephens by 102 to 96; whereupon the anti-Bullock Republicans, of whom there existed several, and the Democrats, afraid that if they persisted in supporting Stephens Brown might actually be elected, caucused, and agreed on Joshua Hill as a coalition candidate, electing him on the second ballot by 110 to 94. It was at the mo-

[18] *MC,* May 19, 1866; March 11, 17, June 30, 1867; *Richardson,* 40.

ment anything but Brown, for Brown had been the only Democrat of real prominence to collaborate with the Republicans. And Hill, with his Unionist background, had better coalition possibilities than Stephens. The incident showed that Stephens was being regarded somewhat in the light of a has-been; and so for four years his name was not presented for any public office. He assumed the role of Elder Statesman. And he wrote a book.

Already in 1865, while he was at Fort Warren, he had been approached by a publisher inquiring whether he would write anything; and during 1866 there came several other such approaches. A collection of his speeches and letters had been edited and published in 1866 by Henry Cleveland. The subject for a book was there; so was the impulse to justify his ways to men; and his decision, made in December 1866, was an inevitable one. The greater part of 1867 was taken up with the work of writing the first volume, his nephew John Grier Stephens acting as amanuensis; and in late December he went to Philadelphia, where J. R. Jones, his publisher, was located, to correct proof, for in such matters he was outrageously meticulous. Until the middle of February he remained, living with Jones, staying indoors most of the time because of the intense cold, getting his exercise by walking two miles a day in Jones' parlor, and suffering a fall on the ice on one of his rare excursions into the streets. Leaving Philadelphia, he went to New York and Boston, where he spent a few days with Mrs. Salter. In both cities he had numerous visitors, being regarded as something of a curiosity. Oliver Wendell Holmes called on him in Boston; Henry Ward Beecher in New York. He could always draw people to him; and he liked the fuss they made. During his visit to Washington in 1866 he had attended one of Grant's receptions, and had attracted much attention from radicals and Democrats alike,[19] at least partly by reason of his appearance. A reporter interviewed him in Washington in March 1868, as he was going homeward, and wrote of him as "Tall, excessively thin, stooped at the shoulders, with a small, boyish face, bright, glittering eye, silvery hair . . . a soft felt hat worn negligently on the back of the head, a carelessly tied cravat under a rolling collar, and a swallow tailed coat," remarking that he seemed nervous, swinging his leg and getting up frequently to walk to and fro across the room.[20] At that time the first volume of the book, which Linton had suggested should be called *History of the Causes of the Civil War in the United States, with its Leading Proximate Effects,* was not yet out, but it appeared soon after.

There was another volume to go, at which he worked through the rest of 1868, though it was not easy. "I fear," he wrote at the end of the year, "I am beginning to grow old." [21] Since the close of the war he had not been at all well and, more than that, was always tired. "I can hardly walk about," he constantly complained. His appetite declined; and Eliza, his cook, whose art was notorious among all who had ever been guests at the Hall, could do no more than feed him chicken wings and coffee. In 1868 the trustees of the University of Georgia offered him the chair of the history of political science at two thousand dollars a year, probably as a result of the publication of the first volume of the *Constitutional View of the Late War between the States;* but after some hesitation he declined, partly on the grounds of his uncertain health.[22]

"Alex. Stephens," said the Memphis *Sun* of February 16, 1869, "was severely injured, on Sunday last, by a heavy

19 *MC,* February 9, 23, March 2, 4, 1868; April 8, 1866.
20 New York *Herald,* March 17, 1868.
21 *MC,* December 14, 1868.
22 Ibid., January 8, 12, 1869.

gate falling on him. We sincerely hope his injuries are
not of a serious character." He had been walking along the
Raytown road, about a mile from Liberty Hall, and had
taken hold of a large iron gate opening on a pasture he
wished to cross, not noticing that the gate was only leaning against the posts. He tugged at it and it fell upon him.
After the first terror had subsided he managed to crawl
out from under it and walked halfway home and was then
taken the rest of the way in a wagon. Linton was at first
disposed to think this accident a mere hiatus; but the
hiatus lasted the rest of Stephens' life. He was never again
able to walk without assistance.[23]

The rest of the year was spent in bed, with occasional
hobbling about on crutches, finishing the second volume
of the book. He was hardly ever left alone: old friends came
in crowds to spend days with him—Richard M. Johnston
down from Baltimore, where he was running a rather un-
orthodox private school; Toombs and Brown; his friend
of Confederate days, Thomas Semmes. And young Hidell
and old O'Neal were always there for talk or whist. After a
few weeks he could sit up for four or five hours a day, in a
chair or on the edge of his bed; but his left hip was badly
injured, and in spite of sulphur baths, steam baths, and
various kinds of manipulations that he tried at one time
or another, he was unable to get further than crutches and
a roller-chair. Added to his already intolerable load of
suffering—bladder stones, rheumatism, poor digestion,
migraine, intense susceptibility to changes in temperature,
neuralgia, and all the rest—it was the crowning touch that
logically should have killed him. But he seemed to be un-
killable.[24]

[23] Ibid., February 18, 1869; *Richardson, 304*, has a little Negro boy with
him when the accident occurred, but his own story told two days after
the event makes no mention of any companion. A little Negro boy, of
course, makes any Southern story more romantic.
[24] His letters to Linton and Hidell during this period are full of ref-
erences to his illness.

Hidell, his quondam secretary, was working with him on the book, and in December went to Philadelphia to supervise the setting up in type, sending back to Stephens the proofs as they were pulled, for the latter's corrections. Having little else to do, his revision became fanatically precise. The second volume was published in May 1870, and at once showed that people were wearying of constitutional disputation by dropping in sales far below those of the first volume. Stephens, undaunted, was already gathering material for a *School History of the United States,* for a South Carolina publisher—his aim being "to keep our children from further imposition as well as dependence upon Northern primary books." [25] At the same time gas lights were being installed at Liberty Hall. Time was marching on.

The first volume of the book, bought, as Jones suggested, by many because they thought it would have stories of battles in it, sold extremely well for a thing of its kind.[26] The war was only three years distant; Stephens had been prominent. The book had a name and a past to recommend it. But what it dealt with was not popular. The book was essentially a defense of Stephens' doctrine of state rights and of the abstract validity of the right of secession. The first volume provided an exposition of the basic position; the second, more narrative in character, was a review of national politics before the war and a personal justification of Stephens' course during it. In an effort to enliven the

25 *LC,* M. J. Kenan to A.H.S., October 10, 1870.
26 By November 1, 1870, 87,572 copies of the book had been sold, 67,193 of the first volume alone. The public had discovered by the time the second volume appeared that the battles the book contained were exhibitions of intellectual shadow-boxing, and the attendance thenceforward declined. At twenty-five cents a copy in royalties, Stephens made almost $22,000 out of the venture, even so. But he could not understand why sales dropped off after 1870, and at times suspected J. B. Jones, the publisher, of indifference, if not outright dishonesty. Their correspondence (in *LC*) grew somewhat strenuous toward the end.

subject-matter, he cast the book in dialogue form, the dialogue taking place at Liberty Hall between himself and a set of straw men whom he systematically knocked down. Only when it is seen—as Stephens himself must unconsciously have seen it—as his *chanson de geste,* does the book attain proper meaning. His battles, with rare exceptions, were intellectual, verbal, forensic, not physical; they were his substitutes for physical power; and so his book might be expected to be a song in celebration of the articles of faith for which he fought, and a personal epic of the fight itself. This book is the framework of a private myth.

In any other view, it is an intolerably dull book, and rightly so. Linton made some critical remarks about the introduction, whereupon Stephens, who always listened to Linton, made a *volte-face* from his former enthusiasm and said: "I became disgusted with . . . the whole work. . . . Writing is not my forte." [27] Except for his prison diary, he was correct; but at the moment there seemed nothing else remaining for him to do, and therefore he went on writing at odd intervals during the rest of his life.

As a defense of a position the book is minutely reasoned and perhaps logically foolproof; but as with all personal epics, it fictionalizes history. Stephens could never learn that it made no difference whether or not the Constitution of 1787 was a compact between the representatives of the sovereign people of thirteen states, and America at that time was "a Conventional nation not a national nation." He could not understand that the United States in 1860 or 1870 was, whether anybody liked it or not, becoming a national nation by reason of the operation of centripetal forces before which a sheet of paper, however sacred, was simply a sheet of paper trying to stop a flood. He could not comprehend that while the people of each state might theoretically be the ultimate sovereigns, the power of

27 *MC,* February 13, 1868.

geography and industrialization was rendering their sovereignty, as one reviewer of the first volume put it, obsolete—and irretrievable. He was outraged at the word "obsolete": "What," he demanded, "is to become of the country when the sentinels upon the watch towers of constitutional rights . . . give up the question as obsolete?" [28] He was not blind: he saw the tendency; but he thought he could defeat it, and passionately wished to. "We are tending to centralization," he told the New York *Herald* reporter in 1868. In fighting to preserve the happiness of the individual from being destroyed by a massive, impersonal power that cared nothing for individuals, he was absolutely right, as we, fighting the same fight, well understand. His error lay in supposing that the impersonal power could be successfully combated by an invocation of a set of political assumptions that, by this time, had lost all basis in fact. The railroad and the telegraph, both which he championed in their infancy, were forcing changes in political structure, changes that lay more and more in the direction of integration and centralization than in that of localism; and the solution lay rather in the controlling of the centralized machinery of government than in its reversion to the shape of 1787.

It was not surprising that the book met with some caustic reviews, quibbles on constitutional points; nor that Stephens promptly replied to the critics and gathered his replies and their reviews into a volume published in 1872, called *The Reviewers Reviewed.* There were some sympathetic notices, such as those in the *Nation* and the London *Saturday Review.*[29] And the book had its praiseworthy aspects. It was calm and dignified in tone, and had none of the ill temper and peevishness that marred Jefferson Davis'

28 *PHS*, A.H.S. to Hidell, June 9, 15, 1868.
29 *Nation*, VIII, 399–400; *Saturday Review* (London), XXVII (1869), 395–6.

Rise and Fall of the Confederacy. If it was doctrinaire, it
was not written out of spleen.

V

The admiration for Grant that Stephens had conceived at
the Hampton Roads conference persisted long afterward,
and very likely contributed something to his political extinction. When, in 1868, Grant was elected President over
Horatio Seymour, even though Stephens was a Democrat and a Georgian and had supported Seymour, he was
not much disappointed; and though Grant's political in-
eptitude became quickly public gossip he still called him
a "wonderful man." He probably dissociated Grant from
the Republican party; for by the end of 1870 the acts of
that party had struck him rather nearly. In 1869 and early
1870 the Ku-Klux Klan and its imitators attained their
highest peak of activity in the South. Terrorism, violence,
sometimes even murder, aimed at the intimidation of
Negro voters, were practiced in large areas of the deep
South. Congress, in 1870, to stamp out these societies,
passed a law committing the whole problem to the Federal courts, empowering Federal marshals to enforce the
Fourteenth and Fifteenth Amendments. Ku-Kluxism was
made a felony. Conservative Southerners were violently
opposed to the hoodlum method of getting Negro votes
because they knew they themselves would be made to feel
the retaliation that was sure to come; and Stephens argued
that the best thing the Southern people could do was "to
obey the laws as expounded by those who have power to
enforce them," [30] a position not far from what Brown's
had been in 1866.

In December 1870 the election for half the state legislature took place. On election day Linton, in Sparta,

[30] *MC,* November 7, 1868; March 13, 1869; *PHS,* A.H.S. to Hidell, January 26, 1869.

charged that a number of Negroes who had not paid their previous year's poll tax, as ordered by the Constitution, were being nevertheless permitted to vote; and when the election managers opposed his contention he had them arrested and jailed. The incident created a considerable stir; and in January, at Bullock's instance, a Federal marshal arrested Linton on charges of having violated the Enforcement Act by "intimidating" and "hindering" the process of election, and ordered him to appear at Macon on January 23 to answer the charges before a Federal commissioner. This Linton did, delivering a long and closely argued speech in his defense, in the preparation of which Alexander gave him a good deal of advice, contending that the Fourteenth and Fifteenth Amendments were legal nullities because ten states were unrepresented in the Congress that passed them, and had ratified them only under pressure; and that even if the amendments were legally binding, the Enforcement Acts were nullities, because the Fifteenth Amendment enjoined the states from denying the right of suffrage to any individual on three grounds only: race, color, or previous condition of servitude; and omitted hundreds of other grounds upon which it could legally be denied; and that furthermore the Fifteenth Amendment operated only upon states and not on individuals. These latter arguments were legalistic quibbles concocted for a purpose; the first was the most telling. The charge against Linton was taken to the Savannah District Court, where it was finally quashed, having come to no serious issue, though both brothers were profoundly concerned over it and regarded Linton as a martyr on the altar of "liberty and constitutional government." [31]

While this incident was taking place, another came to plague Stephens. The mismanagement of the Western &

[31] *MC*, Mary Stephens to A.H.S., December 21, 1870. Linton's speech is in Waddell: *Linton Stephens*, 331–46.

Atlantic Railroad by the Bullock crowd had grown so flagrant by the summer of 1870 that in October a bill providing for its lease to a private company passed both houses of the legislature by good majorities. Soon after the bill became law it was rumored that Joseph E. Brown, always on the right side of everything, was organizing a company to bid for the lease. Working with him was one H. I. Kimball, a very good friend of Bullock's, an amiable gentleman who had swindled the state in various ways. Under the terms of the bill the leasing of the road was left to the Governor, for the Democrats who forced it through knew they could not do so without giving the Bullock ring at least one plum.

Stephens was still on good terms with Brown, perhaps because he disliked Hill, who had been leading the only opposition to Brown worth mentioning; and early in December, hearing of the proposed lease, he wrote asking Brown whether he might be admitted into his company. Brown, with the same thought, wrote to him a day later; [32] and when, on December 27, the list of members of Brown's company was published, together with the news that it had been awarded the lease over the bid of a rival company headed by A. K. Seago and Foster Blodgett, Bullock's erstwhile friend, but now a little alienated, Stephens' name was down for half a share alongside those of Brown, Kimball, surprisingly, Hill, and still more surprisingly, John S. Delano, son of the Secretary of the Interior, Simon Cameron, Senator from Pennsylvania, and Thomas A. Scott, president of the Pennsylvania railroad. These last-named men were brought into the company at the penultimate moment. A group of Macon railroad men, seeing that J. P. King, president of the Georgia Railroad, was in Brown's company, and fearing future collusions in arrang-

---

32 *MC*, A.H.S. to J. E. Brown, December 10, 1870; *LC*, J. E. Brown to A.H.S., December 11, 1870.

ing the disposition of traffic, made up a company of their own to try to get a half interest in Brown's company. Brown refusing to dicker, they reached out and pulled into their group three men high in government circles, thereby scaring Brown, Kimball and Co. enough to win themselves the half interest they wanted.[33]

The announcement of the lease provoked instant criticism. Hill's connection with it was made a target; for Hill, who had so bitterly opposed any co-operation with the reconstructionists, had just publicly announced that the time for resistance had ceased and that unopposable power must only be acquiesced in. This somersault, followed by Hill's joining in an economic venture with the very men he had been denouncing, caused many to think that a bargain had been consummated. Toombs thought so, and anxiously asked Stephens what the extent of his involvement with the lease actually was. Stephens, a little surprised to find himself connected with a transaction so controversial, publicly announced his surprise in the Augusta *Constitutionalist* on January 5, 1871. To Linton, who shared Toombs' doubts, he defended what he had done as "voluntary upright honest & honourable." Three days later he completely changed his mind, and in another letter to the *Constitutionalist* withdrew his name from the company and turned his share over to the state. He had just heard from Seago that the Seago-Blodgett company had bid ten thousand dollars more per month for the road than Brown's had, and was convinced that Bullock's refusal to grant the road to the highest bidder was pure fraud. The fact, as Brown himself was quick to point out, was that the Seago-Blodgett company had tendered the Governor security they had no right to give, and he had no alternative but to award the lease to Brown.

Stephens' withdrawal merely added to the odious con-

[33] Thompson; *Reconstruction*, 247–50.

structions that were being put on the whole affair; and there were some who thought he was trying to wash his hands before it could be discovered that they had been dirty. Others, however, guessed he had been included in the lease as a blind, to "disarm suspicion." The truth probably was that he had, at the distance of Liberty Hall, his judgment perhaps a trifle clouded by his physical sufferings, thought Brown's venture a good one, and had gladly accepted the latter's invitation into the company. He trusted Brown, feeling that despite many "great errors" in his character there were "excellencies" that overshadowed them. He did not know who his partners were to be, nor what the terms; and when Seago, who doubtless wanted revenge, told him that he had offered a higher bid than Brown, not mentioning the matter of invalid security, this fact, coupled with Toombs' and Linton's warnings, served to impel his decision to get out of the thing as quickly as he could. It was the first irregular financial adventure he had ever become involved in; and his morality in financial matters was extremely strict. He was naturally impulsive, and made decisions often hastily. Had he tarried to learn the facts he might not have been so rash.[34]

"How I do want the control of a paper," he was wishing about this time. The campaign of 1872 was in the offing, and the chance existed that a Democratic President might be elected. After coquetting awhile, through his old friend J. Henly Smith, with the Atlanta *Intelligencer*, he received an offer from J. M. Speight, proprietor of the Atlanta *Sun*, of a half interest in that paper. The partnership was formed on May 17 and announced on June 15.

34 *J&B*, 501; *MC*, January 3, 1871; J. E. Brown in Atlanta *Constitution*, January 11, 1871; Columbus *Enquirer*, January 15, 1871; *LC*, A. K. Seago to A.H.S., January 9, 1871. Pearce: *Hill*, 224–30, and Thompson: *Reconstruction*, 250–4, weigh the evidence and summarize the affair.

His first editorial appeared on June 27.[35] He called himself the "political editor," and at once began filling the columns of the paper with a fantastic volume of polemic. Smith acted as business manager and general factotum, carrying a considerable burden, since Stephens almost never went to Atlanta, but stayed at home with his friends and his dogs, criticizing Smith from there. The *Sun* became a losing venture from the start, and even though Stephens bought Speight out completely in December 1871 and worked Smith nearly frantic all through 1872, it became increasingly evident during 1872 and 1873 that the paper could not be kept going in competition with such shrewdly managed journals as the *Herald,* then being co-edited by Henry Grady, and the *Constitution.* Even the *Herald* at this time was losing money, and it was far from being as stodgy and constitutionally minded a paper as the *Sun.* The relationship between Stephens and Smith was a source of constant irritation to both. Stephens was interminably fussy, for the paper was his hobby; Smith was a neurotic to begin with, and toward the end became almost hysterical, for the paper was his bread and butter. Each man kept accusing the other of misunderstanding him, until Smith, who could not endure it any longer, resigned at the end of 1872. Then it was only a question of time. The *Sun* was merged with the *Constitution* in June 1873; and while it had been in his hands Stephens had managed, through its pages, to keep himself from being elected to the Senate.[36] The paper had lost money; there were a good many people in Atlanta who held Stephens' promissory notes; and Toombs, when he heard that his

35 *LC,* J. H. Smith to A.H.S., March 31, 1871; *MC,* May 6, 1871.
36 In *LC* are scores of scribbled notes from Smith to A.H.S., attesting to the former's desperation and the latter's relentless prussianism. A psychoanalyst might advance some suggestive reasons for Stephens' perpetual obsession with clean copy.

friend was going to have a hard time to pay them off, went the rounds, bought up every note, and with a flourish dumped them into Stephens' lap.[37]

Grant as a President had shown himself a failure. His good qualities and weak had been systematically exploited by a clique of venal, power-grasping men such as America had not seen before. The Republican party was rotting at the top. Most of the great scandals of the Administration had not yet been exposed, but the pot, in 1871, was bubbling well, and on the point of boiling over. Certain Republicans, chief among them the Governor of Missouri, B. Gratz Brown, Carl Schurz, and Lyman Trumbull of Illinois, had revolted as early as 1870, styling themselves "Liberals," opposed to the misgovernment of the radical Republican ring. These men gathered other men about them, reformers and philanthropists and politicians, Horace Greeley, Theodore Tilton, Horace White, and others, all hoping to stop Grant from obtaining a second term. For this purpose it would be advantageous to co-operate with the Democrats.

The Democrats were also thinking of co-operation. They had been so badly beaten in 1868 on a platform of opposition to reconstructionism that the temptation to do a little straddling in 1872 was more than they could bear. A movement, called the "New Departure," to recognize the Thirteenth, Fourteenth, and Fifteenth Amendments as matters of fact and no longer open to debate came rapidly into favor with the Northern Democrats, and during 1871 its compromise, common-sensical qualities began to appeal to Southerners who were tired of waging war upon reality.

Stephens, notwithstanding that Clement Vallandigham, an old acquaintance and one of the leaders of the wartime Copperheads, was among the New Departure's sponsors,

[37] R. M. Johnston: *Autobiography,* 132–3.

immediately attacked the movement through the *Sun,* and was supported by H. V. Johnson, Toombs, and Linton, but by few others. For him there could be no compromise with Republicans despite his earlier remarks about obeying the laws. He would obey but go on protesting, and he did. He declared that he was above all a Democrat,[38] but declined to say that he would follow the majority of his party in the direction it appeared to be taking. His assaults upon the compromise movement brought him into controversy with the editors of several other newspapers, including the New York *World,* which on September 2 administered a stern rebuke, accusing him of an "inability to appreciate any other public opinion than that of his immediate neighborhood"—of being, in other words, a provincial, which he probably was.

As usual with him when he had taken a stand, he refused to budge. In January 1872 the leader of the Liberal Republicans issued a call for a national convention to meet in May. This convention duly met amid great enthusiasm, and promptly did the wrong thing: faced with Lyman Trumbull, Charles Francis Adams, Judge David Davis, and Horace Greeley as possible choices for the Presidency, it unhappily chose Greeley, who was of all the least eligible. The Democrats, who had postponed their convention until July to see what the Liberals would do, were somewhat embarrassed. Greeley the Democrat-hater, Greeley the abolitionist, Greeley the On-to-Richmond boy, was the Liberal candidate. To swallow him would be an intense humiliation, yet what else was there to do? To act independently would be to court defeat; and in any event Greeley would be preferable to another four years of Grant. Democrats North and South strained hard, but the pill went down. The young Georgia Democrats, Stephens learned, would take Greeley over Grant any day. He only

38 Atlanta *Sun,* August 30, 1871.

stiffened his stand, opposing both candidates, and advocating, in the event that the Democratic convention nominated Greeley, that the Georgia Democrats nominate their own man and sink with him. Linton, in a powerful speech in the state Capitol on June 13, attacked both men, saying: "I believe that everybody admits that Grant is a Centralist; and how anybody can doubt that Greeley is just as intense a one and more able, is a matter of amazement to me"—to which Hill replied the following night in a retort that even won Toombs' admiration, defending the coalition by saying that under it the Southern Democrats yielded merely the point that reconstruction was an accomplished thing, while gaining immeasurably from the added strength the Liberals would furnish.[39]

The Baltimore convention recognized the inevitable and nominated Greeley; but Stephens persisted in opposition, calling a choice between Grant and Greeley one between hemlock and strychnine.[40] Some of the stubborner Democrats at Baltimore had held together and called a convention to meet at Louisville on September 3. Stephens watched this movement carefully; and wrote the platform adopted by the Georgia delegation.[41] At Louisville, Charles O'Conor of New York and J. Q. Adams III were nominated. O'Conor declined, but the convention adjourned without withdrawing his name. Stephens, though warned he and his paper were "doing great damage to the State democratic party, and to Greeley—more than the Grant papers are—" [42] did not deviate an inch. He stuck by O'Conor and the "Straights," as they were called, being bitterly opposed by the majority of Democrats. Almost every other ex-Confederate had declared for Greeley:

39 *LC*, P. Thweatt to A.H.S., May 6, 1872; Atlanta *Sun*, June 14, 1872; Pearce: *Hill*, 247–51.

40 Atlanta *Sun*, August 20, 1872.

41 Ibid., August 21, 1872.

42 *LC*, P. Thweatt to A.H.S., August 18, 1872.

Hill, Brown, Wade Hampton, Braxton Bragg, Fitzhugh Lee. Stephens was quite alone, save for H. V. Johnson, who was out of politics, and Toombs, who, powerless and unrespected, was degenerating into a chronic alcoholic whose opinions nobody listened to. After a fantastic campaign Stephens' loneliness became even more profound when the results were known. Greeley carried the state with 75,896 votes; Grant came next with 62,485, carrying Stephens' home county; [43] and O'Conor trailed far behind with 3,999 votes. It was reminiscent of 1860. A few days after the election the *Sun* announced it had "never been deluded into the fallacy that there was a probability of Mr. Greeley's election," [44] thus excusing itself for what many had stigmatized as apostasy. It was fortunate that O'Conor's vote was so insignificant as it was.

Yet for some time before the election its outcome had been a matter of utter indifference to Stephens; his own future, political or otherwise, even more so. For some years, ever since 1868, Linton's health had been bad. His business was extensive, his family large; and the pressure of duties of one sort or another gradually began to tell upon him. An extremely conscientious and nervous man, he would not leave a thing half-done or delegate it to others when he could do it himself. Now in the spring of 1872 he was still further burdened, for he had been appointed by Governor Smith as counsel for the state in the investigations then going on of the frauds committed by the Bullock ring. He spent a great deal of time in Atlanta, rushing home every so often to attend to the things that had to be done there.[45] Alexander could not help him; for he himself was still suffering the aftereffects of his accident. So Linton went on doing what he could, driving himself, sick,

43 Statistics in Atlanta *Sun*, November 7, 1872.

44 Ibid., November 10, 1872. But it tried hard enough to beat him all the same.

45 Waddell: *Linton Stephens*, 366–8.

tired, depressed, haunted with thoughts of death. His morbid vein was as deep as his brother's, and it had not dried as Alexander's had done. He was all his life emotionally unstable, a manic-depressive who would weep on the slightest provocation, his moods rising and plunging with unpredictable rapidity. The speech against Greeley was his last great effort. Returning from Atlanta, he spent a few days at the Hall with his brother. Richard M. Johnston, Alexander's biographer, was there, and was struck, as he afterward remembered, by the harmony of thought and feeling that marked the relations of the two.[46] The three men talked, played euchre or whist on the back piazza, or went driving through town, or teased Stephens' various dogs, for whom his affection was always enormous, while the lazy summer sun rose and fell, rose and fell. On July 1 Johnston and Linton left for Sparta. A few days later Alexander had an attack of bladder stones which left him weak and a little depressed. He lay in bed in the front room of the house, reading newspapers and writing editorials for the *Sun,* or on crutches made his way about the grounds, a tall, gaunt, white-haired figure, glimpsed by passengers in railroad cars, or children going by along the road, awkwardly swinging himself across the shaded lawn, his servant Harry gravely walking with him, or perhaps in his roller-chair sat on the front piazza and soaked up the warm noon light. Forty miles away, in Sparta, Linton too lay in bed from the 5th to the 14th of July, when he died. The cause was given as a congestion of the bowels and lungs.[47]

The news was carried to Crawfordville; and time, for a moment, jolted and held still. Stephens, when he was told, reacted as he would have done to a blade thrust into his

46 *J&B,* 511–12.
47 Atlanta *Sun,* July 16, 1872.

body. He cried out aloud, and then was silent. It was all over; and so much was over. *Dove sono i bei momenti di dolcezza e di piacer.* . . . Where was it gone, the past? This was the thing for which he had steeled himself his whole life long: and yet how could one hope to render oneself proof against the loss of half one's self? He had seen so many die whom he had loved: his father, his step-mother, two brothers, and a sister; and yet they were not Linton, and what they had meant to him was not what Linton had meant. "In Linton," Johnston wrote to a friend, "was his brother and his son. . . . I never knew one man to love another as he loved Linton." [48] In Linton, too, was his wife: the tenderness and passion he showed for Linton was that he had never been able to bestow on any woman. Linton had known everything he knew; he had known whatever Linton knew. Nothing was secret be-tween them: they saw no shadows in each other. And now it was all ended. Something unspeakably priceless was finished; and its passing, like the passing of all beautiful things, hurt savagely. "Why am I permitted to live?" he wanted to know; and it would have done no good to tell him it was for the same reason Linton had been permit-ted to die.

For days before and after Linton's funeral he lived in dreams, thinking of the past, of the first time he had seen Linton, of Linton at Cambridge, or in the legislature, or opening a law office, or Linton married, or in the door-way of his cell at Fort Warren, or Linton two weeks ago, saying good-by. Linton's widow, Mary, came to see him soon after the funeral: he could only speak his brother's name again and again. Friends and relatives came to offer their grief to assuage his own: but it was useless. Tributes to Linton were numerous and heartfelt. The state Demo-

48 Ibid., August 3, 1872.

cratic convention adopted resolutions of condolence; the citizens of Hancock County, Linton's own, did likewise.[49] But what was sympathy? For Stephens the best part of his life was gone; and he was sixty. With luck he might survive a few more years. How different they would have to be, and how empty compared with those that now were gone!

[49] Ibid., July 25, 28, 1872.

CHAPTER SIX

Age (1873-83)

"NOTHING heals the wounds of the heart so promptly . . . as useful activity," wrote Herschel Johnson: [1] and by the fall of the year there was activity enough to engross Stephens' mind. He had rallied in time to continue his "straightism" through the election; before the month was out he had begun to count his chances for the senatorship that would fall vacant when Joshua Hill's term was out. The race for this office showed early signs of becoming quite hot. Benjamin Hill, despite his practical political isolation, was a hopeful; so was John B. Gordon, one of Brown's closest friends; and so, at the end of November, was Stephens. When his candidacy was announced, there were varied reactions, some of admiration, some of disapproval. His health was generally thought to be too precarious to admit of his holding high office.[2] As if to disprove this rumor, he appeared in Atlanta in December, where, on the 20th, he delivered a speech defending his course in respect of the late election, indignantly denying the charge of being a Bourbon,[3] an epithet just then gaining currency. It generally meant those ex-Confederates who, like Stephens, refused to accept the New Departure, and might therefore be classed as irreconcilables. It became perverted during the following decade to apply to

[1] *LC*, Johnson to A.H.S., July 24, 1872.
[2] Covington *Enterprise* in Atlanta *Sun*, December 3, 1872.
[3] Atlanta *Sun*, December 22, 1872.

a small ring of politicians, notably Gordon, Alfred H. Colquitt, and Brown, who were supposed to be running the state for their personal benefit.

The election was scheduled for January 22, 1873, but before that date Hill, Stephens, and Gordon all arrived in Atlanta, and each addressed the legislature, Stephens speaking on the 18th. He talked for two and a half hours, mainly in vindication of his Confederate record, which was beginning to haunt him, and again upholding his position on the Presidential election. Excitement ran extraordinarily high, even for Georgia, during these days: pools were sold on the outcome of the balloting; and Stephens' friends were claiming 57 votes for him on the first ballot.[4]

Their predictions were good. On the first ballot Gordon had 93, Stephens 56, and Hill 31; after which the legislature adjourned to the 22nd, while the managers of each candidate scratched backs and pulled wires all night long. The effect displayed itself next day, when on the second ballot Gordon dropped to 87 and Stephens climbed to 71. Hope for victory was not unwarranted. But the Hill men, realizing their candidate could not win, and wishing, probably because of the old unpatched feud, to beat Stephens at all costs, began swinging to Gordon; and after a two-ballot deadlock Gordon, amid great confusion, captured the seat by 112 to Stephens' 86.[5]

"The pressure for Mr. Stephens was tremendous," commented the *Herald,* which had supported Gordon. "His vote," said the *Constitution,* "was simply wonderful, and could have been evoked by no other public man under the same circumstances." His defeat was widely ascribed to his course during the Presidential campaign. He had

---

[4] Augusta *Constitutionalist,* January 22, 1873; Augusta *Chronicle and Sentinel,* January 21, 1873; Savannah *Daily Advertiser,* January 23, 1873.
[5] *Avery,* 506; Augusta *Chronicle,* January 23, 1873.

disobeyed the party; and the party was in the hands of the Smith-Gordon group. But the vote he did receive showed that he still had a following that respected him; and it showed too that it might not be wise for the party hierarchy to let him drop back into political obscurity. A meeting, at which Toombs presided, was called at the Kimball House that same evening; and a large group of legislators and private citizens requested him to run for the House of Representatives in his own district, the 8th. The three candidates already in the field immediately withdrew, and he was offered a practically unanimous election, which he at once accepted, being elected on February 26.[6]

It was a sop; and at times one wonders whether he recognized it as such through the pleasant haze of his love of the House. That he was happy there is beyond doubt; but that he was ever satisfied with the job is less certain. Taliaferro County had been kept in the 8th district at his own request when a reapportionment was made in 1871 —and he may even then have had a notion of returning sooner or later to Washington. At any rate, here he was. The "little irrepressible human steam engine, with a big brain and scarcely any body," had returned.[7]

He was there, in his roller-chair, in the open space just under the Speaker's desk, until November 1882, the strangest figure in the Capitol since John Randolph. A description of him that is almost classic survives. "A little way up the aisle," wrote a newspaper correspondent in 1876, "sits a queer-looking bundle. An immense cloak, a high hat, and peering somewhere out of the middle a thin, pale, sad little face. This brain and eyes enrolled in countless thicknesses of flannel and broadcloth wrappings belong to Hon. Alexander H. Stephens, of Georgia. How anything so small and sick and sorrowful could get here all the way

6 Atlanta *Constitution*, January 23, 1873.
7 *Avery*, 499–500; Pendleton: *Alexander H. Stephens*, 386.

from Georgia is a wonder. If he were to draw his last breath at any instant you would not be surprised. If he were laid out in his coffin he need not look any different, only then the fires would have gone out in those burning eyes. . . ." [8] By any criterion of ordinary physiology he should not have been there at all. He was sick; he was tired; he was old. And because of this, and because he came from the South, his last nine years in the House were largely ineffectual.

These nine years were not for him. There were new powers at work and they had no patience with constitutionalism. Theirs was an economic politics. These were the years of the Grangers and Greenbackers, of Tweed and the Whisky Ring, of the Star Route Frauds, of the strikes of 1877, years of the rise of modern industry, years of the conquest of America by the powers that controlled coal, steel, and oil, years of the growth of cities and the creation of an industrial class, years of enormous immigration. And in all this there was little room for a man left over from an earlier age, an age so distant it seemed almost geological, an age with other ends and other means, other problems and other values. Such a man, tolerated, perhaps even admired, was regarded as vestigial. There was nothing for him to do. He might understand what was taking place, but if he was, as Stephens was, against it, he was deliberately out of the main stream, and therefore relatively powerless. The lever of his influence glanced off wherever he tried to set it down.

And so the last nine years saw little happen. At first he spoke rather often, and in his first session made two long speeches, one on December 11, 1873, in defense of what was known as the "salary grab," a law passed at the previous session, increasing the salaries of Congressmen and making these increases retroactive, so that each man had

---

[8] Quoted by Pendleton, op. cit., 386–7.

taken home with him upon adjournment a bonus of five thousand dollars. The outcry was so vehement that when Stephens arrived, a bill to repeal the increases was already introduced. He could see nothing wrong with what had been done, and told them so. He thought the pay of what he termed the "brains" of the government—including the President, Executive heads, and Supreme Court—was ridiculously low, and put himself on record as favoring a salary of one hundred thousand dollars for the President and fifty thousand dollars for the Chief Justice. Since he had not got a penny of the bonus, his action might be interpreted as extremely high-minded, which it probably was; but he at once heard from Georgia that his position was frowned upon. A few, however, as high-minded as himself, approved, among them L. Q. C. Lamar, whose affection for Stephens was always great and tender.[9]

His other speech that session, delivered on January 5, 1874, had to do with the so-called "Supplementary Civil Rights Bill," a pet measure of the late Charles Sumner, designed to ensure the Negro equal treatment in inns, theaters, and public conveyances. Stephens wrote his speech out, which he rarely did, except on occasions of great importance. He violently opposed the bill, growing at one time so passionate that he had to apologize: "Excuse me, sir; please pardon something to an ardent nature." He admitted that "the chief end of all government . . . should be the protection of rights"; but denied utterly that Congress had the power to go over the heads of the states and set up a code of municipal legislation designed to act directly on the citizens of those states. He cited the recent decision of the Supreme Court in the Slaughterhouse cases, which held that the "privileges and immunities" clause in the Fourteenth Amendment re-

9 Speech in *Congressional Record*, II, 152–4. *MC*, L. Q. C. Lamar to A.H.S., December 18, 1873.

ferred only to the privileges and immunities of citizens of
the United States *as such,* and did not bring the protection
of civil rights from the state governments to the Federal
government. Besides this, he argued, it would be inex-
pedient to thrust any such law upon the people of the
South. Let the whole problem be left to the states, to be
settled according to the dictates of necessity and common
sense; otherwise all those passions awakened by the war,
which had just begun to subside, would once more be
aroused, with what results no one could prophesy.[10]

After this he made but one extensive speech, and that
in 1878. Most of his time in the House was spent in routine business, presenting petitions and introducing relief bills, and attending to what patronage he could get.
He had scarcely the strength to do more. He was given no
committee appointment of consequence, being on the
Coinage Committee for some time, and reporting from
there several bills aiming at the conversion of the gold coinage to a metric standard, none of which received even passing consideration.[11] His solitary speech, delivered from a
roller-chair on February 12, 1878, was in a way a considerable tribute—it might almost be called a tribute to his
memory rather than his presence. He was requested by the
painter F. B. Carpenter and by the two houses to make
some remarks upon the occasion of the presentation to Congress of Carpenter's painting of the signing of the Emancipation Proclamation. James A. Garfield spoke first; Stephens followed. His praise of Lincoln was that of an old
friend: "He was warm-hearted; he was generous; he was
magnanimous. . . . Every fountain of his heart was ever
overflowing with the 'milk of human kindness.' " But he

10 Speech in *Congressional Record,* II, 378–82.
11 45th Cong., 1st sess., H. R. 4190; 46th Cong., 1st sess., H. R. 410 and
411.

spoke extemporaneously, and the speech gradually disintegrated into a rambling lecture whose burden was that
slavery had not been an unmitigated evil, but had had
much of good about it. It was the speech of a sick old man,
and excited derision in some ex-Confederates, not for its in-
coherence but for its having been delivered at all. But in
the North it was well received as "an old man's heart-ut-
terance," with "the almost sacred quality of a confession";
and Stephens was assured that he "stands higher in the
estimation of his Northern brethren than ever before." [12]
Yet a few months later these same Northern brethren,
aided by some Southern, prevented him from speaking
in the House for ten minutes against the proposal of
Clarkson N. Potter, a New York Democrat, to appoint a
committee once again to delve into the disputed Hayes-
Tilden election of 1876. At the time of that election Stephens, though convinced of the fraudulent character of the
returns from Florida and Louisiana, had urged on the
excited Southern Democrats moderation and good sense;
and when the Electoral Commission had decided in favor
of Hayes, he immediately acquiesced in the decision. In
February 1878 he published an article in the *International
Review,* defending the Constitutional arrangement for
election of the President. For him the question was closed;
and when Potter, doubtless for political purposes, tried
to reopen it, he could see no sense in such a course. On
May 16, 1878 he asked for ten minutes to give his views,
but Potter forced an adjournment. When Potter's resolution was passed, Stephens was absent from the House;
but he announced next day that had he been there he
would have voted against it. It was an unpopular course

---

[12] Speech in *Congressional Record,* VII, 971–2; New York *Express* in
Augusta *Chronicle and Constitutionalist,* February 16, 1878. Jubal Early
was highly disgusted with the speech.

to take, being easily subject to misunderstanding; but his reputation remained unshaken, and he was again returned to Congress.[13]

His personal popularity never flagged; and his rooms at the National Hotel, where he always stayed when in Washington, were continually crowded with visitors. Every Sunday he dined eight or ten people. With numerous men of prominence in governmental circles his relations were cordial and sometimes politically useful; through Hamilton Fish, the Secretary of State under Grant (with whom Stephens never ceased to be friendly), he obtained minor posts for some constituents; and for a time he was cultivated by Secretary of the Interior Delano and Thomas A. Scott;[14] but his lack of power at home apparently soon caused them to drop him as unprofitable.

II

These were years of more suffering than he had ever known, and yet somehow he managed to keep himself cheerful and resigned. His sensitivity to changes in temperature became so acute that he had to have a special car always at his command when he traveled by rail.[15] From December 1873 on, there were months at a time when he was unable to leave his rooms and go to the Capitol. All through 1874 he was ill with neuralgia, surrounded by "a platoon of doctors"; and in the summer, despairing of recovery, he tried to decline to run again for Congress, but was nominated in spite of himself.[16] 1875 was little better: he was constantly troubled with stones in the bladder,

---

[13] *Congressional Record*, VII, 3502, 3530. *LC*, R. C. Humber to A.H.S., June 12, 1878. A.H.S.'s article in *International Review*, V, 102–13.

[14] *LC*, J. S. Mosby to A.H.S., December 5, 1873; H. Fish to A.H.S., February 28, 1874; Delano to A.H.S., March 16, 1874; T. A. Scott to A.H.S., December 5, 9, 1874.

[15] Thomas E. Watson: *Sketches: Historical, Literary, Biographical, Economic, etc.* (Thomson, Ga., 1916), 11.

[16] *LC*, I. S. Fannin to A.H.S., August 3, 1874.

against which vegetable tonics, cold-water syringes, and mineral waters seemed to do little. In 1876, as the result of an exposure that to a normal man would have meant nothing, he had an attack of pneumonia from which few of his friends supposed he would recover. Nine months of the year were taken up with the fight for life; and in some miraculous fashion he survived, though there were some premature reports of his death. All through this year he lived on muriate of ammonia, morphine, bromides, tincture of gentian, quinine, yellow jessamine, and cinchonidia; for it was impossible for him to sleep without being drugged, and he suffered at times such pain that he screamed without knowing afterward that he had uttered a sound.[17] And from this time on, it became necessary for him to have drugs administered at rather frequent intervals—a practice, indeed, that had been intermittently followed ever since he was a young man.

It was not always so bad as in 1876, however; and when he was in fair condition he had a regular schedule of activity, rising at nine, being dressed by Harry, or, after Harry's death in 1881, by Alex Kent, having breakfast, then rolling himself out on the piazza to talk or play whist with the guests who were invariably there, resting from eleven to twelve, when he would have dinner, followed by more reading or conversation; after which there would be supper, dictation of correspondence, and bed at ten o'clock. Liberty Hall was remodeled in 1876, widened and redecorated. Stephens lived most of the time in his bedroom, which had been moved to the ground floor at the right of the entrance: a small rectangular room looking out over the downsloping front lawn, toward the railroad and town, fitted up with a great bed, a table in front of the bed, a lamp on the table, a medicine-closet crammed with tinctures and potions, bottles of every possible shape and size,

17 *LC,* letters from Dr. H. H. Steiner, his personal physician.

a green carpet, and a large engraved portrait of Toombs. Here he could lie and doze or read, hearing the rumble of trains across the bridge, or the songs of birds in the early morning, or the creak of wagon wheels upon the sandy road in front of the gate, or the cries of children on long summer afternoons, or the barking of his dogs, with Harry's voice commanding silence, or the clang of church bells in the evenings; and here, as he watched the sunlight stretch and creep along the walls, and listened to the grandfather clock in the next room strike off hour after hour, he could yield to memory, surrender to the past, and in his mind be talking with Clay or Webster or Calhoun, conferring with Douglas, or going to Montgomery, or defending liberty against Jeff Davis, or speaking for the Compromise —piecing together, hour by hour, out of his ambition and his submerged sense of failure to achieve the fullest measure of ambition, a great and private epic history of America, and somewhere near its center himself as hero, wrestling with hydra-headed Tyranny; himself, often beaten, never vanquished; an antique Roman, a Spartacus, a St. George whose armor was the Constitution. And here, weaving this web of wishes, constructing this unconsciously distorted monument which to him was unchallengeable truth, he was happy.

Life was rather pleasant after all; and then there were so many people with him from day to day—the advantage of having a house so near the railroad—that even when, as in 1879, he was unable to move because of agonizing attacks of neuralgia, he was not lonely or unamused. In the course of the last thirty-odd years he had attracted a large clustering of friends of the not distinguished, nonpublic sort, men and women who cut no prominent figures, but for various reasons were congenial. They were as strange as he. Most of them lived at some distance from Crawfordville, and his relations with them consisted largely in letter-writing. There was Henry Cleveland, his one-time biographer, a local product, who was soon to come inexplicably to hate him; there was Samuel J. Anderson, whom he had known back in 1849, a Georgian who had emigrated to New York, atheist and bohemian, dabbling in literature and politics, drifting, after the war, from one job to another, growing steadily poorer, until on Christmas Eve of 1874 he put a pistol to his head and committed suicide, having failed once before to kill himself with poison; there was Andrew H. H. Dawson, an Alabama lawyer whose acquaintance with Stephens began about 1851, and who also traveled to New York, a pious and effusive man whose love for Stephens was unequivocally that of a dog for its master; there were scores of others, ghostly shadows lost in time, glowing feebly when impinged upon by the finger of Stephens' friendship: Peterson Thweatt, the fat little ex-Comptroller-General of the state, garrulous and comic; a physician named C. P. Culver; a very dusty politician named Dudley M. DuBose, who served one term in Congress and lapsed back into anonymity. . . . And there was James R. Randall, who had come closer than anyone save Mrs. Howe to being the Rouget Delisle of the Civil War, author of "Maryland, My Maryland"—now prosaically editing the Augusta *Constitutionalist;* and there was Paul Hamilton Hayne, who had been rejected for military service on account of his ill health, quietly living at Groveton near Augusta, and discovering that in some mysterious way he was coming to venerate the strange old man at Crawfordville; and there was Herschel Johnson, in retirement at Sandy Grove, grown pessimistic and profoundly pious in his age. . . . There were also women, like Sarah A. Lawton of Savannah, who felt themselves morbidly drawn to him because of the fascination of his helplessness, and wrote, like her: "I have loved you many years," and hoped, with her, "that you love me." These were women who longed to mother him, to "minister" to his "slightest wish," to turn down his pillow or to bring him food.[18] Such hosts of hangers-on, disciples, friends, flattered his old age and kept time full.

But his power was diminishing, even at home; the fact was unmistakable, election statistics notwithstanding. Only in 1874 and 1876 was there a named candidate opposing him, and on both occasions his majorities were huge. In 1878 and 1880 his name was not contested.[19] Yet Tom Watson, then a young man, while frankly idolizing the old bundle of cloth and bones in the roller-chair, said of him after his death: "Those who only heard Mr. Stephens after the Civil War, could form no conception of what his power had been," and described a meeting at his own home town of Thomson (in the 8th district) in 1873, when Stephens had spoken during his first campaign. "The audience was small and not enthusiastic"; and the slender, pallid speaker had to cling to the pulpit rail—he spoke in a church— during most of his speech.[20] His talents were waning; and there were many who remembered his behavior in 1864 and 1865 and did not forgive. People listened to him, but they thought—and his appearance helped them think—of a man who had died in 1865. On the 4th of July 1875 he delivered an address in the car-shed at Atlanta, and was cheered time and again before he spoke; but few remembered what he said that hot, sultry day. One sentence had some ring of the old passion for justice in it: "No one, however high, has any rightful power to wrong another, however low . . ." [21] and he meant it, and had tried to live by it. His servants could testify to that.

His name remained, but that was almost all. Following the reclamation of Georgia from the reconstructionists, the

18 Correspondence from all these obscure friends is in *LC*.
19 Cf. *Tribune Almanac*, 1874, 1876, 1878, and 1880.
20 Watson: *Sketches*, 5–6.
21 Atlanta *Daily Herald*, July 7, 1875.

Democratic party had come into pretty secure political domination of the state. The Solid South was at hand. But where there is no opposition, there is faction. The Democrats had no sooner got rid of the Republican menace than they began to bark at one another; and their barking came about in this wise: The party leadership and with it the government of the state was at this time concentrated in a small ring of efficient, powerful, shrewd men, chief among whom were Joseph E. Brown, who had made the right friends as soon as he perceived that Bullock was becoming a trifle passé; Alfred Holt Colquitt, born in 1824, the son of the old antebellum Senator Walter T. Colquitt, a man who had taken little active part in politics before the war, had served in the Confederate army, was a licensed Methodist preacher, a temperance leader, and at one time president of a Sunday-school convention; and ex-General John B. Gordon, next to Longstreet Georgia's most popular living contribution to the Civil War, now United States Senator. These men were not agrarians; they were industrially and financially minded. Brown had become rich since the war, as a real-estate manipulator and as president of the Western & Atlantic Railroad and the Dade Coal Company. Colquitt and Gordon had tried to imitate Jay Gould on a smaller scale by organizing a twelve-and-a-half-million-dollar railroad syndicate with the object of running a line from Atlanta through Birmingham to the Mississippi. They were men who knew what they wanted; they were the dynasts of Georgia. On each of them at one time or another, whether fairly or unfairly, the taint of corruption alighted.

During the administration of James M. Smith, who had been re-elected Governor in 1872, a revolt against the domination of Democratic politics by this small group flared up in the piedmont counties. It was an agrarian revolt, springing from roots similar to, if not identical with, those that fed the contemporaneous Midwestern farmers' uprisings, the Farmers' Alliance, the Grangers, and later the Populists. As the Western movement was directed against the tyranny of Eastern capitalists, so the Georgia Independents rebelled against their own oligarchs. Their leader was William H. Felton, a physician-preacher-politician of inexhaustible energy blessed with a wife even more vigorous than himself. In 1874, when L. N. Trammell, a minor figure in the party machine, was nominated as the Congressional candidate from the 7th district, Felton, responding to the indignation of his fellow farmers, who had not wanted Trammell, named himself as an independent candidate and so fiercely denounced Trammell as a corrupt Bullock-Brown Democrat that the latter was withdrawn and another man substituted. No matter: for Felton won that year, and won twice again, in 1876 and 1878.[22]

Felton's insurgency was, even so, not serious for a time. When Governor Smith, in 1876, decided not to run again, Colquitt, whose popularity had been growing steadily, was nominated and swept into office by an enormous majority. The wave of good feeling that accompanied his election did not last long. One of the first things he did was to endorse $260,000 worth of bonds of the Northeastern Railroad, an act that, though perfectly proper and safe, was not very good psychology, for it awakened some ugly memories. The tumult attendant upon the endorsement was so persistent that Colquitt demanded and received an investigation of the entire matter by a legislative committee, the result being his complete vindication. But after that there was a field day for turning up the stones of government to look for bugs. From 1878 to 1880 Colquitt was made the target of incessant abuse; and his entire ad-

22 *Brown,* 298–9, 306–7; C. V. Woodward: *Tom Watson, Agrarian Rebel* (New York, 1938), 68–72; *Avery,* 513.

ministration, from the Comptroller-General to the keeper of the penitentiary, was busily investigated.[23]

In the face of such attacks it was almost certain that Colquitt would seek renomination in 1880. The year opened with an unfortunate mistake on his part when he appointed Brown to fill the unexpired term in the Senate of Gordon, who, though just then re-elected, had chosen to resign. Independents and Republicans shrieked in chorus: "Bargain! Bargain!" The charge was that Gordon had been offered the presidency of the Western & Atlantic by the Louisville & Nashville Railroad, Brown having agreed to leave the railroad for the Senate, while the Louisville & Nashville would become the owner of the Western & Atlantic. Brown actually did not resign and Gordon protested that he had been offered a position in Oregon; but no matter what the reasons, the transaction was an unlovely thing to look upon. Brown had been out of political office since 1865, and knew very well that he could not get himself in by popular vote; therefore this expedient was hit upon: Colquitt would have Brown's and Gordon's support in the coming election; Gordon would have a pleasant job.

The excitement raised by this maneuver persisted through the year. The Democratic convention of August was a weird and wild affair. A desperate struggle over the adoption of a majority or a two-thirds rule, the former favored by the Colquitt men, the latter by Colquitt's opponents, who hoped in the event of its adoption to defeat him, culminated in a victory for the anti-Colquitt faction. For a week they stuck together and kept him from getting the nomination over Thomas Hardeman and Rufus Lester, his nearest opponents; and when all compromise failed, he was merely recommended to the voters by the majority,

[23] *Brown*, 298–9; *Avery*, 550ff. Rebecca Felton: *My Memories of Georgia Politics* (Atlanta, 1911), indicts the "ring" with partisan vigor.

after which the convention broke up. The minority nominated Thomas Norwood, a former Senator; but when all was said and done, Colquitt's innocence and Brown's and Gordon's power were more than enough to swing the election. Colquitt won by a 54,345 majority, and Felton was defeated in his own district.

Now, in all this confusion Stephens maintained a peculiar position. He never lost touch with the regular Democratic organization, yet had at the same time formed a close friendship with Felton. In some obscure fashion the tall, graying doctor, who, according to his wife, sweated so profusely that when he was riding from town to town in his buggy, campaigning, he was obliged after every speech to change his underwear—somehow this man appealed to Stephens. The old man visited the Feltons at their home in Cartersville, and they returned the compliment. "I have been very lonely ever since you left," Stephens wrote to Mrs. Felton after one such visit. By 1881 they were exchanging Christmas gifts.[24] And Stephens had sympathies with the social philosophy of the Independents, saying once: "If ever there is another war in this republic, it will not be sectional, but social. . . . If ever the masses of the people can be made to understand our system of class-legislation, taxes and finance, there will be trenchant reform or frightful revolution." Yet in the main he remained loyal to the party hierarchy, though he silently opposed Colquitt's re-election in 1880, and in the same year clashed in Congress with Gordon over an item of patronage, as a result of which Gordon's influence was felt opposing his re-election to the House.[25]

His intermediate position made him suddenly enormously available. Colquitt was due to quit office in 1882,

24 R. M. Johnston to Mrs. Felton, August 16, 1877; A.H.S. to Mrs. Felton, December 24, 1877 and December 26, 1881, in Felton MSS., University of Georgia.

25 Felton: *Memories*, 286; Watson: *Sketches*, 292.

for the term of the governorship had been reduced to two years, and he would not run again; and by the winter of 1881 the leaders were beginning to consider Stephens, who had announced in 1879 that he would *not* be governor of Georgia. He and Brown were extremely good friends again, and spent much time in Washington driving out together.[26] At home Stephens was busy with six secretaries, revising his *School History* into a large general history of the United States; in Washington he went on playing the Elder Statesman, receiving callers, many of them women, in his rooms, or riding out.[27] Tom Watson, about this time quite familiar with him, wrote of him: "His scanty hair was snow-white; he never had a beard. In his pallid face were a thousand wrinkles, little and big. Here and there, on his cheeks, were livid, uncanny splotches. His teeth were broken and black. . . . His neck and head were large, and the chin strong. His eyes were beautiful . . . a very dark brown." In February 1882 he celebrated his seventieth birthday, and flowers came from all over the country; there were guests all day long; the President congratulated him; and a flood of letters poured in from those who knew him.[28]

As early as October 1881, it would seem, the Feltons were thinking of capturing him as the Independent nominee for the governorship.[29] But for some time whether he would do anything decisive or not was in doubt, even in his own mind. Shortly after his birthday in 1882 he wrote to Mrs. Felton: "My mind was made up some time ago never to take any active part in politics again"; and in March he publicly announced his decision not to run

[26] Mrs. John S. Spalding to the writer, June 7, 1945. Mrs. Spalding is Brown's granddaughter.

[27] Felton: *Memories*, 345; *Richardson*, 327.

[28] Watson: *Sketches*, 22; Augusta *Chronicle and Constitutionalist*, February 16, 1882.

[29] A.H.S. to Mrs. Felton, October 18, 1881, Felton MSS.

again for Congress.³⁰ When Hill, who was back in the
regular party, made a vitriolic attack on Felton at the
beginning of the year, charging him with combining with
the Arthur wing of the Republicans for the purpose of
controlling Federal patronage in Georgia, Stephens, asked
his opinion, said he thought the phrase "Africanize the
state," applied by Hill to Felton's intentions, was rather
harsh, but that he was more interested in his forthcoming
book.³¹

Nevertheless the movements in his favor gathered
strength. Regulars and Independents, the machine and the
opponents of the machine, were fighting for him as though
he were a bone. In mid-April Governor Colquitt wrote
saying he would like to see Stephens governor.³² This move
was criticized as another evidence of Bourbon arrogance,
but still Stephens held his tongue and said nothing either
way. After the beginning of May speculation grew rife,
with the calling of an Independent mass meeting in Atlanta
to assemble on June 1. It was suspected that Stephens was
waiting for that meeting to ask him to run before he would
commit himself, though he was warned he could not hope
to get the support of both Regulars and Independents, because the latter represented a coalition between certain
renegade Democrats and a disreputable wing of the Republicans. His silence prompted one paper to interpret
him as saying: "No public man has the right to decline to
run for Governor, unless he is in a very precarious state
of health, and I am pretty well, thank you." Pretty well by
his standards, which were not those of most men. On May

30 A.H.S. to Mrs. Felton, February 21, 1882, Felton MSS.; Atlanta *Con-stitution*, March 10, 1882.
31 A.H.S. to Mrs. Felton, January 10, 1882, Felton MSS. Some of these
letters are quoted in Felton: *Memories*, but Mrs. Felton's violent bigotry
led me to check the original sources. Surprisingly, she does not misquote.
32 Atlanta *Constitution*, April 22, 1882.

6 in Washington he told a newspaper correspondent he was not a candidate for the office.[33]

"I have no aspirations," he had informed Mrs. Felton, but he had suggested he would run if shown that the people would unmistakably desire it. This was too vague; and on May 12 she wrote back, requesting a simple yes or no to the question: Do you want Dr. Felton and his friends to recommend you for the office? In the meanwhile she was being assured by Henry P. Farrow, a Republican leader with whom she and her husband had contacts, that Stephens' interview of the 6th was not really discouraging and that "While some of us might prefer to . . . make him a Republican nominee, yet these things are not hoped for . . ." Farrow declared that he was supporting Stephens in the full knowledge of his being angled for by the Regular Democrats.[34]

Mrs. Felton's letter reached Washington on Sunday the 14th. On the 9th, while coming up the Capitol steps, Stephens had stumbled and sprained his ankle; and for the past few days had been in bed, under the effects of morphine. There was a visitor on Sunday, Emory Speer, Congressman from the 9th district, who, while more conservative than Felton, was nevertheless an Independent. Upon learning the contents of the letter Speer, on his own initiative, drew up, after conversation with Stephens, the text of a telegram, which he had the old man approve, and which he sent to Atlanta the next morning. It read: "To Hon. W. H. Felton, Atlanta, Ga. I hope the committee of Independent Democrats, who meet today, will recommend Mr. Stephens as the people's candidate for governor. I know positively that he will not reject such recommenda-

---

[33] Ibid., May 4, 1882; Augusta *Chronicle and Constitutionalist*, May 9, 1882; Albany (Ga.) *News,* quoted in ibid., May 2, 1882.

[34] A.H.S. to Mrs. Felton, May 7, 1882; Henry P. Farrow to Mrs. Felton, May 8, 1882, Felton MSS.; Felton: *Memories,* 362, 365.

tion and that if elected, that he will be governor of all the people, without regard to party. He will be controlled by no ring. EMORY SPEER." The Independent steering committee, meeting at the Markham House in Atlanta, upon receipt of this telegram issued an address placing Stephens in the field as their candidate, declaring him "practically in the field . . . by the spontaneous voice of the people of Georgia," and called off the convention that was to have met on June 1.[35]

The Regular convention was scheduled for late July; and speculation centered chiefly on the question whether, since Stephens was apparently committed to the Independents, the Regulars would nominate him too. But was he committed? It cannot be supposed that the Regular machine would let him slip so easily into the hands of the opposition. There was little doubt that the Regular nominee, whoever he might turn out to be, would capture the election. And Stephens, whose honesty had almost never been questioned, who had been out of all the unclean water that had run under the bridge since 1872, would make a perfect candidate. It may be that Brown got to work; for a week or so after the meeting in Atlanta Stephens issued a statement denying he had sent or authorized the sending of any telegram accepting the Independent nomination. Though Speer explained to the Feltons, perhaps trying to clear his own skirts, that the denial referred merely to a telegram *alleged* to have been sent by Stephens, and not to the actual telegram sent by himself, Speer, the Independents were furious. H. V. M. Miller, who had signed the address of May 15, decided it would be "impossible to defeat Mr. Stephens' election & unde-

[35] Felton: *Memories,* 366–7. Original of Speer's telegram in Felton MSS. A.H.S.' accident in Washington communicated to Mrs. Ann Mary Coleman, May 9, 1882, in J. J. Crittenden MSS., Duke University. Mrs. Coleman was Crittenden's daughter, and A.H.S. gave her some assistance in writing a life of her father that was published in 1873.

sirable to do so," implying that this course had already been discussed. Felton himself thought that Stephens, under the influence of hypodermics, had forgotten his pledge to Speer and been persuaded by Brown into an outright denial. Mrs. Felton was blunter: "He wants to be governor and has sold himself to the highest bidders." She never again wrote to Stephens, nor he to her.[36]

By the middle of June Stephens was denying he had ever had an understanding with the Independents; though his note to Felton of May 18: "I think you managed matters at Atlanta last Monday admirably," certainly conveys the impression that an understanding had existed.[37] And when the delegates to the July convention gathered in Atlanta on the 19th, the old man was there in his roller-chair to receive them,[38] having left Washington for the last time some weeks before. On the last day he and Richard M. Johnston had gone out for a last carriage drive around the city where so many of his days had been spent, and whose citizens, as the carriage rolled slowly by along the warm bright street, might casually or otherwise have raised their eyes from usual tasks and glimpsed the pallid face and blowing hair and a hand extended, covered with a black silk gauntlet. Callers at the National Hotel that day were numerous, and every one of them, as he or she departed, took away a gift, a small memento to be looked at, eight

36 Felton: *Memories*, 369–70. Speer to Mrs. Felton, May 27, 1882; H. V. M. Miller to Mrs. Felton, May 25, 1882, Felton MSS. A little later Stephens wrote to L. N. Trammell, a leader of the Regulars: ". . . you who got me into the present position must see to it that your objects shall not be thwarted . . ." (A.H.S. to Trammell, June 1, 1882, Trammell MSS., Emory University). This sounds very much as if Stephens was embarrassed by his betrayal of the Independents and wanted definite assurance that the Regulars would nominate him. The whole thing would otherwise have looked a little silly. In point of fact, if it did not reveal quite nakedly Stephens' senility, it would be distinctly comic as an episode.

37 Atlanta *Constitution*, June 18, 1882; A.H.S. to Dr. Felton, May 18, 1882, Felton MSS.

38 Atlanta *Constitution*, July 19, 1882.

months later, with sharpened consciousness, and shown to friends with the words, a little proud, a little sad: "He gave it to me with his own hands last July. . . ."

The convention was almost a religious revival. It opened amid great excitement on the 20th. Stephens' only competitor for the nomination was A. O. Bacon. The first order of business was the rejection of the two-thirds rule and the substitution of the majority rule, which was accomplished without much difficulty. As soon as this preliminary stage-setting was done, one delegate after another got to his feet, begging to be recognized so that he might have the privilege of nominating Stephens by acclamation. Every time the name of Alexander H. Stephens was mentioned there was wild cheering. But in order for him to receive the nomination unanimously, Bacon would have to withdraw; and so the steam-roller was halted for the night. Next day at noon the delegates again assembled, to hear that Bacon had retired from the race; and then, while men got up on chairs and waved their hats and stamped and yelled themselves hoarse, a ballot was taken: Stephens, 325; scattering, 9; blank, 37. The nomination was thereupon made unanimous.[39] There was perfect discipline; the machine revolved without the slightest friction.

Toombs, asked his opinion of the nomination, was swift, cruel, and possibly jealous. "Mr. Stephens," he said, "must be in his dotage," and he hoped the Independent candidate, Lucius Gartrell, who was being supported by the Republicans, would win the election. The Independents looked on with a fury that was not so silent. "It is a rough old saying," Mrs. Felton wrote to work off her spleen, "that 'offered favors stink,' and we are prepared to say, that the endorsement we as Independent men offered to Mr. Stephens does not smell any better to us than it appears to do

---

[39] Ibid., July 20, 21, 1882. As early as July 4 Colquitt had 127 delegates pledged to Stephens. *LC*, Colquitt to A.H.S., July 4, 1882.

to him. . . . The same crowd that runs the Convict Ring in Georgia, got around Mr. Stephens to induce and flatter him into their control that they might profit . . . on convict labor." She represented Stephens as saying: "If Newt Trammell's press gang don't say I'm a clever fellow—I aint one," and concluded: "Heaven pardon us for ever looking at him!" As the campaign progressed, Felton's speeches became more and more acrimonious in tone; and Stephens for a time after the election considered publishing a complete review of all his dealings with the Independents, but gave up the idea because "mud throwing with a parson is perfectly abhorrent to me." [40] It was as well that he refrained, for he might have learned a few distressing facts.

During September he made a leisurely jaunt through the state, speaking in Atlanta, Macon, Columbus, and last of all in Augusta, where one man who saw him riding through the streets in a carriage said: "Little Alec will surely die when this excitement is passed." [41] He did not need to fight very hard, though he himself was pessimistic, saying: "Our friends are too confident and relying too much on a big majority. . . . Gen. Gartrell will get a much bigger white vote than is generally credited to him. . . ." There was once again opposition to Stephens on the grounds of his war record; and he feared the Federal money-faucet was being turned on to aid the Independents.[42] His speculations about Gartrell's vote-getting ability were not altogether inaccurate. Gartrell of course leaned heavily on the Negro vote; but when the tumult and the shouting had died on October 4, it was evident that he had received a good many white votes as well. Stephens' vote was 107,-253; Gartrell's, 44,896, Stephens thus receiving 70.43 per

[40] MS. sheet in Mrs. Felton's hand, undated, in Felton MSS.; *PHS*, A.H.S. to Hidell, October 27, 1882.

[41] Augusta *Chronicle and Constitutionalist*, October 4, 1882.

[42] A.H.S. to Trammell, August 19, 1882, Trammell MSS.

cent of the total vote cast. He carried 130 out of 137
counties, and those he lost, such as Fannin, Bartow,
Pickens, and Towns, were Independent strongholds. All in
all, his showing was very good, perceptibly better than
Colquitt's in 1880.[43]

He should never have considered the office. He was
seventy, which for him was ninety; he was constantly ill;
his strength was gone; his memory failing.[44] The duties of
the governorship and the strains of having to deal with
astute politicians should not now have been his. He probably hesitated at the beginning for some such reason; but
while he never wanted political office, he could not live
without it, and so was always doing what he said he hated
to do; and in this case, when the opportunity arose, sense
yielded to ambition. After a triumphal ride from Crawfordville to Atlanta, he was inaugurated on November 5 in
DeGives Opera House. Toombs, despite his wrath, was on
the platform when he wheeled himself out to face the
vast crowd that had come to see him. His inaugural was
brief and noncommittal. He said only that he entered
office "with no feelings of elation, but rather of deep depression from a profound sense of the weight of responsibility." When the ceremonies were done, the crowd was
permitted to come up on the stage to shake his hand. Then
he was driven through the sunny streets past lines of men
in bowlers, cigar-smoking, handlebar-mustached men, past
ladies in the preposterous fashions of the eighties, holding
parasols up against the heat, to the Executive Mansion. "I

43 *Tribune Almanac*, 1882, gives the vote by counties.

44 It is scarcely odd that after fifty years of almost continual sickness
his mind should have begun to deteriorate. And in these last years his
natural egotism, unfettered by precise recollections, was free to expand
itself. He seems to have spent his time spinning—in all unconsciousness
—a vast legend of American history in which, from 1840 on, he took the
central role. This may have been a compensation for some inner sense of
failure. See the letter he wrote in 1871 reviewing his political career, in
Recollections, 15–29.

should prefer to be beaten," he had told Richard M. Johnston on his last day in Washington;[45] but he knew then that his chances were very good indeed to win. And here he was.

III

The routine, dull, ordinary work indispensable to the governorship, the inescapable round of daily activity, was, especially for a sick old man, a terribly taxing business. There were bills to be examined, explained, and signed; there were proclamations to be issued; reports to be read; commissions to be granted; warrants to be served; rewards to be offered for the apprehension of criminals; and even if one's nephew was near by, in the capacity of Adjutant-General and Superintendent of Public Buildings, and there were several eager young secretaries hovering about besides, the burden could only be lifted, not erased. And there were so many people to see; so many letters to dictate; and there were friends who could not be neglected. And there was criticism to endure as well. By the end of the first month of the term one was being told that too liberal a use was being made of the pardoning power;[46] and when one pardoned Edward Cox, who had been a lessee of convicts for General Gordon—no doubt at Gordon's own insistence—convicted of having murdered an outspoken opponent of the system then current in the state of leasing convicts out to work for the great oligarchs like Joseph E. Brown: when Cox was pardoned, an immediate storm arose, though there were a few who approved.[47] There was altogether so much work to do and so little time in which to do it. And there was still the long history of the United States waiting to be completed. . . .

---

[45] The inaugural is in Atlanta *Constitution*, November 5, 1882. *J&B* (rev. ed., 1883), 551.

[46] *LC*, J. E. Brown to A.H.S., December 22, 1882.

[47] *LC*, anonymous to A.H.S., January 6, 1883.

And then there came the Savannah sesquicentennial; and the Governor was supposed to go and make a speech, for the event was important and demanded his presence; and he traveled all night in a railroad car with a broken windowpane, breathing air that was too chilly and too damp; and arrived at half past seven in the morning; and was driven through great crowds and streets alive with flags and bunting to the Screven House, where there was rest for a few hours; and then one had to receive visitors, a pleasure that could not be done without even though it was so tiring; and then the speech was spoken, a proud peroration on the man Oglethorpe and his courage and vision, and a hopeful glance into the future of Georgia; and one then returned to Atlanta, crossing the state, riding through the February countryside, naked and gray and cold, across the barrens and into the rich foothills, back to the Governor's Mansion.[48]

That was on February 12. In the room at the end of the hall on the lower floor of the mansion work went on for a week or so; but then he began to grow feebler and ill; was seized with attacks of vomiting; for some days could take no food; slept little. He was only ill, and not much notice was taken; no announcement was made, though the news gradually leaked out. By March 3, a Saturday, H. H. Steiner, his physician, having come the day before, it looked as though he would recover. He was taking soup, beef tea, cream and sugar, and retaining them. But after noon of the 3rd he began to weaken once more. Delirium came; and as the eyes in the wrinkled parchment face on the pillows clouded, Steiner sat by the bedside and said sharply: "Mr. Stephens, who am I?" The eyes steadied; the old flame came dimly back; and the high voice whispered: "Why, doctor, how are you?" But then he slipped again: attention would not hold. Yet for some hours the word was

48 Augusta *Chronicle and Constitutionalist,* February 13, 1883.

not spoken; he had been so near so often, and had each time pulled back by the sheer power of his own will. This time, though, they slowly understood that the will itself was gone; was blunted and uncertain; no longer knew itself or its desires. At ten that night Steiner could hold back from saying what he had to say no more:

"The Governor is dying."

John A. Stephens was there; the secretary C. W. Seidell was there; the Governor's aide, I. W. Avery, was there; Steiner and two other doctors were there; Mary Stephens was there. . . . At half past ten a stupor came, awakening from which brought only incoherent speech. He was reliving the campaign of 1855, the anti-Know-Nothing campaign. That pitiful body, transfigured by truth, was riding out once more, as it had so often done in the dim, tangled past, riding to the defense of liberty and justice. Suddenly he said very clearly: "But I carried it individually by six hundred majority"; and John, taking his hand, replied: "Yes, uncle." The long, attenuated, frail body lay on the front of the bed; the face was pale, the eyes half-closed. At two in the morning of March 4 a mustard plaster applied to the wrists brought no blood; a little later the doctors found the feet to be cold; at three o'clock Dr. Steiner, who had been resting, returned; at three twenty-four he leaned over, stared for a moment into the face, and, turning to the others, said: "I'm afraid he is gone." After a few seconds he repeated: "He is dead." Two Negro servants in the hall outside were crying.[49]

All day Sunday he lay in the north parlor of the mansion, dressed in his customary black, while a committee of citizens and legislators met to make preparations for a funeral. "Death," it was noted by one who saw him, "takes

---

[49] Isaac W. Avery: *In Memory, the Last Sickness, Death, and Funeral Obsequies of Alexander H. Stephens* (Atlanta, 1883), 3–9; Augusta *Evening News*, March 5, 1883.

from his face . . . every trace of pain or anguish"; and it was noted that "with the scant, silvered hair brushed back, the real majesty of his head was disclosed, looking strangely broad and high. . . ." His hands, encased in gloves as they had been in life, were strangely "birdlike."

On Tuesday, March 6, the casket was taken to the Capitol, where it lay in state, covered with flowers, in a room lighted only by gas turned down, a room draped in purple and black, in a building draped in purple and black, in a city draped in purple and black, in a state draped in purple and black. . . . The empty roller-chair stood next the casket.

And on Thursday, March 8, after twenty thousand people had viewed the peaceful face, the casket was shut; and at ten in the morning the legislature of the state paid its last tribute. Colquitt spoke; and Toombs, standing by the casket, wept for five minutes before he could begin to speak. He was deeply shaken, for he too was old and about to die. "His life has been an open book—that book the history of his country for the last half century," he said. "He was modest, gentle, refined, learned and eloquent. . . . His whole life was spent in the practice of virtue, the pursuit of truth, seeking the good of mankind. . . ." Brown spoke, saying that "the name of Alexander H. Stephens can never die as long as liberty dwells on earth, and intellect and virtue are honored by the good and the great." H. V. M. Miller called him "the bravest man I ever looked in the face." No one who spoke of him that day omitted the word "virtue."

Then the procession moved through the city to Oakland Cemetery, where the casket would temporarily be interred in the vault of D. G. Cotting, former Secretary of State of Georgia. The estimates of the number of people present ranged from sixty to a hundred thousand. The streets were densely crowded, no matter what the statistics, as the procession, bands playing the Dead March, seven hundred militiamen marching with reversed arms, the hearse, the carriages, the citizens on foot, went slowly down Broad Street and Hunter to the cemetery. The list of pallbearers was curious and significant: James M. Smith and Rufus Bullock, Colquitt, Gordon, and Brown beside Emory Speer and Robert Toombs. At the cemetery members of the Governor's staff carried the coffin to the vault; a choir sang: "How blessed the righteous when he dies"; Bishop Beckwith celebrated the Episcopal ceremony of interment; and the doors of the vault were closed. The sun was going down. Once speaking of his death, he had expressed a wish: "I would prefer being carried alone to the grave by the negroes with torches and be buried at night." The romantic flavor of it would have pleased him.[50]

In Virginia that day the flags were at half-mast; in Vermont the state offices were closed; and in Washington the flag flew low over the Capitol. It was a little while before the people had all left the cemetery.

[50] Avery: *In Memory*, 3, 32; Savannah *Morning News*, March 4, 1883; Augusta *Chronicle and Constitutionalist*, March 9, 10, 1883; Atlanta *Constitution*, March 6, 9, 1883; *Recollections*, 558.

Coda

THEN it was time to judge a life. When the respect and the ceremony of grief are done, measurement may begin. The worst that could be said was said by the New York *Times,* which remarked: "Mr. Stephens seemed very often on the point of becoming great through adherence to a great and sound conviction in the face of overwhelming opposition, but he always failed." The *Tribune* echoed: "He will appear in history . . . as a man of excellent public intentions, though found unfortunately deficient in strength of character at a critical moment." Henry Grady, on the other hand, wrote in the Atlanta *Constitution*: "By the death of Alexander H. Stephens, Georgia loses one of her most illustrious and patriotic sons, and the union loses one of its most liberal and enlightened statesmen, and humanity at large loses a faithful friend and an earnest and faithful counsellor." "His legacy," said the Savannah *Morning News,* "is his love of Georgia, his faith in his country's institutions, his lofty patriotism, his philanthropy and his purity." The Augusta *Chronicle and Constitutionalist* said merely: "He was one of the people." [1]

The difference shown in these estimates was partly a residue left over from the war, which had closed but eighteen years before, and partly expressive of the diversity of reactions shown to an extraordinarily complicated and contradictory character. According to the *Times,* he had ultimately failed because in 1860 he had, while opposing secession, not refused to go with his state or to accept a

[1] New York *Times,* March 5, 1883; New York *Tribune,* March 5, 1883; Atlanta *Constitution,* March 4, 1883; Savannah *Morning News,* March 9, 1883.

political trust under the flag of a cause for which he felt so
little sympathy. What the *Times* misunderstood was that,
though he was extremely averse to the idea of disunion, he
was always prepared to accept it as an ultimate remedy, and
opposed it in 1860 because he did not believe the situation
warranted it. If inconsistency and political cowardice are
to be charged upon him, other acts than those of 1860–1
require pointing to.

His basic political faith was brief and simple, and it
shines, if sometimes brokenly, in almost everything he did.
Liberty under law was his theme and his religion; and no
matter on which side of the fence he was found, it was
always the side he believed would bring liberty under law:
though his notion of liberty was qualified by a firm belief
in moral gradation—the conviction that men were naturally graded according to their mental and moral capabil-
ities, and that the degree of liberty to which they were entitled depended upon their rank in the hierarchy. Since
the Negro belonged, by definition and axiomatically, near
the bottom of the social organism, it was obvious that he
could claim but little liberty—which was the justification
for keeping him a slave. Stephens never denied the edu-
cability of Negroes, and often said that antebellum Southern society's greatest error was its failure to give its slaves
an elementary education, but he shared the common
Southern belief that Negroes could be educated "only so
far and no further," to the limit of their powers, which
were inferior to those of whites.

If he qualified his idea of liberty, he was often wrong in
his efforts to ensure its preservation. He was wrong when
he abetted the passage of the Kansas-Nebraska Act and he
was dead wrong when he pushed the Lecompton constitution through Congress; but his attitude during reconstruction, when it was expressed (and his silences may be excused on various grounds, among them being shrewd

political wisdom), was invariably moderate, well disposed and conciliatory. His opposition to the Mexican War, attributable largely to his hatred of Polk, was historical wrongheadedness, since the acquisition of California would have come with or without Polk. His behavior in 1864 and 1865, and his attitude toward the Davis government, form the least creditable chapter in his career. He was here more intensely convinced than ever that it was liberty under law he was defending; and yet he could not understand that if the war were to be won, great powers must be entrusted to those who had the task of waging the nation's war. His sympathies with those who suffered were greater than his devotion to the cause for which they suffered; and when he saw or thought he saw the little good the war might do being neutralized by executive incursions upon civil liberties, he could not remain silent. He was conservative to the last, fighting a mistaken battle for conservatism.

He always, and with pride, called himself a Jeffersonian and a democrat; and his philosophy of government, except where it was twisted by his view of slavery, was distinctly agrarian in tone. He hated centralized power in any shape; he wished always for less rather than more government; he never wavered in defense of civil rights. On the other hand, he was no Jeffersonian egalitarian, with his firm belief in natural gradation; nor did he subscribe to any Lockean theory of natural right, believing as he did that political rights were created by law alone, and not by God. Aristocracy, democracy, feudalism, agrarianism, worship of progress—his theory of government nibbled at them all.

His political life was long, almost forty-seven years; and his power was at times considerable; yet in the final assessment he accomplished little. When he was right he was nearly always in the minority; when he was wrong he sometimes achieved wrong results, as in 1854, 1857–8, and

1864. He was neither party politician, like Colquitt, nor opportunist, like Brown; he had a line, and hewed to it, regardless of where it led. His talents were capacious, but his judgment, of both men and events, was bad. "Times change and men often change with them, but principles never!" was his faith—and it sounds like Wilson's "Ideas live; men die"—and where he too often erred was in the application of the principles he held. What he lacked, in a word, was wisdom.

As a Southerner he steered a difficult course between Unionism and separatism. First of all a Georgian—a Southerner—he was always prepared for the second eventuality; but in a vague way a lover of America and fanatically in love with the Constitution, he was always ready to conciliate in good faith so that the Union might not be destroyed unless it were absolutely necessary. This was why he talked loudly when he did; and it was why he stood by Douglas and non-intervention in 1860. But he was in blood and bone a provincial, and the Union never meant to him what it did to Webster or Lincoln. The realest part of the world for him was Georgia, and he never knew any other half so well.

Of the strange triumvirate that ruled Georgia in antebellum days, he was probably the strangest and the greatest. He was certainly the most loved, as his life after the war would show. Cobb, the hedonist, the fat Machiavel, died in comparative obscurity in 1869; Toombs, almost blind, his once magnificent body ruined by chronic alcoholism, grown into an arrogant, cynical old man, died practically unmourned in 1885. Neither is remembered as Stephens has been; for he, though as abnormal as they, was somehow more lovable. And Cobb, if not Toombs, resented it and felt for him a contempt he did not trouble to conceal, especially in later years, a contempt founded perhaps on Stephens' physical frailty as well as on his emotional instability. It was the contempt of the bland schemer for the man who could not scheme with a straight face.

All his life Stephens wanted to be great, wanted it desperately, though he loathed the whole mad scramble in the mud that was the race for greatness. But toward the end this passion seems to have somewhat abated, just as after 1864 his terrifying melancholy disappeared. There may be a connection between the two. If, as has been suggested, his depressive moods were the expressions of an inability to reconcile himself to his physically handicapped position in society, perhaps their disappearance signifies that at some point, or over some length of time, he managed finally to come to terms with himself and to accept his fate. And since his intense desire to be great, as well as his pride and occasional arrogance, came largely out of a wish to overcome the extreme limitations nature had put on him, once he had achieved peace with himself there would be no longer a great pressure urging him always on to prove himself to the world. Such an explanation may be too easy. And it does not answer the question of why and how he did manage this conquest of himself. That it did occur in 1863–5 is fairly clear. But by what agency, unless it was Christianity—for during the war he became increasingly devout and remained so till death—is impossible to fathom. It may be that he suddenly and simply came to believe that he *was* great. His "reconstruction" of history in terms of his own importance lends color to this supposition; for an easy and quite unconscious mode of resolving such a conflict as he seemed to suffer from is the construction of a past in which one's failure is replaced by great success. And his poor memory—which in this case would have been made even poorer by the desire to reconstruct the past itself—made it almost impossible for doubt to creep in.

His father, his half-brother, and his physical infirmity

were the three great determinants of his character. His
unbending insistence on justice (*Fiat justitia, ruat cœlum,*
was a favorite phrase with him), his veneration for law,
his truthfulness, his rectitude, can all be traced to that
stern schoolteacher who reared him. And Linton, who, he
often said, more resembled his father than any of the
other children, was more important to him than any other
person. Linton was as necessary to him as air. Linton was
the pivot on which his whole world turned. Linton was
the recipient of all the love he would have given the
woman he needed but could never know. With the sexual
element left out, his love of Linton was that of a man for
a woman. Everything he did was done for Linton; if Linton disapproved it fell to ashes; when Linton was not with
him, or had just gone away, he was miserable and lonely;
to make Linton happy was the great end of his existence.
And this was why Linton's death was so terrible for him.
The prop he had leaned upon for sixty years was kicked
away from under him, and he had to learn to walk alone.
He had not thought he would be able to do it, but he did,
and was even happy.

Though in public life and private dealings he could be
dictatorial and overbearing, especially when his reasoned
opinions were questioned—when the armor of intellect he
wore against the poverty of his body was pierced, and he
was threatened with being reduced to nothing but a peculiar character instead of a great mind—though in his
later life he acquired the peevishness and crotchety behavior of the old, yet the general and essential generosity
of his nature was never dimmed, and the attitude of all
who really knew him was one of respect and love. "Thy
soul is golden if thy head be grey," Paul Hamilton Hayne
once wrote him in a poem; and from men he befriended he
received time after time the tribute of profound affection.
"For yourself," one wrote, "my love—love as pure as hu-

man heart can own." His servants felt the same: "I have
never known a time when I wanted to see you so much—
My prayers are in your behalf dear Master," on one occasion wrote his slave Travis; and his body servant Harry,
who served him with singlehearted devotion from the early
1850's to his death in 1881, signed all his letters: "Your
true friend until death"—and meant it.

His generosity was proverbial. At Liberty Hall there
was a room kept always ready for any tramp who might
come by and want a place to spend the night. The number
of young men he financed in their college careers is estimated at between fifty and a hundred. After the war he
held law classes at the Hall for poor young men who
wanted to study for the profession (and their facilities for
study if they worked with him were considerable, since his
law library alone comprised some 1,500 volumes, and his
miscellaneous collections 5,000 more). Money he was always lavish with: when a poor young sculptor attracted his
attention, he commissioned a bust of himself and paid far
more for it than it was worth. Together with his generosity
went an expansive hospitality. Liberty Hall was so named
because, as he said, "I do as I please here, and I expect my
guests to do the same." In Washington in antebellum days
he was in great demand at social functions, and spent
much time at the dinners of Senators, Representatives,
Cabinet members, and Presidents, and going on excursions with Toombs and other friends. He enjoyed an
evening's conversation, liked the stimulation of good company—perhaps, indeed, because they offered him moments
of escape from the brooding he was too often tempted to
indulge in. His love of children was enormous, and it was
reciprocated with the addition of considerable awe. All
the children of the family—his great-nephews and great-
nieces, who spent much time at the Hall—stood in awe of

the strange old man who rolled himself here and there about the house. One of his firm convictions was that pie was good for children; and if any of them disliked it they were made to eat it anyhow. And they did, and without protest, because they had been taught that anything Uncle Ellick ordered was to be done. Occasionally these children by whom he was surrounded made shrewd comments about him: Linton's little daughter Becky once remarked to her father: "Papa, if Uncle Ellick was a school teacher, his children wouldn't learn anything." "Why not?" "Because he'd tell them everything," she said. And she was right.[2]

His mind was interesting rather than extraordinary. The *Constitutional View* and some of his better speeches demonstrate that he could push an argument with a fair degree of cogency; but he was in no sense an original thinker. He was nurtured, among other books, on the Bible, Pope, Aristotle's *Politics,* Blackstone, Dickens, Bulwer-Lytton, Carlyle, Scott, Sterne, Smollett, Rabelais, Fielding, Cicero, Herodotus, Shakespeare, Byron, and Burton. His acquaintance with literature other than the English and Latin classics was relatively slight: his attitude toward literature was "moralistic" in an eighteenth-century way, and he always admired eighteenth-century writing for its "moral elegance" and its "chastity of style." For himself, as has already been suggested, he was an incorrigible romanticist who believed profoundly in almost every shibboleth of his time, and with especial fervence in "progress." He was a pessimist in theory—his view of human nature and the fall of man was Calvinist in its intensity—but an absolute optimist in his dealings with men. He was constantly being astonished at the capacity of individual men for dishonesty, cruelty, and selfishness; yet he invariably behaved as if all men were angels. Therefore he was often intolerable, be-

2 *Richardson,* 271.

cause when they behaved like men, he insisted on their being angelic, and condemned them for a failure that was in the end his own.

As a writer he was undistinguished. He had little sense of form or style so far as he himself was concerned; his speeches and books are longwinded and sometimes turgid, and never altogether happy in their choice of language. His letters, scrawled in a peculiar cramped and tortured hand, especially so after the Cone episode of 1848, were the things he really enjoyed writing—he often wrote twenty letters in a single evening—and they are much more readable than any of his set prose.

Had he been more stable, he would have been a great man. As it was, his nature was abnormally impulsive and made him do many things he would not have done had he been a better master of himself. But he loved the truth and did his best to learn it. His honesty was absolute; his vision much in error. That he lived as long as he did is the greatest wonder. In the end it was not so much sickness as simple overwork that killed him. He drove himself so hard that mind and body became strained beyond coherence, and disintegrated like the shay. But it was fitting they should have endured as long as they did, so that he might die Governor of Georgia. The office was a compliment that touched him more than any other could, being given as it was by the people he loved. He had come from the people, as so many of the political leaders of his generation had done, and according to his lights he died serving them. *"Non sibi, sed aliis,"* and despite his errors it was true.

He had been so lavish with money that his estate was cumbered with debt. By his will, made in 1881, old Quinea O'Neal, the Ordinary, was given a permanent home at Liberty Hall; his cook Eliza, Harry's widow, was given the cabin she then occupied; and $2,000 was left to Lin-

ton's children. These were the main provisions; but there
were many others, for he had remembered everyone.[3] But
when all the debts were totted up, it became apparent that
Liberty Hall would have to be sold at sheriff's auction. So
that it might not fall into the hands of those who had no
love for it or respect for what it symbolized, a corporation
called the Stephens Monumental Association was formed,
among whose members were many of his old friends; and
when the property and house were sold on June 3, 1884,
the Association purchased them. A year later, on June 10,
1885, a cold, rainy day, the casket was removed from the
vault in Oakland Cemetery, placed in a zinc case and a
massive oak box, put aboard a special train in which rode
Governor McDaniel and the ubiquitous Brown and Colquitt, and brought to Crawfordville; where at four in the
afternoon, while three thousand people from Taliaferro,
Greene, Hancock, Wilkes, and Warren counties—his
neighbors, his closest friends—looked on, the bones were
finally laid to sleep in his own land.[4] On May 24, 1893 a
statue carved in Italy by an Italian sculptor who had never
seen the living man was unveiled beside the grave. And
years after, in 1914, Linton's body was brought from Sparta
and buried with him.

[3] This information was obtained from a paper written by Robert G.
Stephens, Jr., deposited in Liberty Hall.
[4] Augusta *Chronicle,* June 11, 1885.

Bibliographical Note

MANUSCRIPTS

ENOUGH remains of Alexander Stephens' correspondence to indicate that its volume must have been enormous. Stephens loved to write, and spent pages upon pages talking about himself and his affairs to one after another of his many friends. His letters therefore form the most important source of study for his personality. Of all collections, easily the most interesting and revealing is that containing his letters to Linton (and many from Linton to him), which, having been for some time in possession of Mother Claude Stephens, Linton's daughter, is now deposited in the library of the Manhattanville College of the Sacred Heart, New York. There are a little over 3,000 items in this group, dating from 1834 to 1872. Stephens wrote Linton nearly every day, sometimes twice a day, and with an intimacy and candor he showed few other men. As a result, these letters have enormous psychological value; to read them consecutively is to follow a man about the world in the course of his daily life. Their historical value is slighter but still considerable. Johnston and Browne made considerable use of them in writing their biography; but since they made it a practice to "edit" all the letters they printed, I have preferred to quote from the originals.

In the Pennsylvania Historical Society's manuscript collections is a group of about 250 letters from Stephens to his secretary of the war years, William H. Hidell, dating from 1859 to 1883. Here again psychological exceeds historical importance. At Emory University, Decatur, Ga., are about 20 unenlightening letters; but in the L. N.

Trammell, J. P. Hambleton, and Jefferson Davis papers at Emory are other Stephens items of greater value, mostly from the war and postwar years. Duke University, Durham, N. C., has some Stephens letters in a separate collection, and others in its J. J. Crittenden, T. J. Semmes, and C. C. Jones papers, of which those written to Semmes during 1862–4 reinforce one's ideas about Stephens' political thinking in those years. The Illinois Historical Society has 5 letters, including the invitation tendered Stephens by his Congressional colleagues to a testimonial dinner in 1859. In the Department of Archives and History, Atlanta, are preserved the Governor's Minutes and Letterbooks for 1882–3, together with some letters and photographs. The manuscript of Stephens' prison diary, and also the originals of the letters printed in Phillips' collection of *Correspondence,* were, until last year, in the hands of Dr. Robert G. Stephens, Washington, Ga. I have no idea what has become of them since that time; nor was I able to consult them. There are about 5 letters from Stephens in the William H. Felton papers at the University of Georgia, Athens, which are of considerable importance.

In the office of the Clerk of the Superior Court of Taliaferro County, Crawfordville, Ga., are drawers containing somewhere near 600 letters written to Stephens between 1835 and 1845, concerned mainly with his legal practice. The largest single group of Stephens manuscripts extant is that in the Library of Congress, at one time owned by Mrs. Mary Holden of Atlanta, and in 1937 purchased and given to the Library by Mr. Bernard M. Baruch. This collection comprises roughly 7,000 items embracing Stephens' general correspondence between 1834 and 1883. Its bulk falls between 1865 and 1880, but the small group of antebellum letters is of high quality. As a complement to the Manhattanville collection, it is of inestimable value, illustrating as it does the daily grind of the Congressman and Vice-President, and furnishing whole correspondences from a score or more of Stephens' friends, as well as bills, solicitations, advertisements, and letters from slaves and servants. Since this collection was not available for reading during 1943–4, I had the good fortune to study it in a microfilm copy made by the University of Texas for its Ramsdell collection of material relating to Southern history. Any errors in transcription, therefore, which may have crept in may be laid to the fact that the film is not of uniformly good quality, and in some instances could not be improved even by the help of photographic enlargement.

PRINTED CORRESPONDENCE, SPEECHES, ETC.

One of Ulrich B. Phillips' most valuable contributions to the historiography of the South was his editing and publishing of *The Correspondence of Robert Toombs, Alexander H. Stephens, and Howell Cobb,* (Washington, 1911) as Volume II of the American Historical Association's *Annual Report* for that year.

In Dunbar Rowland's ten-volume compilation of Jefferson Davis' papers, *Jefferson Davis, Constitutionalist* (Jackson, Miss., 1923), and in Series I and IV of the *Official Records,* are the texts of Stephens' exchanges with the Confederate President, as well as other relevant documents. Percy S. Flippin: *Herschel V. Johnson, State Rights Unionist* (Richmond, 1931) contains many letters from Johnson to Stephens. *Benjamin H. Hill, His Life, Speeches and Writings* (Atlanta, 1893) has the Stephens-Hill duel correspondence of 1856. Henry Cleveland: *Alexander H. Stephens in Public and Private* (Philadelphia, 1866) has some important letters and many speeches; while R. M. Johnston and W. H. Browne: *Alexander H. Stephens* (Philadelphia, 1878, revised edition, 1883) make extensive quotations from the Manhattanville letters. James D. Waddell:

A Biographical Sketch of Linton Stephens (Atlanta, 1877)
uses the same source for quotations from Linton's letters.
An important letter from Stephens to a friend, written in
1854, is in the *American Historical Review,* VIII, 91–7.

OFFICIAL DOCUMENTS

The old standby of all political biographies is of course
the *Congressional Globe* (28th–35th Congresses), and later
the *Congressional Record* (43rd–47th Congresses). The *Official Records of the Union and Confederate Armies* contain much pertinent matter. Then there are the *Journals*
of the Georgia House of Representatives and Senate for
the period of Stephens' service, and the *Journals* of the
Confederate Congress (Washington, 1904–5, 58th Cong.,
2nd sess., Sen. Doc. 234). *The Confederate Records of the
State of Georgia,* edited by A. D. Candler (Atlanta, 1909–
11), provide the background of controversy for 1864.
House Repts. 3 and 275, 34th Cong., 1st sess., and House
Rept. 377, 35th Cong., 1st sess., give Stephens' own words
on the Kansas affair.

BOOKS BY STEPHENS

Stephens' magnum opus is the *Constitutional View of the
Late War between the States* (Philadelphia, 1868–70, 2
vols.). *The Reviewers Reviewed* (New York, 1872) is a
collection of attacks upon it, with his rebuttals. There
were three editions of his *Compendium of History of the
United States* (New York and Columbia, S. C., 1872); and
three of the *Comprehensive and Popular History of the
United States* (Baltimore, 1882). His prison diary was
edited by Myrta L. Avary as *Recollections of Alexander H.
Stephens* (New York, 1910).

BIOGRAPHIES, AUTOBIOGRAPHIES, ETC.

Biographies of Stephens are somewhat disappointing.
Johnston and Browne, already mentioned, is a mine of in-

formation but a horrifying example of history or art. Louis Pendleton: *Alexander H. Stephens* (Philadelphia, 1907) is better thought out, but contains little not already in Johnston and Browne. Eudora Ramsay Richardson: *Little Aleck; the Life of Alexander H. Stephens* (Indianapolis, 1932) defies comment, its amiability being exceeded only by its fatuousness. Henry Cleveland (op. cit., *supra*) and Mrs. Avary (op. cit., *supra*), Gamaliel Bradford, in *Confederate Portraits* (Boston, 1914), and Burton J. Hendrick, in *Statesmen of the Lost Cause* (Boston, 1939), all have interesting sketches of Stephens. Isaac W. Avery, who was the Governor's aide in 1882–3, wrote a pamphlet about his death: *In Memory, the Last Sickness, Death, and Funeral Obsequies of Alexander H. Stephens* (Atlanta, 1883). Lucian L. Knight: *Alexander H. Stephens, the Sage of Liberty Hall* (Athens, Ga., 1930), is of little value.

Waddell's biography of Linton, mentioned above, is the only one. Ulrich B. Phillips' *Robert Toombs* (New York, 1913) is good on politics, disappointing as a personal study. Of Howell Cobb no biography exists, and his life must be pieced together out of various sources. Among biographies consulted, especially useful were Ann Mary Butler's *Life of John J. Crittenden* (Philadelphia, 1873), Haywood J. Pearce's *Benjamin H. Hill, Secession and Reconstruction* (Chicago, 1928), C. Vann Woodward's *Tom Watson, Agrarian Rebel* (New York, 1938), John W. DuBose's *Life and Times of William Lowndes Yancey* (reprinted New York, 1942, 2 vols.), Claude M. Fuess' *Daniel Webster* (Boston, 1930, 2 vols.), George R. Poage's *Henry Clay and the Whig Party* (Chapel Hill, 1936), Robert D. Meade's *Judah P. Benjamin* (New York, 1943), Roy F. Nichols' *Franklin Pierce, Young Hickory of the Granite Hills* (Philadelphia, 1931), Raymond B. Nixon's *Henry W. Grady, Spokesman of the New South* (New York, 1943), Rembert W. Patrick's *Jefferson Davis and His Cabinet* (Baton

Rouge, 1944), Laura A. White's *Robert Barnwell Rhett, Prophet of Secession* (New York, 1931), and Carl Sandburg's *Abraham Lincoln, the War Years* (New York, 1939, 4 vols.).

Percy S. Flippin's biography of H. V. Johnson, cited above, aided in analysis of the antebellum years. Louise Biles Hill: *Joseph E. Brown and the Confederacy* (Chapel Hill, 1939) is excellent, but incomplete as biography. Of books about Jefferson Davis, William E. Dodd's *Jefferson Davis* (Philadelphia, 1907) is probably the best. H. J. Eckenrode: *Jefferson Davis, President of the South* (New York, 1923), Allen Tate: *Jefferson Davis, His Rise and Fall* (New York, 1929), and Elisabeth Cutting: *Jefferson Davis, Political Soldier* (New York, 1930) are interesting but inadequate.

Richard M. Johnston's *Autobiography* (Washington, 1890) gives an estimate of Stephens by one who knew him intimately. The same may be said for Herschel V. Johnson's "Autobiography" (in *American Historical Review*, XXX, 311–36). Rebecca Felton's *My Memories of Georgia Politics* (Atlanta, 1911) is full of venom and interest. U. S. Grant's *Personal Memoirs* (New York, 1895, 2 vols.) and W. T. Sherman's *Memoirs* (New York, 1875, 2 vols.) deal briefly with their authors' contacts with Stephens, as does at greater length Tom Watson's *Sketches: Historical, Literary, Biographical, Economic, etc.* (Thomson, Ga., 1916). Thurlow Weed's *Autobiography* (New York, 1883), Gideon Welles' *Diary* (Boston, 1911, 3 vols.), James K. Polk's *Diary* (Chicago, 1910, 4 vols.), and Jefferson Davis' *The Rise and Fall of the Confederate Government* (Richmond, 1938, 2 vols.), and John A. Campbell's *Reminiscences and Documents Relating to the Civil War during the Year 1865* (Baltimore, 1887), all touch upon various points in Stephens' life.

Mary J. Windle: *Life in Washington* (Philadelphia,

1859), Virginia Clay-Clopton, *A Belle of the Fifties* (New York, 1905), John W. Forney: *Anecdotes of Public Men* (New York, 1873–81, 2 vols.), and Henry W. Hilliard: *Politics and Pen Pictures at Home and Abroad* (New York, 1892) give glimpses of Stephens and of the social world in which he moved in antebellum years; for the war years the same function is fulfilled by John B. Jones' *A Rebel War Clerk's Diary* (New York, 1935, 2 vols.), Mary B. Chesnut: *A Diary from Dixie* (New York, 1929), Eliza F. Andrews: *The War-time Journal of a Georgia Girl* (New York, 1908), and Sara A. Pryor: *Reminiscences of Peace and War* (New York, 1905).

BACKGROUND SOURCES

Stephens' life was long, and he participated in much history. The background of his career is therefore inexhaustibly treated in American historiography, and the following list must be suggestive merely. An excellent bibliographic guide to the period 1812–83 (indeed, to the whole of American history) may be found in S. E. Morison and H. S. Commager: *The Growth of the American Republic* (New York, 1942, 2 vols.)

On Stephens' antecedents and the Georgia of his youth, especially helpful were Harry H. Hain: *History of Perry County, Pennsylvania* (Harrisburg, 1922), Grace G. Davidson: *Early Records of Georgia* (Macon, 1932, 2 vols.), Garnett Andrews: *Reminiscences of an Old Georgia Lawyer* (Atlanta, 1870), George R. Gilmer: *Sketches of Some of the First Settlers of Upper Georgia* (New York, 1855), Ellis M. Coulter: *College Life in the Old South* (New York, 1928), Lucian L. Knight: *Georgia's Landmarks, Memorials and Legends* (Atlanta, 1913–14, 2 vols.), Augustus B. Longstreet: *Georgia Scenes* (New York, 1840), George G. Smith: *Story of Georgia and the Georgia People, 1732 to 1860* (Macon, 1900), Emily P. Burke: *Reminiscences of*

Georgia (Oberlin, Ohio, 1850), Richard M. Johnston: "Early Education in Georgia" (in *Report* of the Commissioner of Education for 1894–5, House Doc. 5, pt. 2, 54th Cong., 2nd sess.), and Basil Hall: *Travels in North America in the Years 1827 and 1828* (Edinburgh, 1830, 2 vols.).

The political history of antebellum Georgia in its national aspects has been masterfully treated by Ulrich B. Phillips: *Georgia and State Rights* (Washington, 1902). Richard H. Shryock: *Georgia and the Union in 1850* (Philadelphia, 1926) is an excellent detailed study. The background of Stephens' first political attachments is studied in E. M. Carroll: *Origins of the Whig Party* (Durham, N. C., 1925), and A. C. Cole; *The Whig Party in the South* (Washington, 1913). Economic aspects of Southern society are treated in John G. Van Deusen: *The Ante-bellum Southern Commercial Conventions* (Durham, N. C., 1926), Robert R. Russel: *Economic Aspects of Southern Sectionalism* (Urbana, Ill., 1924), and Ulrich B. Phillips: *A History of Transportation in the Eastern Cotton Belt to 1860* (New York, 1908). Ralph B. Flanders: *Plantation Slavery in Georgia* (Chapel Hill, 1933) is a very judicious book. Arthur F. Raper's *Tenants of the Almighty* (New York, 1943) provides much useful information on cultural and economic conditions in antebellum middle Georgia. Adiel Sherwood: *A Gazetteer of the State of Georgia* (Athens, 1827, reprinted 1937) and George White: *Statistics of the State of Georgia* (Savannah, 1849) provided pertinent figures.

George F. Milton: *The Eve of Conflict: Stephen A. Douglas and the Needless War* (Boston, 1934), Edward Channing: *History of the United States* (New York, 1912–25, 6 vols.), and James F. Rhodes: *History of the United States from the Compromise of 1850* (New York, 1927–8, 9 vols.) give old and new interpretations of the antebellum struggles in Congress. Dwight L. Dumond: *The Secession*

Movement, 1860–1861 (New York, 1931) and Emerson D. Fite: *The Presidential Campaign of 1860* (New York, 1911) study those crucial years in a general view.

James G. Randall: *The Civil War and Reconstruction* (Boston, 1937) is the best one-volume work on the period. On the internal affairs of the Confederacy, most useful were Frank L. Owsley: *State Rights in the Confederacy* (Chicago, 1925), Albert B. Moore: *Conscription and Conflict in the Confederacy* (New York, 1924), William M. Robinson: *Justice in Grey: a History of the Judicial System of the Confederate States of America* (Cambridge, Mass., 1941), Nathaniel W. Stephenson: *The Day of the Confederacy* (New Haven, 1919), and Georgia L. Tatum: *Disloyalty in the Confederacy* (Chapel Hill, 1934). John C. Schwab: *The Confederate States of America, 1861–1865* (New York, 1901) deals mainly with economic affairs.

Ellis P. Oberholtzer: *A History of the United States since the Civil War* (New York, 1917–37, 5 vols.), Matthew Josephson: *The Politicos* (New York, 1938), and L. M. Hacker and B. B. Kendrick: *The United States since 1865* (New York, 1943) are only three of many general histories of the new America. There is no good study of the postwar history of Georgia. Clara M. Thompson: *Reconstruction in Georgia* (New York, 1915) is good as far as it goes. Isaac W. Avery: *The History of Georgia from 1850 to 1881* (New York, 1881) is called "The history of Joe Brown's Georgia," but is not without value. Alex M. Arnett: *The Populist Movement in Georgia* (New York, 1922) and Robert P. Brooks: *The Agrarian Revolution in Georgia, 1865–1912* (Madison, Wis., 1914) are valuable analyses of postwar Georgia agriculture.

PERIODICALS AND NEWSPAPERS

Of articles in periodicals, a few that were of some use were Thomas P. Govan's "Banking and the Credit Structure in Georgia, 1810–1860," in *Journal of Southern History*, IV, ii, 164–84; Judson C. Ward's "The Republican Party in Bourbon Georgia," ibid., IX, ii, 176–209; Francis T. Long's "Richard Malcolm Johnston, the Maryland Years," in *Maryland Historical Magazine*, XXIV, iv, 305–24, XXV, ii, 270–86, and XXVI, i, 54–69; James H. Bass' "The Georgia Gubernatorial Elections of 1861 and 1863," in *Georgia Historical Quarterly*, XVII, iii, 167–88; Horace Montgomery's "The Solid South Movement of 1855," ibid., XXVI, ii, 101–12; and Paul Murray's "Agriculture in the Interior Part of Georgia, 1830–1860," ibid., XIX, iv, 291–312.

Where such a plenitude of other, more reliable sources exists, as is the case with the antebellum period of Stephens' life, newspapers are rather irrelevant; but for the years after 1872, when the correspondence with Linton ceases and other correspondences dwindle, newspapers were found to be of considerable value. Those consulted were the Atlanta *Constitution*, 1873–83, the Atlanta *Daily Herald*, 1873–83, the Atlanta *Sun*, 1871–3, the Augusta *Chronicle and Sentinel*, 1868–70, 1873–83, the Augusta *Constitutionalist*, 1873–83, the New York *Herald*, 1876, 1882–3, the New York *Times*, 1883, the New York *Tribune*, 1883, and the Savannah *Morning News*, 1848, 1864, 1873–83.

Index

NOTE: Where no state designation is given following a place name, the place may be assumed to be in Georgia.

[*i*